Ever Present Love

365 Days of Discovering Jesus in the Gospels

BroadStreet
PUBLISHING

BroadStreet Publishing® Group, LLC
Savage, Minnesota, USA
BroadStreetPublishing.com

Ever Present Love: 365 Days of Discovering Jesus in the Gospels

Copyright © 2018 Brian Simmons and Gretchen Rodriguez

978-1-4245-5668-7 (faux leather)
978-1-4245-5669-4 (e-book)

The Passion Translation®, Copyright © 2018 Passion & Fire Ministries, Inc.
The Passion Translation® is a registered trademark of Passion & Fire Ministries, Inc.

All Scripture quotations are from The Passion Translation®. Copyright © 2014, 2015, 2016, 2018 by Passion & Fire Ministries, Inc. Used by permission.

Stock or custom editions of BroadStreet Publishing titles may be purchased in bulk for educational, business, ministry, fundraising, or sales promotional use. For information, please email info@broadstreetpublishing.com.

Cover design by Chris Garborg at garborgdesign.com
Interior design and typesetting by Katherine Lloyd at theDESKonline.com

Printed in China

18 19 20 21 22 5 4 3 2 1

Introduction

The Gospels provide us with more than information; they bring us to discovery. The gospel message is a message of good news—wonderful news that must be shared with everyone on the earth. This passionate devotional will bring you to the feet of Jesus Christ in wonder and worship. The historical facts of His life live through the pages of the Bible, and each day you will find Jesus loving the broken, restoring the bruised, and healing the hearts of men and women. So many truths are waiting for you each day as you examine the life of Jesus.

The love of God doesn't come in spurts. It is constant, eternal, and ever present. Jesus embodied the love of God when He took on human form. How grateful and how blessed we are now, to be able to see what love looks like!

Jesus is love with skin on. He walked, talked, and exuded the ever present love of God wherever He went. To follow Jesus is to follow in the footsteps of this great love. To miss the message of love is to miss the gospel message: "For God so loved the world" (John 3:16). That message begins with a love for every human being, a love that cannot be fully described. And believing that message is not simply believing the facts of Jesus' life; rather, it is believing in the love that sent Him into the world.

May you experience a measure of the ever present love of Jesus as you turn the pages of this book. May each day become a discovery of how great and vast His love is *for you*!

You will see Jesus through a lens of love as you read each devotion. Consider it a daily journey into the heart of Jesus. He will not disappoint.

Be blessed, my friend, on this exciting excursion into the heart of God!

Brian Simmons

January

Your New Beginning

This is the scroll of the lineage and birth of Jesus,
the Anointed One, the son of David and
descendant of Abraham.

Matthew 1:1

A new beginning! Jesus comes into our lives and gives us a new start. The One who had no beginning loves to help us start over. Our failures are never final, for grace overcomes every obstacle.

Did you notice two names that are linked to Jesus? David and Abraham. Both had failures that impacted them for the rest of their lives, yet God restored them. God gave them a "do-over," a new beginning. So many times our guilt convinces us that God will never use us, speak to us, or show us a miracle—all because we have a failure in our past. But in God's eyes, we don't have a history; we only have a destiny. And that destiny is full of hope and glory. Let this day be the first day of your new beginning!

Lord Jesus, there is no one who loves me like you do. I give you my heart today. Take me into a new beginning, where nothing of my past matters. I want a relationship with you that never fades even if I fail. Show me again your love that overcomes every obstacle.

Reality

In the very beginning the living expression was
already there. And the "Living Expression" was
with God, yet fully God. They were together—
face to face, in the very beginning.

John 1:1–2

There's so much mystery in the kingdom of God—such depth available for us to discover. Jesus, the eternal, creative Word is the divine expression of all that God is. He's with God yet is God. He's a part of the Trinity, and yet Father, Son, and Holy Spirit are also separate. Some things make no sense to the natural mind. We can't grasp many of the truths of the Bible with our understanding; they must be absorbed by our spirits, until truth resonates so clearly, it cannot be denied. The tangible reality of what we cannot see, yet know to be true, is hard to explain with words.

We were created for the unimaginable, the wild, the unexplainable. Though we may not understand it, it's become very real. Mystery intrigues us, excites us, and draws us closer. We're often left with more questions, but these questions pull us like a magnet as we seek to know Him more.

Jesus, the mystery of your kingdom fascinates me. I want to know in my heart what I cannot understand with my mind. I want to come face to face with the One who lives inside of me. Make yourself so real to me that momentary doubts or questions don't stand a chance.

Expressions of Love

And through his creative inspiration this
"Living Expression" made all things, for nothing
has existence apart from him! Life came into being
because of him, for his life is light for all humanity.

John 1:3–4

All of creation displays God's sovereignty. Nature gives us glimpses into His glorious existence. To think that He loves us and wants to continually remind us of His nearness by surrounding us with bits and pieces of His beauty is astounding. Everything that was, is, and is to come stems from Jesus, our eternal expression of life and love.

Yet nothing exemplifies this incredible love more than when Jesus became a man and saved us. Light invaded darkness and the darkness was powerless to extinguish it. Even now, this One who is light shines into every dark place with hope and truth. As we bathe in His glorious light, dark shadows of heaviness, sickness, and disillusionment fall from our shoulders. We become illuminated with the glory of Life Himself. If we would simply look with expectation, we would see the expression of His love all around us.

✢

Jesus, shine your light into my life today. Illuminate my thoughts with the glory of your truth. Spark hope where I've allowed discouragement. Ignite my faith as I yield shadows of fear to your holy fire. Enflame my heart with passion to know you, as you know me. Thank you for expressing your love for me so consistently.

Still Speaking

At the same time, a voice spoke from heaven,
saying: "You are my Son, my cherished one,
and my greatest delight is in you!"

Mark 1:11

It seems ironic that Jesus needed encouragement. Yet here we read the Father's declaration of who Jesus was and how the Father felt about Him. "You are my Son, my cherished one, and my greatest delight is in you!" God wasn't speaking to bystanders at the river; the booming voice of the Father spoke directly to His Son.

When Jesus was tempted in the desert by the enemy, satan tried to confuse Jesus' identity. It may sound unbelievable that the Son of God could ever doubt who He was, but Scripture tells us that He was tempted as we are (Hebrews 4:15). God gave Him what He'd need during temptation—He reminded Him who He was. The same is true for us—God knows exactly what we need, when we need it. If you're in need of encouragement, reach out by faith and receive it. God loves to speak to us!

Jesus, speak to me and encourage me the way the Father did for you. Help me to tune out every other voice and hear yours only. I have more faith in your ability to speak to me than in my inability to hear you, and I believe that you love me.

Jesus Comes Bursting Through

And this Living Expression is the Light that bursts through
gloom—the Light that darkness could not diminish!

John 1:5

*N*o matter how dark and gloomy things are, Jesus can
turn things around in an instant. When you've been
going through a trial and weariness is weighing you down, it's
tempting to become negative and angry. The enemy loves to
remind us how bad things are. He wants us to be consumed
with despair. The good news is that hopelessness and glory
cannot coexist!

Stir up your praise and find things to be thankful for.
Dance around the room and do the opposite of what melancholy wants you to do. Shake off heaviness and become
fascinated with Jesus. Let Him love you and breathe life into
the darkest places. The enemy may be attacking you, but
Jesus' light shines brightest in the darkness. Trials are opportunities to see God do amazing things! Don't run from trials;
find Jesus in the middle of them. Laugh in the face of them.
Allow them to build patience. Let these trials become some
of your greatest victories!

✦

*Jesus, no one cares for me more than you do. You're faithful,
and I believe you're working behind the scenes on my behalf,
right now! Come. I'm expecting your light and joy to burst in.
Thank you for loving me so well.*

Promise Keeper

They were both lovers of God, living virtuously
and following the commandments of the Lord fully.
But they were childless since Elizabeth was barren,
and now they both were quite old.

Luke 1:6–7

When the Lord has access to our hearts, the heavens are open over our lives even when promises are delayed. Zechariah and Elizabeth had waited for the blessing of children for many years. It's easy to imagine them in their old age, wondering why, after serving the Lord faithfully, they'd be denied this gift. Little did they know that the blessing of their son was so significant, he'd need to be born at precisely the right moment. John would be a forerunner for Jesus. A moment in time so precious to God, it would be recorded in history for all to read. He wasn't withholding the blessing to punish them; He was guarding their promise to bless them extravagantly.

Let this story encourage you. Keep your heart open and never stop expecting, regardless of how long you've waited. The Lord has not forgotten you. Shake off the doubt and get excited! He never walks away from His promises.

Lord, today I choose to believe despite what I see. You're faithful, and I'm anchored within your promises. You will fulfill your word, and I will see your blessing in my life. I trust in your perfect timing. I relinquish every care and will simply enjoy being with you.

Fixated on Jesus

He entered into the very world he created,
yet the world was unaware.

John 1:10

The entire world is surrounded by the brilliance of the One who created it. Even our bodies testify of the wisdom of our Creator, yet many live in spiritual blindness, oblivious to His hand upon their lives.

As Christians, we recognize the Lordship of Jesus in our lives, but we have to do more than acknowledge His omnipotence. We need to yield to Him in continual connection. It's time to become aware of our Creator in every decision, every moment, every conversation, and every thought. When we're aware of Him, it changes our lives. Sin's no longer an option—relationship with Him becomes our priority. When we receive His love and intentionally focus on Him, it's easy to walk in freedom. We don't look for excuses to yield to our flesh when we're fixated on Jesus. Let's become so mindful of Him that when we look in the mirror, we see Him reflected in our eyes.

✣

Jesus, I want you to be the center of my life. When I sense the gentle nudge of your Spirit, may I never dismiss it. Teach me to look for you in every person, to seek your wisdom in every decision, and to be aware of your presence in everything I do.

This Love

> But those who embraced him and took hold
> of his name were given authority to become
> the children of God!
>
> *John 1:12*

You are not an orphan. When you invite Jesus to be Lord of your life, you've made the decision to accept the family name. Thus begins your journey as a child of the King. From now on, you're eternally connected to God's love. Because of Jesus, nothing in the entire universe can separate you from this love. His arms have wrapped around your past, present, and future, bringing them into perfect harmony and making you whole. Every provision for your life exists inside of Him.

Jesus defined you by your identity in Him, even before you understood who you are. You're loved with perfect, unselfish, and inexhaustible love that has nothing to do with your past nor is it based on behavior. He loves you, simply because He does. From now on, you have the privilege of living in wondrous awe of your loving Father, every day.

Jesus, I love being a part of this family! I never knew I could be loved so extravagantly. You never demand my love in return—you're crazy about me, no matter what. Teach me to love this way—able to love and accept others even if they don't know how to love me in return.

He Knows Your Name

Then David and Bathsheba had a son named Solomon,
who had a son named Rehoboam, who had a son named
Abijah, who had a son named Asa, who had a son
named Jehoshaphat, who had a son named ...

Matthew 1:7–8

Y ou are significant—known by name and celebrated by all of heaven. The One whose breath fills your lungs has sealed your identity and welcomed you into the most royal family. You're not just one of an innumerable number of people who He occasionally remembers. You have the attention of the Father, Son, and Holy Spirit at all times.

All that you are, every thought, dream, fear, and question, has His attention. He's taken the time to count every hair on your head, tattooed your name in the palm of His hand, and knows every tear you've cried. Jesus knows you better than anyone ever will. He sees everything about you and calls you beautiful.

Jesus, you know me more completely than I know myself, so there's no need to hide who I am or what I think and feel. You see through every disguise. When I look into your eyes, I see myself reflected in the perfection of your love. When I hear you call my name, I'm reminded of who I am—a child of the King, significant to the One who matters most.

Embracing the Impossible

Many will rejoice because of him. He will be one of the
great ones in the sight of God.

Luke 1:14–15

Like many of us at some point in time, Zechariah had a hard time believing the promise of God. It probably seemed impossible to an old man that not only would he and his wife conceive but that their future son, John, would become "one of the great ones in the sight of God."

Jesus sees our lives through the lens of perfected reality. A frame of reference that contradicts circumstances. Though His promises for us may seem too fantastic to accept, that's precisely what the life of faith is about—reaching, believing, and embracing the impossible. Faith erases the boundaries. It creates unlimited possibilities by removing natural understanding from the equation and placing Jesus as the source. Nothing is too difficult for Him, and when we choose to trust Him despite what we see, the impossible suddenly becomes possible.

Jesus, I choose to believe. I invite the atmosphere of heaven to surround me and permeate every thought that doesn't agree with your truth. I relinquish every mind-set that contradicts your nature. You are good, and you have created me for an amazing purpose. Help me to see things the way you do and to embrace a life of unlimited possibilities.

A Beautiful Path

"Clear a straight path inside your hearts for him!"
Mark 1:3

The mountains you face, even those within your own soul, crumble as dust when Jesus is the passion of your life. When you cry out for His love to purify every part of you, nothing remains the same. Humble yourself and invite His glory to cleanse you. Soon you'll notice peace has replaced anxiety, and temptation has been conquered by a holy desire to live undefiled.

When you clear a path for His love to bloom, weeds of complacency and doubt disappear. As you look into His eyes, His love frees you from indifference and your life becomes a garden of beauty. The boundaries between heaven and earth become blurred and you live in continual communion with the One who gave His all for you.

Jesus, I'm done hiding. I want nothing to do with sin. I don't want to be a lukewarm Christian. Illuminate the dark crevices of my soul with your glory. I want to live in the light of your presence forever, with nothing hindering our connection. I am yours—totally and completely.

In His Timing

But the angel reassured him, saying,
"Don't be afraid, Zechariah! God is showing grace
to you. For I have come to tell you that your prayer
for a child has been answered."

Luke 1:13

Jesus is moved by the desires of your heart. Those things you've spent years crying out to the Lord for have not gone unnoticed. Perhaps it seems like He's forgotten or that this one area just isn't important to Him. Be encouraged—delay is not the same thing as denial. Unless the Lord has clearly told you no, then it's simply a matter of waiting for His perfect timing.

Zechariah was an old man and his prayers for a child had probably ceased many years before his petition was granted. Like him, our answers may not come at a time that seems ideal. Life may have stolen our zeal for what once captivated our hearts, when suddenly, God decides we're ready. God's way seldom makes sense to our natural mind. Despite our restlessness, He isn't stressed about meeting our deadlines.

Jesus, I believe you hold all things together in perfect wisdom and release your blessings when you know the time is right. While I wait, I will devote myself to following you and allowing my heart to be fully captivated by your glory. Let my heart flow in rhythm with yours. With perfect tempo, orchestrate my life.

Unveil My Eyes

And so the Living Expression became a man and lived
among us! And we gazed upon the splendor of his glory.

John 1:14

*H*ow amazing it must have been to see Jesus face to
face, the way we see each other. Though it's rare for
Jesus to reveal Himself in bodily form today, we can see His
glory in a different way—with the eyes of our heart. Though
our natural eyes may not see Him, our spirits perceive something
unmistakable.

As we still ourselves and whisper His name, He rushes
in to meet with us, peeling back the veil that clouded our
view. Peace floods the ground where anxiety and stress grew
like weeds within our soul. Our hearts become overwhelmed
with the sheer enjoyment that only His presence can bring.
We feel inspired, astounded, and utterly undone by the reality
of His touch. As we turn our focus to Him, His love will fill
our vision and consume our hearts.

*Jesus, I want to experience the radiance of your smile and look
into your eyes. Breathe upon me now as I still my soul and turn
my attention to you. Let me see you more clearly—to know
you and live with unveiled vision and deeper revelation.*

JANUARY 14

Straight into My Heart

Moses gave us the Law, but Jesus, the Anointed One,
unveils truth wrapped in tender mercy.

John 1:17

When Jesus instructs us, it kisses our hearts with mercy and truth. Even the pain of correction, when He reveals our sin, draws us closer to Him. The fires of purification are cleansing and redeeming—revealing our great need for our loving Savior. They burn within us, stoking the embers of devotion that cannot be feigned.

Unlike man, when Jesus highlights our sins, it isn't for the purpose of condemning or punishing. It's a call to redemption, where we exchange the yoke of sin, guilt, and shame for a yoke of holy union. No adherence to religious duties or rules will ever change us. We can act right, say the right things, and behave in a way that makes us appear righteous, but only the invitation to true repentance sets us free.

✣

Jesus, thank you for seeing past the disguise and straight into my heart. Your presence creates a burning desire to walk in the ways of purity and wholeness. I yield myself to you fully and ask that you would empower me with your grace to walk before you with a pure heart.

Always with Me

Listen! A virgin will be pregnant, she will give birth
to a Son, and he will be known as "Emmanuel,"
which means in Hebrew, God became one of us.

Matthew 1:23

Astounding! To think that God in all three forms—Father, Son, and Holy Spirit—loves us enough to see things from our perspective and become a man is wondrously confounding. Jesus doesn't smile at us from a distance, unaware of what it's like to be human. Instead, God became one of us—dwelling with the frailty of man.

Today, Emmanuel remains with us, and in us. The Creator of all that was and ever will be never leaves us. He knows our coming and going before we even take a step. Every aspect of our life is important to Him.

Right now, pause and allow yourself to be filled with awe and wonder. Ponder the power of the One who lives inside of you. Look in the mirror and see Him smiling through your eyes and igniting your heart.

Jesus, I'm more confident in your love for me than anything else in this world. I will worship you from the depths of my spirit and never take this love for granted. Thank you for understanding my struggles and unveiling the work of your Spirit in my life. Your mercy is so beautiful to me.

Eating Locusts

John wore a rough garment made from camel hair,
with a leather belt around his waist, and he ate locusts
and honey of the wilderness.

Mark 1:6

*L*ocusts are a symbol of intimidation—the things in our lives that try to scare us out of our inheritance. John ate intimidation for lunch and so can we! We aren't weak and wounded cowards who let the enemy steal what's rightfully ours. We're strong and healthy representations of Jesus. Our weapons of warfare are powerful when we fight our battles from a posture of victory.

Like John, we not only fill our bellies with the very things the enemy tries to keep from us, we know the importance of enjoying the Lord's sweetness. Honey is a biblical metaphor for the sweetness of holy revelation pouring forth from God's Word. True revelation uncovers the enemy's plan and shows us how to effortlessly stop him in his tracks. When you know who you are, many battles are won by enjoying a meal with Jesus and laughing at His banqueting table.

Jesus, your kisses prepare me for battle. Your Spirit within me causes me to triumph. I am who you say I am—fearless. I eat intimidation for lunch! Today, I allow the Word to steady my soul and infuse me with faith. I step into the victory you've won on the cross.

The Lion and the Lamb

The very next day John saw Jesus coming to him
to be baptized, and John cried out, "Look!
There he is—God's Lamb!"

John 1:29

The Bible says that Jesus is both the Lion and the Lamb (Revelation 5:5–6). He is wild and powerful, tame and docile. He's the One who fights our battles one moment and embraces us beside still waters in another. He's the sacrifice and the reward. A source of tenderness and unmatched strength.

Jesus exemplifies the perfect balance between things that seem to be contradictory. His nature encompasses all that's perfect and holy. We were created in His image, which means this nature, this perfect balance, dwells within us. When we tap into His character, the tension between meekness and power actually settles us. We aren't afraid to be brave and set boundaries, nor are we uncomfortable to be tender and meek. Jesus is the best of both, and as we grow in His likeness, we discover that we are too.

Jesus, I love the many ways you speak to me and encourage my heart. You always have something new for me to discover about you and about myself. Help me to embrace who I am while knowing which part of your personality should shine forth from me at any given moment. Let all I do be seasoned in love and saturated with holiness.

Dreams in the Night

When Joseph awoke from his dream, he did all that
the angel of the Lord instructed him to do.

Matthew 1:24

Every aspect of our life is precious to Jesus. He's the keeper of our hearts and the administrator of our dreams. He loves to speak to us in our dreams, and we should lift our faith for Him to do so. Guidance, correction, warning, and countless other things are revealed when we sleep. Children of God should expect to hear from Him.

Dreams are powerful tools when we take the time to seek His interpretation. They can show us when we're off track or how to pray into trials. They're so powerful, even the devil tries to nudge his way into them. But when our hearts are toward the Lord, nightmares can be used to our advantage—strategies to pray against the enemy's plans. Take the time to pray into every dream and seek understanding. Jesus alone is the Lord of our sleep.

Jesus, I love when you speak to me in my dreams. Set a watch over my soul as I sleep tonight. Set your angels to protect the images that stream through my mind. I want every aspect of my life to be in tune with your Spirit. Speak, Lord, I'm listening.

He Lifts Our Burdens

She said with joy, "See how kind it is of God to gaze
upon me and take away the disgrace of my barrenness!"

Luke 1:25

Jesus bore your shame and longs to lift your burdens.
Though others may look at what you've done or define
you based on your past, God sees your inner beauty—the
real you. He exchanged your imperfection for His perfection
and calls you beautiful. You're worth everything to Him.

The shackles that once bound you to heavy weights of
disgrace, guilt, and shame have been unlocked by the kindness of the One with nail-scarred hands. No longer do you
carry the stigma of your past. Perfect love has awakened
your heart, wiped away your sin, and set you free. Once you
embrace the truth of who you are, you won't strive to prove
it to anyone. You will be at peace with who you are. Infused
with confidence that doesn't need validation from anyone
other than Jesus.

*Jesus, as I meditate on the kindness of your love, I'm gloriously
overcome with gratefulness. I want to spend my life searching
the depths of your reality and peeling back the layers of your
love. I am no longer defined by my past. You have made all
things new.*

Contagious Love

The very next day John was there again with two of
his disciples as Jesus was walking right past them.
John, gazing upon him, pointed to Jesus and said, "Look!
There's God's Lamb!" And as soon as John's two
disciples heard this, they immediately left John and
began to follow a short distance behind Jesus.

John 1:35–37

*J*esus has called us to partner with Him in ministry and champion the calling of others. It's our privilege to point people to Him and not take it personally when His Spirit leads them away from us. Everything we teach our natural or spiritual children or those we mentor should highlight the importance of their dependence on God more than man.

Let's always remind those who look to us for counsel and support that their relationship with Jesus is the priority. Give them grace when they make mistakes, teach them to hear His voice, and always direct them to a place of intimacy with Jesus. When we send healthy, confident people who understand their identity into a confused world, they'll release beauty into chaos and set the world ablaze.

Jesus, help me to impart confidence and humility into everyone who learns from me. Give me grace to never put my desires for them above yours. Thank you for entrusting me with your cherished ones. May my love for you be contagious, always leading them to you, the One I love.

Believe

"Not one promise from God is empty of power,
for nothing is impossible with God!"
Luke 1:37

Within God's promises is the power to cause them to come to pass. Every word that flows from Him is infused with the very life of His Sprit. It isn't only trustworthy, it's the literal substance of truth. Power for us to wield in the face of opposition.

When we take Him at His word, we're setting ourselves up for victory. Whether we're standing on a Scripture, a promise He's given us through prophecy, or whispers to our hearts, our agreement with Him seals the deal. Sure, He could fix everything without our help, but He's teaching us the power of walking in harmony with Him. The Lord gives us the opportunity to have a part in our breakthrough. Keep His promises before you. Speak them. Sing them. Remind yourself of every word He's declared over you. He's faithful, and what He said is true.

Jesus, your words are my lifeline. By them I'm tethered to unwavering hope and unrelenting faith. Every promise is true and full of life—it rewires the way I think and unites my heart to yours. May I always be known as one who dares to believe the impossible is possible with you.

What Do You Want?

Then Jesus turned around and saw they were
following him and asked, "What do you want?"
They responded, "Rabbi (which means, Master Teacher),
where are you staying?" Jesus answered,
"Come and discover for yourselves."

John 1:38–39

Jesus loves to get straight to the point. He asks questions to reveal the intent of our hearts. It isn't our actions that mean the most, it's the motivation behind them. Many follow Christ, but few take the time to know where He abides and become one of His closest friends.

This is what He's asking when He turns to His followers and says, "What do you want?" He wants us to recognize our own desires and motives. If all we want is an answer to prayer, a touch of healing, or to experience deliverance, then we only need to receive by faith what has already been granted. But for those who want something more, who want to linger with Him and remain close, it takes a conscious decision. The choice is ours. The invitation to press in and discover Him for ourselves has been extended.

⁜

Jesus, I'm seeking you for who you are; not only for what you can do for me. I want to know what you're doing so I can partner with you the same way you did with the Father when you were on this earth. I want to discover for myself the treasures of living every moment with you.

Loving Ourselves

Nathanael was stunned and said, "But you've never
met me—how do you know anything about me?"
Jesus answered, "Nathanael, right before Philip came to
you I saw you sitting under the shade of a fig tree."

John 1:48

We all long to be seen. Known. Understood. Celebrated. And sometimes we forget that we are—known by the One who knows us better than we know ourselves. He loves us. Likes us. Continues to see the best. Can you sense Him now? He's standing right beside you, enjoying you. Smiling at you.

Sometimes we look in the mirror and close ourselves off to our own hearts. We get caught up in all of our quirks and shortcomings and forget to celebrate ourselves. It's time to think as highly of ourselves as Jesus does. It's time to laugh louder, stand taller, love harder, and smile bigger. It's time to stop being ashamed of our imperfections, because it's what allows Jesus to shine more brilliantly through us. If Jesus can see us—truly see us—and still call us friend, it's time for us to embrace ourselves with the same unashamed approval.

Jesus, let your unconditional acceptance of me unravel every lie I've ever believed about myself. I'll no longer hide behind walls of insecurity. I won't be afraid to see my imperfections; I will smile despite them. You see me, every part, and I'm okay with it.

Favor

"Great favor is upon you, for you have believed every
word spoken to you from the Lord."

Luke 1:45

The favor of the Lord is upon you, simply because you're
His child. Like every loving parent, He enjoys blessing His
kids. But if you don't believe you have the advantage in life,
you may be missing out. Gifts are meant to be unwrapped.

This is the mind-set of an orphan: "Good things happen
to everyone but me," "Doors always shut in my face," or "I
can't ever catch a break." It is not the mind-set of a child of
the Most High. Don't settle for tattered rags when you've
been offered royal garments. Align your words, attitudes, and
thoughts to His. Agreement with the Lord changes things
and causes favor to be attracted to you. Shake off the past. A
new day is upon you, if you'll only believe.

*Jesus, your plans are designed to prosper me and give me a
future filled with hope. You are the favor that clothes me and
the power that makes me strong. Bless me with connections,
wisdom, and courage. Unlock destiny within me, lift the ceiling that has stunted my growth, and open doors that no man
can shut.*

A Soft Answer

Nathanael sneered, "Nazareth! What good thing
could ever come from Nazareth?" Philip answered,
"Come and let's find out!"

John 1:46

As Jesus' beloved bride, it's important to dispense His presence into every situation—especially those that are filled with animosity. How we respond when people voice their ignorance is vital to their breakthrough. An answer that demonstrates grace and tenderness, has the ability to draw people to Jesus.

Instead of putting up walls and rejecting those who haven't encountered the Lord, let's lead them to discover His ever present reality. When we choose not to get defensive, even when they sneer and mock, it keeps us open to hear God's heart. It also alleviates tension and helps soothe their troubled soul. Compassion inspires us to reply to their intellectual questions like Philip did—leading them to the One who knows exactly what they need.

Jesus, I want to represent you well and live above reproach. When people voice the hardness of their hearts, help me to respond with compassion and power. May I always speak the truth in love and release your fragrance into every situation. Let my words refresh the souls of the weary, and my actions convey your mercy.

Uncontainable

"My spirit bursts with joy over my life-giving God! For he
set his tender gaze upon me, his lowly servant girl."

Luke 1:47–48

Nothing stirs us to praise more than when we remember where we've come from. When life left us bruised, broken, and feeling unlovable, Jesus pulled us close and declared our worth. He exchanged His perfection for our imperfection and called us beautiful.

Though once crippled and wounded, we now soar on the wings of praise. We're courageous and strong because His love has conquered every fear. A fountain of grace and mercy has unlocked our souls and flows from our lips with songs of uncontainable joy! Our testimonies of His great deliverance become the floors we dance upon. Heaviness cannot stick around when we shift into praise. Take time today to remember all He's done. Let praise catapult you straight into His presence!

✢

Jesus, I'm not sure how much of your glory my body can handle, but I want to find out. Flood every part of me with your magnificent splendor, until nothing exists that doesn't reflect you. Let hope rise within me and praise overtake me as I turn all of my attention to you!

Holy Devotion

"Now we can boldly worship God with holy lives,
living in purity as priests in his presence every day!"
Luke 1:74-75

What an honor it is to live our lives from a position of holy devotion. Even now, as your heart turns to Him, He's there with you—captured by your love. Your desire to live in purity and holiness pleases Him, even if you're not always successful. Jesus isn't standing with arms crossed and a stern look on His face. He's smiling at you. Delighting in the worship of your lovesick heart.

The Lord seeks those whose hearts are loyal to Him, and your consecrated life has become His delight. He isn't put off by your immature love. Jesus knows your heart, so stand before Him in confidence. He's moved by your desire to please Him. Guard your walk and fill your life with righteous pleasures. He's paid a great price for you. You were created to love and be loved in the most fulfilling way.

Jesus, all that I am is yours. I've devoted my life to becoming one with you, thinking like you, loving as you do, and discovering what moves your heart. I want to stand before you with a pure heart—radiant and beautiful in the deepest parts of my being.

A Lifestyle of Holy Visitation

"The splendor light of heaven's glorious sunrise is about
to break upon us in holy visitation, all because the
merciful heart of our God is so very tender."

Luke 1:78

Jesus is the manifestation of heaven, and He wants to give you a holy visitation every single day. Though you live in a world filled with darkness and chaos, that's not what shapes the life of a child of God. You were created to experience a lifetime of encounters with Jesus, and He alone must be the reality that shapes your life.

Meeting with Him and knowing His tangible presence is not a one-time event. It's not reserved for special occasions or for those who live perfectly. Your relationship with Jesus is based on His mercy alone. His tenderness draws us to Him and stirs cravings that can only be satisfied in His presence. Stir up your passion and make Jesus your priority. Take Jesus breaks—momentary pauses to acknowledge Him throughout the day and tell Him how much you love Him. Spend time with Him every day.

❖

Jesus, only you can satisfy the yearnings of my soul. Right now, no matter how I feel or what's happening in my life, I turn my affections to you. Increase my passion for you until I'm consumed by nothing else. I want to live fascinated by your presence.

The Wilderness Season

Afterward, their son grew up and was strengthened
by the Holy Spirit and he grew in his love for God.
John chose to live in the lonely wilderness until the day
came when he was to be displayed publicly to Israel.

Luke 1:80

There's such a beautiful thing about the time of separation. When, despite our calling or any desire for public ministry, we're set apart to grow in love with Jesus. This is the time we're strengthened by the Holy Spirit—when we learn firsthand of His faithfulness and recognize our great need for His leadership.

The wilderness season is lonely. At times it feels as if we're suffocating in a prison of delay. We often view these times as setbacks or roadblocks to our future, but that's not how Jesus sees them. To Him these moments are precious opportunities to discover our identity. Jesus is more concerned about the condition of our hearts than He is about our ministry. He doesn't want to give us something that can ruin us. The sooner we embrace the lessons of the wilderness, the more fully we'll emerge from them as mature brides.

Jesus, I yield to your timetable. Do a perfect work in me as I surrender every desire into your care. Be my everything so that nothing can steal my affection. Teach me, counsel me, and refine me so that in holy confidence I'll go forth into all you have for me.

Because He Loves You

Jesus and his disciples were all invited to the banquet,
but with so many guests in attendance, they ran out of wine.
And when Miriam realized it, she came to him and asked,
"They have no wine, can't you do something about it?" Jesus
replied, "... My hour of unveiling my power has not yet come."

John 2:2-4

It's amazing that Jesus told His mother Miriam that it wasn't time for His power to be unveiled to the public, yet He still performed the miracle of turning water into wine. Scripture doesn't record a lengthy conversation. It only states that after Jesus said it wasn't time, Miriam told the servants to follow His instructions. She obviously believed He'd do this miracle simply because He loved her. The story reveals that Jesus did exactly as she'd asked.

What an amazing example of confident faith! Miriam didn't beg and plead her case; she asked once and then behaved as if her request was granted. Jesus changed His plans because He loved her. Though God's timing is perfect, there are occasions when He'll change the timetable because we ask. Never underestimate your relationship with the One who loves courageous faith.

Jesus, I want to be so confident in our relationship that I not only pray outrageous prayers but believe you'll grant them. Flood me with confident faith that moves your heart. Your outrageous love makes me bold.

You Are Significant

"And you, little Bethlehem, are not insignificant among
the clans of Judah, for out of you will emerge the
Shepherd-King of my people Israel!"

Matthew 2:6

Look in the mirror. What do you see? Hopefully you
see what Jesus sees. A beautiful demonstration of
glorious mercy. A vessel of honor and importance. A person
created in the very image of God. Someone worthy, brave,
holy, and loved.

Never let anyone make you feel insignificant. Even the little town of Bethlehem became a city of famed importance.
Never accept the lie that you have no value. You're worth
everything to God. He sees everything you do and listens to
every word you say. God doesn't mark you by your failures,
weaknesses, what you do, or how you appear. To Him, you're
perfect. Even the angels stand in awe of you. You are God's
masterpiece—priceless, created with intention, designed to
awe the masses. You, my friend, are significant to the One
who matters most.

✛

*Jesus, I am beautiful and gloriously made in your image. Every-
thing about me is wonderful, because it reflects you. I am
worthy. Loved. An extravagant masterpiece formed by your
hands. I shake off any lies that contradict my value. To you,
I'm perfect.*

February

Look Past the Price

> Falling to the ground at his feet they worshipped him.
> Then they opened their treasure boxes full of gifts and
> presented him with gold, frankincense, and myrrh.
>
> *Matthew 2:11*

Love will always be tested. More than words that carelessly fall from our lips, love embraces difficulties and rises above the harshest conditions. The suffering love of Jesus is our pure and perfect example. The gift of myrrh did more than prophesy of Jesus' coming sacrifice; it spoke of true surrender for those who would follow Him.

Jesus is the Man of Sorrows who calls us alongside Him, even in His suffering. Every believer must do more than embrace His blessings. We must be willing to acquaint ourselves with the burdens of His heart. The commitment to follow Him anywhere and pay any price will have plenty of opportunities to be proven. When we're not afraid to lay aside our will for His, we joyfully surrender every thought, action, and desire, because we know His ways are higher.

Jesus, I'm all in! Your extravagant and costly love has paved the way for me. Total surrender to your will far outweighs anything I could ever forsake. Nothing compares to knowing you. I willingly release anything that could hinder our connection and look beyond the sacrifice to you, the One I love.

Peace

"Glory to God in the highest realms of heaven! For there
is peace and a good hope given to the sons of men."

Luke 2:14

At the birth of Jesus, the angels sang their praise—God had brought peace and hope to mankind. This wasn't a declaration limited to one day, it was a proclamation of the heart and intent of God for us forever. Peace has always been the plan. Yet peace cannot rule our lives unless we let it.

It's a lot of work to be upset. Constantly rehearsing a problem requires a lot of effort. Our minds endlessly run in frantic circles trying to find a solution. But when we're anxious, it's almost impossible to hear the Lord. Clinging to stress is like gluing our thoughts to a demonic inventory of all that could go wrong, even if it's completely ridiculous. Nothing good ever comes from living that way and it's not your portion. From the moment of Jesus' birth, peace and hope have been granted to you, but it's up to you to embrace it.

Jesus, when I'm tempted to yield to fear and doubt, help me to remember that you're my peace and hope. The moment stress tries to smother me, remind me to refuse it and to settle my thoughts on you. Anchor me in your peace and nourish my spirit with your love.

The Mystery

But Mary treasured all these things in her heart
and often pondered what they meant.

Luke 2:19

God's ways seldom make sense to the natural mind. That's because the wonders of God's kingdom aren't meant to satisfy the wisdom of man. They're meant to fill us with awe. To draw us closer to the mystery by reminding us of the One whose power and love confound the intellect. To leave our mind out of it and do what Mary did—ponder these things in our hearts and wait for God to unravel the meaning in *His* timing.

When the mysteries and promises of God seem too hard to believe, lean into them. Lean into the One whose birth was cloaked in mystery. Whose life sustains you, even now. Accept with your heart what your mind and circumstances push you to reject. Ponder with expectancy this God who holds every promise and keeps it safe, just as He did for Mary.

Father, I honor you for the promises, the mysteries, the unfathomable things that make no sense and yet are. When I'm faced with challenges to my faith, help me to lean into the peace that passes all understanding and to treasure your promises. I believe I'll experience the birth of my miracle, just as Mary did.

Rescuer

"For today in Bethlehem a rescuer was born for you.
He is the Lord Yahweh, the Messiah."

Luke 2:11

Jesus has never been afraid of our messes. He's not only the Savior of the world but *your* Savior. Your Rescuer. The One who mercifully steps into every situation and makes His presence known, simply because He loves you. Not even your biggest mess is too much for Him to handle. He was born for this. He was born for you!

With tenderness and compassion, Jesus pulls us out of every pit, whether we dug them ourselves or not. He doesn't lecture us and drive us to change by giving us a guilt trip. Instead, He rescues us by loving us into wholeness. He reminds us of who we are and what we're capable of when we are united to His will. Our Rescuer knows exactly what we need.

⁂

Jesus, thank you for always coming to my rescue. No matter how many times I find myself in a mess, you always come. You always save me. You continually encourage me. You brush off the dry, dusty remains of chaos and fill me with hope. Thank you for being my constant companion and friend.

Tuned In

> And this is the message he kept preaching:
> "There is a man coming after me who is greater and
> a lot more powerful than I am. I'm not even worthy to
> bend down and untie the strap of his sandals."
>
> *Mark 1:7*

With profound revelation, John the Baptist prophesied of Jesus' coming. By divine inspiration, he understood Jesus in ways few others did. For those who had ears to hear, an opportunity to step into the waters of divine destiny was available.

John's message made no sense in the natural. He was tapped into truth that had no earthly explanation. It was as if he was in tune with the very presence of Jesus on the earth and had experienced the fiery touch of the Holy Spirit, which had yet to be poured out. You've been offered the same chance—to know what few others know, to encounter Him in ways no one else has. There's no limit, no restriction on how close to the Lord you can be. Take the most incredible testimony of encountering Jesus and press in to discover even greater things for yourself.

Jesus, I'm not satisfied with hearing about what other people have experienced or what others have heard from you. I want to know you for myself. I want to see the One I read about. I want to experience the reality of you with me, right now.

Alone with Jesus

The next morning, Jesus got up long before daylight,
left the house while it was dark, and made his way to
a secluded place to give himself to prayer.

Mark 1:35

Our relationship with the Lord should take precedence. Prayer must be more than a religious duty. As people who understand our need for Jesus, our alone time with Him is a necessity we cling to. We recognize that when we're in tune with Him, we become the best version of ourselves.

In the quiet of His presence, peace drowns out confusion. As we meditate on His Word, we're flooded with wisdom and revelation. When we acknowledge the stirring in our spirits to pray for someone or something, our intercession changes things. With songs of worship, we pour out love and encounter His. Each day, let's do whatever it takes to seek the Lord's face. Let's lavish Him with our devotion and wait for His fire to fall upon our hearts.

Jesus, when busyness feels like it's cluttering my life, give me grace to stop and find your presence. My desire is to stay close to you at all times and set time aside to be alone with you. I need you, and I'll do whatever is necessary to adjust my life and keep time with you a priority.

The Gift of Faith

They went up on top of the house and tore away the roof
above Jesus' head. And when they had broken through,
they lowered the paralyzed man on a stretcher right
down in front of him!

Mark 2:4

Radical faith tears away anything that separates us from our answer and puts us face to face with Jesus. Holy boldness rises within, and suddenly the thing that seemed insurmountable not only feels possible, but it becomes undeniably certain.

This assurance is greater than hope. It's not induced because we've talked ourselves into believing. It's a level of faith that comes as a gift from the Holy Spirit. It's so out of the ordinary, so confident, and so strong that it causes us to do things we wouldn't normally do. With absolute certainty we find ourselves doing or saying something, knowing God has already guaranteed our victory. All of us have a measure of faith that we must exercise and wield. However, if we find ourselves facing a seemingly impossible situation, we can ask the Holy Spirit to anoint us with a gift of faith.

✦

Jesus, faith has found its home inside my heart. You've proved to me that impossible things are possible for the person who trusts in you. Teach me how to stand in the midst of turmoil and fear with unwavering faith. Demolish every fear with your powerful love and let me experience the gift of faith rising from within.

Supernatural Life

"For the natural realm can only give birth
to things that are natural, but the spiritual realm
gives birth to supernatural life!"

John 3:6

Y ou are more than what you see. Though you live and interact within the natural realm, your spirit is alive and active at all times within the unseen realm around you. You're a triune being—spirit, soul, and body; created to experience the fullness of life in the spirit. As you seek to remain aware of His presence, the movement of the Spirit will become a compass that guides your life.

Reach past the veil of this world and grasp the hands of the One who created you. His touch will strengthen you, enabling you to live each day with courage, hope, and healing. To live a supernatural life means embracing the power of His Spirit, allowing it to affect the way you see every situation, because you see it from heaven's perspective. By faith, you pull the promises and reality of God's kingdom into every aspect of your life.

Jesus, I'm not content to live a mundane life. I want my feet planted firmly in the reality of heaven, so all I do and say reflects the truth of who you are in my life. Help me to live the best life imaginable—one filled with wholeness in every part of my being.

Undefiled

"Why is it that someone like Jesus defiles himself
by eating with sinners and tax collectors?"
Mark 2:16

The Pharisees leaned heavily upon reasoning. They depended on their interpretation of Scripture more than the voice of the Father. When they saw Jesus hanging out with sinners, they reacted to the first thought that popped into their heads—if Jesus was truly holy, He'd protect Himself from defilement. How little they knew the God of the Scriptures.

Holiness flows from the inside out. It isn't contaminated by what swirls around it. When something within us is tempted by what we see, that's when we need to pay attention. For example, if a Christian struggles with perversion, he or she shouldn't minister to girls who were rescued from sex trafficking. However, for the person who doesn't struggle, even when surrounded by vulgarity, they hear the Holy Spirit's instructions and can set those girls free. Protecting ourselves from defilement means using wisdom and being led by the Spirit. It doesn't mean hiding our light from the very ones who need it.

Jesus, cleanse me with your holy fire. Let there be no darkness hiding in my soul. I want to be a pure vessel so I can minister with compassion and power to those who are bound by the enemy. Come, examine my heart.

Right on Time

For the Holy Spirit had revealed to him that he would not
see death before he saw the Messiah, the Anointed One
of God. For this reason the Holy Spirit had moved him to
be in the temple court at the very moment Jesus' parents
entered to fulfill the requirement of the sacrifice.

Luke 2:26–27

God is setting you up for your moment of breakthrough.
It may seem like you're not in the ideal situation for His
promises to come to pass, but the God of time and space
knows no limitations. He's faithful to place you exactly where
you need to be at precisely the right time. You will not miss
your hour of visitation.

Keep doing what you know to do. Never stop believing.
Like Simeon, who walked with the Spirit of holiness, keep
yourself before the Lord. Stay in a place of worship and
expectancy, knowing that delay and denial are not the same
thing. The ever present One is with you, even when you
don't realize it. Your destiny is safe in His hands.

*Jesus, sometimes it feels as if your promises have become a
faint memory. Though I don't understand all of your plans, I
choose to believe they will unfold before me with orchestrated
perfection. You are the Author and Finisher of my faith, and
in the end, I know you'll make everything right. I will remain
steadfast and rest in your faithfulness. You are always right on
time.*

Eternal Love

"For this is how much God loved the world—
he gave his one and only, unique Son as a gift.
So now everyone who believes in him will never perish
but experience everlasting life."

John 3:16

God's commitment to you is extravagant and unending. His love is incomprehensible yet thoroughly satisfying. It reaches through time and devours the most heinous sin. Jesus isn't offended by your past; He's with you in the present, and He's already seen your future. He knows everything about you and still longs to be with you. Though He proved it once from a blood-soaked cross, His love will continue to be revealed throughout eternity.

Never forget the price He paid. Remind yourself frequently how important you are to Him. Heaven's cherished One sacrificed Himself just to be with you. Pour your heart out to Him and discover what moves His. Spend your life getting to know the One who is the very definition of love.

Jesus, I'm undone; struck with awe because of this love that has wrapped me in eternity and kissed away my pain. I can do nothing more than fall prostrate before you and worship. It will take forever to discover the treasures of your love—it has become my beautiful obsession.

Stillness

"For the spirit-wind blows as it chooses.
You can hear its sound, but you don't know where it
came from or where it's going. So it is within the
hearts of those who are Spirit-born!"

John 3:8

You were created to feel His touch—to sense His voice as it rises softly from the depths of your being. The mystery of His presence is unmistakably real, but in order to experience it, you must be intentional. Don't shy away from stillness. Set time aside to wait in the Lord's presence, even if it feels uncomfortable at first and you hear nothing. The truth is that stillness is teeming with spiritual activity.

Be still. There is beauty in silence. Let every breath become a movement of worship. Find yourself in the midst of Yahweh. Still your mind and yield every thought to His holy presence. He is with you right now. See Jesus gazing at you with eyes of love, lifting you above your circumstances as He soars on the wings of spirit-wind. You were created for the holy, outrageous, and indescribable.

⁜

Jesus, I posture my heart before your presence. Overtake every thought so that I'm focused on only you. I feel the presence of heaven—brushing against my skin and refreshing me with gusts of tangible love. Your presence is intoxicating. Everything I desire is found in you.

Unrestrained

"He will submerge you into union with the Spirit
of Holiness and with a raging fire!"
Matthew 3:11

This isn't a tame love. The One who roars with holy passion and whose eyes blaze with fire isn't timid. His love for you is outrageous! Hell cannot quench it. No enemy can block its path. It's the kind of love that gave everything in order to be with you, forever.

The path of the cross leads us into the depths of God's nature. It's unyielding, uncompromising, and radically excessive. It sees even the slightest movement of our hearts toward Him and rushes in with billowing waves that overtake us and drown every contrary thought. It never ceases in its devotion and commitment to us, even when we lose our way.

Today, let His beauty rise within. He is with you, in you, and your union with Him is felt most profoundly in times of stillness.

Jesus, thank you for this gift of love that leaves me utterly undone and completely overjoyed. Nothing thrills my heart more than to know how much you love me. You poured out pain and suffering as a sacrifice of pure love, and I gratefully drink from its overflowing cup. I'm intoxicated with the joy of knowing you.

Suddenly

Then suddenly the voice of the Father shouted
from the sky, saying, "This is the Son I love,
and my greatest delight is in him."

Matthew 3:17

There's such comfort in knowing that regardless how long we've waited for promises to come to pass, our "suddenly" will come. Waiting is our opportunity to tap into faith. It's our chance to offer sincere praise to God—adoration that isn't based on whether He's fulfilling our every whim. Waiting offers us time to know Him for who He is. It creates character, maturity, wisdom, humility, and depth. It always precedes breakthrough, and though we don't like it, it's a necessary precursor to greatness.

Maybe you've tarried for a long time. That open door, perfect mate, or promotion feels like it will never come, but it will. In the Lord's perfect timing and with a voice that no one can ignore, He'll shine the spotlight of favor upon you. Suddenly things change. Suddenly the door opens, and the opportunities come. No matter how many years you've waited, stay humble and never stop believing. Your *suddenly* will come!

Jesus, I trust in your love for me and your perfect timing. While I wait for my promises to be fulfilled, help me to embrace the lessons you're teaching. May each day of my life delight your heart and unite me to your will.

It's Time to Be Free

"But those who love the Truth will come out into the
Light and welcome its exposure, for the Light will reveal
that their fruitful works were produced by God."

John 3:21

Step into the light of His presence. Come face to face
with the God of purity and truth. There's no need to
hide yourself beneath a cloak of pretense—those eyes of fire
that search your soul see it all. Drop the façade; let it fall to
the ground like a cumbersome burden. It's time to be free.

The Lord's correction ushers in the grace we need to face
our weaknesses and overcome temptation with His strength.
We must courageously invite His presence to search us. As
we stand before Him, His glory lights up the shadows of
darkness, revealing areas that need our attention. We never
need to fear His searching gaze. His correction is freeing;
it releases us from lies that seek to hinder our walk. What a
privilege it is to live before His holy presence.

*Jesus, I invite the radiance of your presence to examine me
today. As you shine upon the areas that need your mercy, strip
away the lies that I've tried to hide behind. I stand before you
today, confident in your love, ready to learn from you, and
excited to grow in the light of your glory.*

You Are Beautiful

> Then God's audible voice was heard, saying, "My Son,
> you are my beloved one. Through you I am fulfilled."
>
> *Luke 3:22*

When God publicly declared His love for Jesus, it was also a prophetic declaration of His love for you. You are loved and cherished just as much as Jesus. When the Father looks at you, He's fulfilled. You, despite your weaknesses and with all your imperfections, are the one He adores. Let this revelation sink in deeply: you have ravished the heart of God.

That's the power of the cross—Jesus took your nature upon Himself and, by the resurrection, gave you His. You look just like Jesus and bring the Father the same fulfillment that the Son does. You are the joy of angels. Sealed by the Holy Spirit. This all-powerful, all-knowing, mysterious, and eternal God is moved by your love. You are beautiful.

Jesus, I'm in awe of your perfect love. Of the sacrifice that mysteriously unlocks the chains of darkness and makes me just like you. To think that I move the Father's heart the way you do leaves me undone. Nothing but the blood could ever beautify me that way. Come enjoy my offering of love today.

Perfect Counsel

"For the one who is from the earth belongs
to the earth and speaks from the natural realm.
But the One who comes from above is above everything
and speaks of the highest realm of all!"

John 3:31

Listening to wise counsel is essential to our Christian growth. Others who are more seasoned in the Lord than we are may see areas of our lives that are prone to deception. We need each other, and God loves to bless us with people who will help us on our journey. However, all wise counsel should point to Jesus and not create dependency upon man.

It's important to seek prayer, support, and direction from others, but ultimately, we must have a relationship with the Lord for ourselves. We must know His voice and learn to discern His wisdom for our lives. Counselors, mentors, pastors, and leaders are prone to error simply because they're human. Take the time each day to seek the wisdom that only comes from above. Jesus is speaking; we only need to surrender our thoughts and listen.

Jesus, meet with me today and speak words of wisdom and perfect counsel. I yearn to know your voice so well that I never question what you say. Teach me to wait upon you with expectancy and rest patiently in your faithfulness. Speak to me and wrap me in the power of your life-changing words.

More than Words

As Jesus was walking along the shore of the Lake of
Galilee, he noticed two brothers fishing: Simon and
Andrew. ... [He] said to them, "Come follow me and
I will transform you into men who catch people instead
of fish!" Immediately they dropped their nets and left
everything behind to follow Jesus.

Mark 1:16–18

What caused Simon and Andrew to walk away from
their fishing business and follow a stranger? Jesus
didn't exactly use eloquent words or spend a lot of time trying to convince them. After all, most fishermen don't want to
catch people. Yet they left everything behind to follow Jesus.

When Jesus enters our lives, He comes with much more
than words. Though He speaks to us through people or a
message, it's the tangible anointing behind the words that
draws us to Him. Jesus loves to woo us in ways much more
profound than words can express. Even now, as you're reading these words, you probably sense the presence of God
tugging on your heart—drawing you into the awareness of His
love for you. Never dismiss these moments—they have the
ability to change your life.

*Jesus, I sense you drawing me into love. Help me to never
ignore the gentle tugs of your Spirit inviting me to spend
time with you. Like Simon and Andrew, I want to be quick to
respond to your voice when you call.*

An Outward Façade

Everyone was watching Jesus closely to see if he would
heal the man on the Sabbath, giving them a reason to
accuse him of breaking Sabbath rules.

Mark 3:2

Jesus did a number of things on the Sabbath that religious leaders had a problem with. They chose rules and
rigidity over compassion and mercy. They enforced the law
of God so harshly that it actually inhibited what He wanted
to do.

The rules we now follow flow from a heart longing to
obey God. The Lord's not fooled by outward service that
seeks to please man. Obedience is a posture of the heart
based on relationship with Jesus. It doesn't focus on the way
a person dresses, how they style their hair, or what movie
they watched. Purity doesn't have to conform to man's ideas.
Though it can be seen on the outside, it mustn't start there.
Anyone can portray something they're not, but Jesus is concerned with the heart and we should be too.

*Jesus, help me not to judge a person based on what I see on
the outside. I want to remain humble, knowing that if it wasn't
for mercy, I'd be lost to sin. Thank you for never requiring me
to wear a mask of religious piety. May my desire to obey you
be true—stemming from a pure heart and not an outward
façade.*

Living Words

He answered, "The Scriptures say: Bread alone will
not satisfy, but true life is found in every word, which
constantly goes forth from God's mouth."

Matthew 4:4

When Jesus was tempted by the enemy, He left us
with valuable tools for our own arsenal. One of
our greatest weapons is knowing what God has said and is
currently saying. His words become a foundation to stand on
when the world feels like it's shaking under our feet.

Jesus points out that the words continuously coming from
our Father's mouth give us life. In addition to studying the
written Word, it's vital we hear His voice. We were created
to hear Him. To be intimately acquainted with Jesus as the
Living Word. Never doubt your ability to hear Him, even if
you're currently feeling like He's silent. Often He uses seasons of silence to stir our passion so we'll press in for more of
Him. It may take time, but as you turn your focus away from
your struggle and to the One who longs to satisfy you with
His voice, you will hear Him.

*Jesus, speak to me. I'm listening. Touch my mind and help me
to still my thoughts. Thank you for loving me and speaking to
me even now. I rest in your love and release my cares to you. I
reject the lie that I cannot hear you. I believe.*

Finding Jesus in Trials

Afterward, the Holy Spirit led Jesus into the lonely
wilderness in order to reveal his strength against the
accuser by going through the ordeal of testing.

Matthew 4:1

The wilderness, those seasons of life that are difficult and lonely, isn't designed for your destruction. It has the potential to reveal untapped strength by teaching you first-hand about God's faithfulness. During this time, it often feels as if the Lord is hiding, but He isn't. He's drawing you closer, pulling you into the secret chambers of His presence where the weakness of man collides with God's amazing grace.

When we choose to speak His truth in the face of intense trials, our words of faith illuminate the darkness. In response to even our feeblest whispers of love, Jesus greets us with open arms. The storms of life, especially the ones that bellow within, fade into the background when we're tucked into His presence. Nothing will separate us from His love.

Jesus, I know what it's like to experience breakthrough. I've seen your faithfulness in my life many times. Come and let your love shine brighter than the darkness of this season—illuminating my soul. Though I cannot see your hand, I know it remains wrapped around mine. Even in the silence, you are good.

The Fountain of Your Love

Soon a Samaritan woman came to draw water.
Jesus said to her, "Give me a drink of water."

John 4:8

Jesus, the Living Water of God, thirsted for the refreshing devotion of a Samaritan woman. Today, Jesus continues to be satisfied by the sincere devotion of a passionate soul. For all eternity, He'll find pleasure in the love of His bride. Our life, pure as a garden spring, flows into Him and thrills His heart.

As you pour out your life to Him in worship, devotion, and dedication, you become a continuously flowing fountain of living water. In turn, He saturates you with Himself, drenching every part of your being with His Holy Spirit. There in the garden of your heart He dwells, enjoying the beauty that's found no place else. The presence of God inside of you will never run dry.

Jesus, come and drink from the abundance of my love. Let my surrendered life satisfy you at all times. Meet with me. Saturate me with your presence and pour out a deluge of love that cascades over my soul and sets me free. Let me become a refreshing drink, which not only satisfies you but also quenches the thirst of weary souls around me.

Know Who You Are

> But Jesus said, "Go away, enemy! For the Scriptures say
> ..." At once the accuser left him, and angels suddenly
> gathered around Jesus to minister to his needs.
>
> *Matthew 4:10–11*

Jesus wants us to understand the authority we have as believers. The examples we have in the Bible aren't there just to teach us how powerful He was when He walked the earth but to demonstrate how we should live as well (see John 14:12–14).

When satan tempted our Lord, Jesus didn't fight him by screaming or throwing holy water. He simply responded to the enemy's twisted facts with truth. He stood in full assurance of His identity and spoke with the authority He has passed down to us. He lived as a man, revealing the power we now carry.

If the enemy has been tempting you, remember who you are. You are a child of the Most High. Turn your attention to Jesus and declare God's Word. You will see the enemy flee!

Jesus, I am who you say I am. I am not weak and hopeless. I am strong, brave, and powerful. In the shelter of your presence, no enemy can touch me, so here I will remain—secure in the safety of your arms. I am confident that the One who is in me is greater than the enemy.

The Reality of Heaven

From that time on Jesus began to proclaim his
message with these words: "Keep turning away from
your sins and come back to God, for heaven's
kingdom realm is now accessible."

Matthew 4:17

What a glorious proclamation! Not only does God not shut us out when we've sinned, His mercy is the doorway to the realm of heaven. A realm that's teeming with life. A kingdom that's equipped with everything we need to live in wholeness—spirit, soul, and body. All that heaven offers has been granted to us because of the goodness of God and the power of the cross.

This is the realm that cannot be seen with natural eyes, but can be accessed by faith. It's right in front of us. Closer than our skin. Like immersing ourselves in a pool of refreshing water, we can dive into His presence, become saturated with His tangible reality. The invitation has been given by Jesus Himself—no matter what's been keeping you from God, it's time to come back. It's time to access His presence and experience the reality of heaven in your life.

Jesus, I want to experience everything you've paid the price for me to have. Thank you for the power of the cross that grants me access to your presence and the right to encounter heaven's glory. I turn to you with all my heart and step into the kingdom of life.

The Written Word

> Next, the Devil took Jesus to Jerusalem and set him on
> the highest point of the temple and tempted him there,
> saying, "If you really are the Son of God, jump down in
> front of all the people. For it is written in the Scriptures
> ..." Jesus replied, "It is also written in the Scriptures,
> 'How dare you provoke the Lord your God!'"
>
> *Luke 4:9–12*

*J*esus, the Living Word, used the written Word to overcome the enemy's temptations. If it was important for Jesus to address the devil with the truth of the Word, then it's vital we do the same. It's imperative we remember that our enemy knows the Word of God, and he'll twist it any way he can to confuse us. He wants us to overthink and analyze anything that doesn't make logical sense, since the kingdom of God itself is beyond reasoning.

Anytime we find ourselves doubting the Word in times of trials and disappointment, we must search for a truth to replace the lie we're tempted to believe. Speak the Word out loud. Meditate on the truths that lighten your heaviness and give you hope. It has the power to transform your mind and change your circumstances.

Jesus, thank you that your Word gives me absolute certainty of your will. Transform my mind with your truth so that it becomes a foundation for me to stand on. As I know and declare your Word, I will be poised to win every battle.

Every Moment

"So tell me this: Why do our fathers worship God
here on this nearby mountain, but your people teach
that Jerusalem is the place where we must worship.
Which is right?" Jesus responded ... "From here on,
worshipping the Father will not be a matter of the
right place but with the right heart."

John 4:20, 23

When we come to Jesus with theological questions that really only serve to placate our minds, Jesus responds with words of life that enlighten our entire being. Life with Jesus isn't a to-do list of righteous deeds. There's no right or wrong time to pray, worship, or enjoy Him. You don't have to wait until you go to church to lavish your love upon Him or to receive the touch of His presence.

When you're washing dishes, lean into His arms, worship Him in the stillness of your heart as you work, and expect His presence to flood your car as you drive down the street. He isn't interested in only spending time with you at specific locations or when you've set time aside to pray. Jesus wants your life to be a habitation for His glory, at all times.

Jesus, I hold nothing back from you. I want to enjoy the fellowship of your love every moment of every day. Teach me to turn my thoughts to you continually and to welcome you into all I say and do. From the posture of a humble and devoted heart, I give you my worship and my life.

Strong to Overcome

That finished the devil's harassment for the time being.
So he stood off at a distance, retreating until the time
came to return and tempt Jesus again. Then Jesus, armed
with the Holy Spirit's power, returned to Galilee, and his
fame spread throughout the region.

Luke 4:13–14

*E*very trial is a divine opportunity for our character to grow. It's a chance for us to discover how truly faithful Jesus is and how strong we are when we're fastened to His love. When our faith is tested and fear looms in the shadows, we can reach for the Light and He will come.

Trials are a launching pad for our glorious transformation. Though the enemy creates them to take us out, Jesus shakes things up and turns things around. Ironically, trials become things we can be thankful for. If it weren't for them, we'd never know how faithful He is. If our love was never tested, we'd never truly know how devoted to Jesus we are. To discover His power, there must first be a need for it. To relish the joy of laughing in the face of adversity, there must be an enemy to laugh at.

Jesus, teach me to fight my battles from the posture of confident trust and perfect peace. Help me to remember that the safest place to be is in the warmth of your glory, where the flames of praise are ignited by your nearness. Your love casts out every fear and fills me with confidence.

The Fragrance of the Brokenhearted

"The Spirit of the Lord is upon me,
and he has anointed me to be hope for the poor,
freedom for the brokenhearted."

Luke 4:18

The tears you've cried in private and the worship you poured out when everything inside felt like it was dying have become priceless gifts to the Lord. Nothing was overlooked. The love you lavished upon Him, though it felt fragmented and lifeless, was actually a beautiful fragrance that He cherishes.

Though the enemy tries to use heartache to break you, it actually has the ability to catapult you into profound encounters with the Lord. Jesus wants to give meaning to your life in ways you've never known. He'll not only heal your wounded heart, but in the process of repair, give you a portion of His own—the very life of Jesus flowing into you. As you invite Jesus into your greatest pain, you'll experience freedom unlike anything you've ever known. It's time for your healing.

Jesus, I release my pain to you. Let me find you in the midst of every memory. I refuse to let sorrow hold me earthbound when I was created to soar with joy. Infuse me with your love and revive my heart with inexplicable hope. I am courageous, beautiful, and whole. I will live in the freedom that's mine.

March

Letting Grace Lead

Everyone was impressed by how well Jesus spoke, in awe
of the beautiful words of grace that came from his lips.

Luke 4:22

To the list-makers, goal-reachers, and perfectionists: You
can check everything off your list and reach every goal
with precision and timeliness, but if it's not merged with
grace, you've overstepped a boundary. Jesus' words and
actions were executed with grace because He wasn't moved
by circumstances but by the Father's leading.

Grace lays the framework for all you say and do. It's a
safety zone that keeps stress at bay. When your mind is at war
with your spirit and your actions are directed by your anxious
thoughts instead of His Spirit, it's time to take personal inventory. Ask the Lord if He's in the center of your to-do list. Stop
assessing your worth by what you do and how well you do
it—Jesus most definitely doesn't define you that way. Let life
flow from a posture of grace, confident that whatever you do
or don't do, you're loved either way.

⸙

*Jesus, your grace positions me for peace and contentment,
even when I mess up. I don't have to do everything perfectly
to be perfectly loved. Forgive me for being critical of myself
and allowing myself to be motivated by fear and rejection. I
will lean into your grace today and follow your leading.*

The Greatest Blessing

> He appointed the Twelve, whom he named apostles. He
> wanted them to be continually at his side as his friends,
> and so that he could send them out to preach and have
> authority to heal the sick and to cast out demons.
>
> *Mark 3:14–15*

The qualifications of every believer to preach, heal the sick, and cast out demons begins when we become children of God. Our training is initiated as we live our lives at His side, as friends.

Jesus has called us, like the apostles, to represent Him with power, mercy, and compassion to the world around us. Without degrees or official titles acknowledged by religious leaders. As imperfect as they were, Jesus sent out those He called friends. The same is true of us—our eligibility isn't based on our religious titles but on the fact that Jesus commissioned us. What an honor it is to be an extension of our Lord on the earth—to see the sick made well and the bound set free. We're not only His representatives but His beloved who live by His side, day by day and throughout eternity. This is the greatest blessing of all.

Jesus, I want to represent you well; to be so completely confident in your Spirit within me that I never withhold prayer to those who need it. Help me to never doubt the power I have as your beloved. Together we will walk side by side, releasing your glory everywhere we go.

Searching

Jesus said to her, "You don't have to wait any longer,
the Anointed One is here speaking with you—
I am the One you're looking for."

John 4:26

We spend so much time searching for something to make us feel alive. Yearning for adventure, romance, careers, children, and a myriad of other things to complete us. Yet, despite our effort, many feel the void may never be filled.

It may feel as if you've been waiting your entire life for that one thing. You may not even know exactly what you're waiting for, but you know you don't have it. You're craving something, but you aren't sure what. Empty, you grasp for anything that may take the edge off this longing that cannot seem to be satisfied.

Jesus is that one thing. He alone is what you're looking for—the substance that fills every void. No mate, money, fame, or adventure alters your life like He can. Turn your attention to Jesus every day and reach for the One your soul truly longs for. You don't have to wait any longer.

✥

Jesus, forgive me for allowing my pursuit of outward things to take priority over spending time with you. You're so gracious and kind, overflowing with provision for my every need. Fill me with your presence. I turn my heart to you—the One my soul desires.

Think for Yourself

Then the Samaritans said to the woman,
"We no longer believe just because of what you told us,
but now we've heard him ourselves and are convinced
that he really is the true Savior of the world!"

John 4:42

As Christians, our entire belief system must be built on a firm foundation. Our convictions cannot be based on what others have told us. We must know the Lord for ourselves. To ask, "What do I believe? And why?" Our beliefs need to be strong enough to get us through the hard times. Seen in the way we live—not for the approval of man, but because of our deep connection with Jesus.

To know Jesus personally is to experience freedom, not bondage. Discovering what's right or wrong shouldn't be a burden placed upon us by human hands. We do or don't do things because, in our relationship with the Lord, we've heard Him for ourselves. We value His Word and study it with the guidance of the Holy Spirit. We not only know *about* Him or live *for* Him; we also encounter Him and embrace Him for ourselves.

Jesus, I want to know you for myself. I want my convictions to be strong and my faith to be true. Bless me with loving mentors who will lead me straight to you. I want to hear you, to sense your leading, and to fill the world with the light of your love.

The Answer to Your Prayers Has Come

But the man continued to plead, "You have to come
with me to Capernaum before my little boy dies!"
Then Jesus looked him in the eyes and said, "Go back
home now. I promise you, your son will live and not die."

John 4:49–50

The promises of God are received by faith. If this man, who pleaded with Jesus to heal his son, didn't rise from his posture of begging and turn with expectancy to see the promise fulfilled, he wouldn't have known that his prayer was answered. He had to believe what Jesus said and act on His instructions.

Too often we persist in supplication without rising in confidence. Instead of prayers of faith, we have venting sessions. We say, "Amen." And we think that if we don't immediately see the answer to our cries, they haven't been answered. The promises of God are true. Though waiting can be hard to endure, it serves as a teacher, instructing us in the ways of unshakable faith. The season between prayer and breakthrough is meant to build our trust, not fuel our doubt.

Jesus, draw me close and whisper words of love that awaken my soul. It seems I've waited for so long for my answers to come. Today I rise in faith that dispels the doubt that has plagued me. You are faithful, and though I haven't seen it with my natural eyes, I choose to believe that the answer to my prayer has come.

How Does He See You?

He appointed his Twelve and gave Simon the nickname
Peter the Rock. And he gave the brothers, Jacob and
John, the sons of Zebedee, the nickname *Benay-Regah*,
which means "passionate sons."

Mark 3:16–17

*H*ave you ever asked Jesus how He sees you? When
He gave nicknames to Simon and the sons of Zebedee, He was declaring who they were in the eyes of God.
Jesus wanted to give existence, purpose, and function to
those who would become His apostles, and He wants to do
the same for you.

Jesus loves to proclaim your worth. He not only sees
who you are at the moment, but He also knows who you'll
become and treats you as if you're already there. He's always
encouraging—reminding you that you're special, even when
you feel dry, weary, and invisible to others. Today, take some
time to ask Jesus exactly how He sees you. Listen as He calls
your purpose into existence. Perhaps He'll even share the
nickname He has for you.

*Jesus, you delight in me right now and don't base your
approval on what I'll become in the future. Yet you also love to
encourage me and remind me who I'm destined to be. Infuse
me with the sound of your voice. Tell me, what do you see
when you look at me?*

The Enemy's Plan Backfires

In the congregation there was a demonized man,
who screamed out with a loud voice, "Hey, you!
Go away and leave us alone. I know who you are.
You're Jesus of Nazareth, God's holy one."

Luke 4:33–34

I once heard a story: A backsliding woman, at a large event, high on drugs and alcohol, went for a walk. Suddenly, a man lurched in front of her. "What're you doing here, *Christian*?" he growled, seething in anger. Though the man didn't know her, the demons influencing him did. Because her life wasn't right with the Lord, the encounter stunned her. The *enemy* reminded her who she was. This one confrontation sent her running back to God!

Honestly, sometimes we have to laugh at the devil! In his non-stop attempts to thwart God's plans, he sabotages his own. The demonized man in this verse received deliverance because the enemy drew Jesus' attention. When the enemy screams in our face, instead of being drawn into a battle, let's laugh! His tactics often give us the fuel we need to stand our ground and see our deliverance come to pass.

Jesus, you can bring deliverance in any situation. Even when the enemy tries to confuse me and steal my attention, you know how to turn things around for my good. You are my rescuer. Instead of fearing the enemy, teach me to laugh in the face of adversity.

73

Our Treasure

"What wealth is offered to you when you feel your spiritual poverty! For there is no charge to enter the reign of heaven's kingdom."

Matthew 5:3

There is nothing purer or more beautiful than when we recognize our great need for God. It creates within our hearts the humble posture necessary to receive the glorious wealth of heaven's kingdom—riches much more valuable than silver or gold.

As children of God, we don't live with our focus on ourselves or what we're lacking. However, when our eyes are fixed on the Lord, His holiness draws us to be like Him. We see Him in His great mercy—this One who is perfect, longing to be with those who are imperfect. It brings us to our knees as revelation pierces our being. We discover that we're created to partake of the bliss of heavenly realities—the very presence of Jesus Himself, the true treasure of heaven.

Jesus, when I taste of your glory, I finally understand—there's nothing that compares to you. There's nothing I could ever obtain that would satisfy me the way your presence does. You are the answer to every prayer I've ever prayed—the treasure all men seek, yet few bow low enough to discover.

The Source

"What delight comes to you when you wait upon
the Lord! For you will find what you long for."
Matthew 5:4

The entire Sermon on the Mount given by Jesus points to an inward position of the heart, regardless of outward circumstances. No matter what we go through, Jesus must be our ever present reality. All that we long for, even during times of sickness, poverty, grief, or temptation, finds its fulfillment in Him. It's our trust in Him—reaching for His presence and releasing every burden to His care—that truly sets us free and releases us from stress.

Often, when things aren't happening fast enough, we scramble to make something happen. It can be hard to be still and give Him full control, but it's the key to experiencing peace in any season. As we learn to seek His face and wait upon Him in stillness, we're taken deeper, beyond the confines of earthly thinking and into a new and glorious way of living.

Jesus, I yield every fear, doubt, and frustration to you. I declare that you're my comforter, provider, and healer. All that I need and desire is found in you. Teach me to still my soul and to wait upon you in trust and expectation. Transform my heart and mind in your presence and fill me with your grace.

Peacemakers

"How blessed you are when you make peace! For then
you will be recognized as a true child of God."

Matthew 5:9

A true child of God isn't known for powerless words
that yield no fruit but for words and actions motivated by confidence in our identity. Knowing who we are in
Christ emboldens us to release the atmosphere of heaven
into every situation. As children of God, we take each circumstance and place the reality of Jesus in the center of it.
This is what a peacemaker is!

Peacemakers take initiative. We don't argue to prove a
point or highlight every wrong. We simply live each day walking out who Jesus is inside of us. When we see sickness, we
release peace with a healing touch. Where there's a spirit
of confusion, we restore peace by taking authority over the
turmoil and communicating with wisdom and serenity. Being
a peacemaker simply means looking for the way Jesus wants
us to release His presence into every situation and doing it.

*Jesus, I want to be known as a true child of God, not because
I need the attention of man but because I want to honor you.
Whether you ask me to stand back and pray or to step in and
do something, I will release your glory and peace into every
situation.*

Shift

> "Master," Peter replied, "we've just come back from fishing all night and didn't catch a thing. But if you insist, we'll go out again and let down our nets because of your word." When they pulled up their nets, they were shocked to see a huge catch of fish, so much that their nets were ready to burst!
>
> *Luke 5:5–6*

Sometimes Jesus asks us to do things that seem totally bizarre. He speaks to our spirits, and all too often we respond by leaning into our analysis of the situation. We rattle off a list of facts when, quite frankly, He never asks for them. He simply gives us instructions that He knows will bless us or others. And though what He asks us to do may seem impossible, all He asks is that we obey.

Peter and the others were probably tired and discouraged after fishing all night. They may not have wanted to man their boat a little longer so Jesus could minister to the crowds from it, but they did. Their reward—about two weeks' worth of fish.

Obedience to Jesus causes a shift in our lives. Things that should take weeks take hours. Circumstances that are going in one direction turn at His command. This is the mystery of obedience, and it doesn't stem from obligation but from our understanding of His love.

Jesus, it's an honor to follow you on this journey. Help me always put your desires before mine—to leave everything behind, knowing I'm actually in the best position to have it all.

To Be Like Jesus

"How ecstatic you can be when people insult and
persecute you and speak all kinds of cruel lies
about you because of your love for me!"

Matthew 5:11

As Christians, we often talk, act, and see things differently than others. At times, our love for Jesus and desire to live in purity can be misunderstood. The enemy loves to cast shadows upon even the noblest intentions, causing others to see us through a false lens. When that happens, keep your eyes on Jesus and your heart pliable in His hands. The way you handle yourself has the ability to affect all who are watching.

Our job isn't to purposefully become objects of controversy but to remain holy vessels of His Spirit. It's an honor to live for the King, but living for Him doesn't mean you separate yourself from others, even when you're misunderstood. It's our love for God and man that transforms people. When we live in humility and don't take offense, we are offering the world a true view of Christianity.

Jesus, remind me to extend grace to those who speak falsely against me, knowing that I too have misjudged people. Help me to step back and get your perspective. Give me wisdom to conduct myself with integrity, humility, and forgiveness. Let me shine with your character at all times. I want to be like you—able to love the very ones who crucified you.

Treasures

"But some of the seeds fell onto good,
rich soil that kept producing a good harvest.
Some yielded thirty, some sixty—and some even one
hundred times as much as was planted!"

Mark 4:8

Tending to the garden of your heart means cherishing and nurturing your relationship with the Lord. When your heart is tender and yielded to Jesus, it's the perfect soil for revelation, wisdom, and faith to grow. As these multiply, priceless treasures of the kingdom are poured out to you—more valuable than all worldly wealth combined.

Jesus has more available for you than you can ever imagine. The power of His promise is alive and true. When given the right environment, His Word thrives and blooms within us. Water it by meditating upon it and declaring its truth. It will lay a foundation for your life and create a floor for you to dance with victory. It opens prison doors and sets the captives free. It is hope, joy, and peace. It is love. It is Jesus.

Jesus, imprint your truth deeply upon my heart. I honor your Word and believe it's powerful enough to change everything that needs to be changed. I will meditate on your promises and tend to the garden of our love. My expectant heart will bubble over with words of faith.

Burnout

Massive crowds continually gathered to hear him
speak and to be healed from their illnesses.
But Jesus often slipped away from them
and went into the wilderness to pray.

Luke 5:15–16

Jesus, functioning in His calling, ministered to massive crowds. The anointing on His life was powerful, and though He knew His mandate and had the grace for it, He also understood His earthly limitations. Jesus not only demonstrated how we should walk in the anointing, but He also taught us how to manage our souls. He paid attention to His needs, as well as the needs of others, by slipping away from the crowds to pray and refresh Himself.

It's vital that we understand our limitations as well. When we're constantly pouring out at home, work, ministry, etc., we need to refuel. There's nothing wrong with stepping away to take care of ourselves. We need alone time with the Lord—to encounter His presence and allow true refreshing and peace to flood our souls. Being sensitive to our needs and taking care of ourselves are to warding off burnout and exhaustion.

Jesus, thank you for offering us real keys to mental and spiritual health. When I start overdoing it and burning the candle at both ends, remind me to take care of myself. You've not only blessed me with your anointing, you've also given me a wonderful and complex body to take care of.

Understanding Truth

He said to them, "The privilege of intimately knowing
the mystery of God's kingdom realm has been granted
to you, but not to the others, where everything
is revealed in parables."

Mark 4:11

You are not a stranger or an outsider. As Jesus' beloved, you can enjoy the blessing of wisdom and understanding. In the secret place of His divine presence, the mysteries of heaven are hidden—unveiled solely to those hungry enough to seek out their truth. Only those who care enough to search out heaven's priceless jewels will find them.

Jesus doesn't withhold heavenly knowledge from you, but He does want you to esteem it and crave the answers it contains. The Bible isn't only filled with truth waiting to be discovered; it's a living and powerful tool for you to wield against the enemy. Spend time reading the Bible, not because it's the religious thing to do but because it's a written account of His ever-unfolding love story with you.

Jesus, as I lean into your Word, let my spirit come alive with understanding. Unfold the story of our love and the victory of the cross to me in ways I never knew possible. Teach me. Let the scales that once hindered my vision, fall to the ground. I want to know you. I want to encounter you through tangible encounters with your sacred truth.

A Taste of Heaven

"Your lives are like salt among the people. But if you,
like salt, become bland, how can your 'saltiness' be
restored? Flavorless salt is good for nothing and will
be thrown out and trampled on by others."

Matthew 5:13

You were created to bring the world a taste of heaven. You're like seasoning, sprinkled by the hand of God strategically upon the earth. The same Spirit that rose Jesus from the dead lives inside of you. You're powerful! A living, breathing example of God's glory.

Every person you meet encounters His presence when they're in your company. To not offer them a glimpse of His glory is to deny them a taste of heaven. Keep your heart open. Pay attention to the people He brings across your path. Be sensitive to the Holy Spirit as He nudges you to pray for someone in the store or to strike up a conversation with a stranger. As you allow Him to care for others through you, you're retaining your "saltiness" and giving them a taste of heaven.

Jesus, teach me to stay tuned into your voice as I go about my day. Help me to be bold and full of compassion everywhere I go. I won't use busyness or my personality type as an excuse to ignore those around me. I want to be the type of person who makes the world a better place.

Troubled

"And the seed sown among thorns represents those who
hear the Word, but they allow the cares of this life and the
seduction of wealth and the desires for other things crowd
out and choke the Word so that it produces nothing."

Mark 4:18–19

What's on your mind? It's important to know. Most of the time we don't slow down enough to really find out what's going on inside of us. We're busy. So focused on our problems that we lose touch with ourselves and with the Lord. Instead of feasting on God, we're choking on our problems—consumed with facts instead of truth.

The Word of God has the power to transform, if given proper place in your heart and mind. When cares become obsessions, they suffocate the truth. If you're feeling over-whelmed, find a Scripture that applies to your situation. Read it over and over again until you can feel it renewing your hope. Then, be still and pay attention to the other thoughts running through your mind, inviting Jesus into each one. Yield each care, praise Him as Lord over impossibilities, and declare His faithfulness.

⁜

Jesus, I yield every thought. I lay every care at your feet. Long to feast upon your love. Wash my mind with truth and refresh my soul. You're the Lord of the impossible. Nothing is too hard for you. Thank you for your Word—alive and powerful within me. I will not lose hope!

Emanate

"And who would light a lamp and then hide it in an obscure place? Instead, it's placed where everyone in the house can benefit from its light. So don't hide your light! Let it shine brightly before others."

Matthew 5:15–16

We are the light of the world. Light that carries power for breakthrough. Light that never stops repelling darkness. We're called to shine. To brighten the world, unafraid of being contaminated by sin and darkness, because we know who we are in Jesus.

Love is the fuel that lights our lamps. When our hearts are ablaze with holy passion, we live for the joy of sharing that light. We remain so engaged with His presence in us that it gushes out wherever we go. We don't spend our energy fighting darkness, we simply to embrace our identity and love well. People are drawn to the light when it isn't fogged by judgment and criticism. We owe people an encounter with Jesus. To brilliantly display the glory that's within us!

Jesus, help me to release hope everywhere I go. The anointing of your glory within me is meant to be shared. Teach me who I am in you so I never doubt what I carry. Let my life awaken others to their destiny, and may my love for you be contagious!

Rise Above

"However, I say to you, love your enemy, bless the
one who curses you, do something wonderful for the
one who hates you, and respond to the very ones
who persecute you by praying for them."

Matthew 5:44

In a perfect world there would be no hatred. Love would be the driving force that quells rage and enables everyone to get along. As Christians, we're called to demonstrate what life in God's kingdom (the true, perfect world) is like. It's our responsibility to love in ways the rest of the world finds difficult. The only way to do that is to tap into God's heart.

When others misunderstand or unfairly judge us, it hurts. When those who were supposed to have our backs become enemies, it's difficult to love. The answer—embrace a truly humble heart and cry out to see these people through God's eyes. It isn't possible to heal every relationship. You may have a deep wound, but forgiving them not only heals you—it may heal the heart of another. The way you respond creates character in you and keeps you free from bitterness. It brings heaven to earth.

Jesus, give me the grace to love those who have wounded me and judged me unfairly. Help me to see them the way you do. Teach me how to love purely, so I can honor you and give the world a true interpretation of Christianity.

Living Testimony

So the man left and went into the region of Jordan and parts of Syria to tell everyone he met about what Jesus had done for him, and all the people marveled!

Mark 5:20

You don't need a theological degree to stand before people and share the love of Jesus. Your life is a testimony of the power and mercy of God. Your family, the people you work with, and those who know you, are the audience you've been given. The ground beneath your feet is the only pulpit you need.

When Jesus radically transforms your life, people notice. You don't have to do or say very much—the evidence is right before their faces. You only need to point them to the One who deserves the credit. Every breakthrough, every time Jesus comes through for you, is an opportunity to tell people about the goodness of God. Let people know what He's done for you. Your life is a testimony—no one can argue that your experiences aren't real. And people are looking for real. Let your excitement overflow and splash on everyone who needs to hear.

Jesus, I want my life to spill over with stories of what you've done for me. Give me the courage to tell everyone how faithful you are. May my testimonies spark hope and faith in all who hear. Let my joy be contagious!

Expectation

"Because the Father loves his Son so much, he always
reveals to me everything that he is about to do."

John 5:20

Jesus brought us a new and beautiful demonstration of connection with God. To know God as Father opens an entirely new way of looking at our relationship with Him. As our Father, we expect to hear Him, to laugh with Him, to be held by Him, and to know what He's up to. Jesus knew how loved He was, and He wants us to live in this same confidence.

The invitation for intimacy with the Father, Son, and Holy Spirit means that we not only talk *to* them, but we also expect to hear *from* them. We understand our place as both children of God and partners with Jesus on the earth. Communication becomes a necessary and meaningful part of life. As we grow from glory to glory, let's anticipate His voice with longing and excitement. It's possible to be as confident in the Father's love as Jesus was.

✦

Jesus, thank you for showing me what the Father is like so I can know Him the way you do. Help me, Holy Spirit, to hear His voice every day. Lord, I'm not content knowing about you—I'm diving into our relationship with all of my heart. Embracing love with joyful anticipation.

Healer

"If you are only willing, you could completely heal me."
Jesus reached out and touched him and said,
"Of course I am willing to heal you, and now you
will be healed." Instantly the leprous sores were
healed and his skin became smooth.

Luke 5:12–13

Before you can experience Jesus as your Healer, you must first believe that it's His will to heal. It's not enough to know that the One who never changes still heals; you must trust that He longs to heal *you*—every part of you.

The story of the leper is one of compassion. Jesus reached out and touched this leper, which was forbidden because of the fear of contamination. He came close to a man who hadn't felt the touch of love in years—shunned by society. This man came to Jesus asking for physical healing, but Jesus knew He needed more than that. The leper not only walked away with smooth skin, but he also walked away having experienced a loving affirmation and a physical touch. Jesus still heals, and His healing touch is personal—meeting every need.

Jesus, thank you for the compassion you show me. Heal every part of me. Infuse every wound with your life-giving touch. Meet with me. Hold me with your timeless and eternal love. I stand upon your Word and embrace my healing today.

Partnering with Jesus

So, Jesus said, "I speak to you timeless truth.
The Son is not able to do anything from himself
or through my own initiative."

John 5:19

One of the greatest mysteries is that Jesus chose to become a man, who without the power of the Spirit could do nothing. But as a man with the Holy Spirit, He gave us an example to follow. All that He did we can do too.

As we partner with Jesus the way He partnered with His Father, we're stepping into destiny. If it was important for Jesus to look to the Father for guidance, so must we. If He drew strength from the Spirit, we should do the same. If Jesus only did what the Father showed Him to do, we must continually look for His direction. Jesus was our example—He showed us how a man could live in power and purity. His blood cleansed us and made us pure, now it's up to us to embrace our identity and live in power.

Jesus, lead me. Just as God anointed you as a man, with the power of the Spirit, anoint me. I look to you for direction and guidance. I want to partner with you to bring the glory of God to the earth. To embrace my identity and walk in the power of your Spirit.

Revelation

"For those who listen with open hearts will receive more revelation. But those who don't listen with open hearts will lose what little they think they have!"

Mark 4:25

The kingdom of God is eternal. With its immeasurable time comes inexhaustible revelation. Most of us agree that regardless of how smart or anointed we are, there's always more to learn. The problem is that with a kingdom as vast and glorious as God's, true revelation is often uncomfortable. It doesn't always fit our limited mind-sets, which means we often reject what doesn't make sense.

The desire to receive revelation from God isn't enough. We must be completely open to His Spirit. Willing to allow Him to download concepts that contradict logic. It's okay to process with the Lord and ask Him for understanding, as long as our hearts are open to what we don't understand. God longs to give us fresh revelation, but what doesn't register with the mind must be embraced with the heart.

Jesus, I cry out for Spirit revelation! I want to know the way you move and how you think. I long to know what you desire and to embrace all that I'm capable of doing with you. Take me from glory to glory as I open my heart to you fully.

Relationships

> "So then, if you are presenting a gift before the
> altar in the temple and suddenly you remember a quarrel
> you have with a fellow believer, leave your gift there in
> front of the altar and go at once to apologize
> with the one who is offended."
>
> *Matthew 5:23–24*

Jesus cares more about relationships than many realize. So much so that He'd rather you withhold His gifts in order to first restore connection to an injured relationship. It's important for the corporate body of Christ to be healthy—functioning in unity and power. Offense can easily turn to bitterness, leaving a wound that weakens the entire body.

God entrusts us with the hearts of others and wants us to take responsibility for the condition of those relationships. If you've offended someone, it's your duty to apologize with compassion and sincerity. If you've been offended, it's your privilege to imitate Jesus and forgive. It may not always be possible or wise to allow that person back into your life but releasing the pain of bitterness and unforgiveness is critical.

Jesus, I want to live in the peace that's beyond understanding. I don't want to hold on to anything that will poison my soul or cause division in our heavenly family. I choose to forgive those who have hurt me, and I will do my part to mend any wounded relationships in my life.

Even in Your Mess

"I have not come to call the 'righteous,' but to call those
who fail to measure up and bring them to repentance."

Luke 5:32

Most of us came to Jesus because we finally figured
out that we didn't have it all together and nothing
we could do would change that. In our great need for something that neither the world nor ourselves could supply, we
humbly received the gift of salvation. We didn't deserve it.
He didn't choose us because we were righteous. He chose
us because He loved us—even in our mess.

Jesus isn't afraid of your mess. As a matter of fact, He's
pretty good at taking messes and turning them into miracles.
If your life doesn't feel like it's measuring up, remember who
you are. Don't let shame, guilt, and condemnation keep you
away from Him. Only the enemy wants you to focus on what
you're not. Jesus called you to Himself and continually calls—
no matter what your life looks like.

*Jesus, I want to live from the perspective of heaven. I want to
see myself the way you see me. You don't focus on my faults,
so I won't either. You believe in me and you're constantly
cheering me on. Even in my mess, you don't just love me, you
like me! By your grace, I am victorious!*

From Glory to Glory

"And who pours new wine into an old wineskin?
If someone did, the old wineskin would burst
and the new wine would be lost."

Luke 5:37

The Ancient of Days flows with the new wine of the Spirit. His wisdom and truth have been established from the foundations of the world and yet He chooses when to unveil them. He is in the past, present, and future. He's always been, and He'll always be.

The truths we learn on our journey aren't meant to lock us into a rigid way of viewing life or spirituality. We're destined to go from glory to glory, not settle. As we grow in the Lord there's a temptation to get comfortable with what we've learned. To lean on our understanding of truth instead of seeking Him for fresh revelation. We mustn't get stagnant, but keep our hearts open to Jesus, yielding old mind-sets in order to embrace greater understanding. His truth gladdens the heart. He is the new wine that flows within.

Jesus, I never want to get stuck in a mind-set that's contrary to the truth of your Word, no matter how right it seems. I want to walk in the light as you're in the light. Help me to live with an open heart, always ready to receive all that you want to pour out.

Rest

Suddenly, as they were crossing the lake, a ferocious
tempest arose, with violent winds and waves that were
crashing into the boat ... But Jesus was calmly
sleeping in the stern, resting on a cushion.

Mark 4:37–38

Every opposition must be met with faith. But what do we do when we've done everything we can and feel like our faith has been hijacked by terrorists? We rest. Rest goes against our fight-or-flight instinct. It feels counterproductive and impractical. Let's be honest—when you're in a battle, resting doesn't come naturally. Yet in this place of turmoil and contradiction, we're reminded of Jesus—asleep in the back of the boat. We learn that the greatest posture of faith is rest.

True faith doesn't need to scream at the enemy, fast for a month, or call an emergency prayer meeting. It's completely convinced of God's love. It simply relaxes, finds its footing, and fixes its eyes on the Lord. It's the state of true surrender and absolute trust—empowered by the beauty of our relationship with the Lord. It's from this place of rest that we know exactly what to do because we hear Him.

Jesus, thank you for teaching me that everything I do must be motivated by faith and not fear. Give me grace to rest in your arms when I find myself in the midst of turmoil. Speak to me and lead me with perfect peace. I say no to fear today and trust in your faithfulness.

In the Waiting

Jesus knew at once that someone had touched him,
for he felt the power that always surged around him had
passed through him for someone to be healed. He turned
and spoke to the crowd, saying, "Who touched my clothes?"
His disciples answered, "What do mean, who touched you?
Look at this huge crowd—they're all pressing up against you."

Mark 5:30–31

The woman in this story had been bleeding for twelve years. That's a long time! I imagine she may have been physically weak and emotionally spent, but she didn't let it stop her. Crowds were all around Jesus, the Living Word, but only she "touched" the Word in faith. Desperate, she did what throngs of others didn't. She drew from the anointing on Jesus and received her healing.

Waiting for breakthrough isn't easy. When you've been battling sickness or believing for some other answer to prayer, what you do while you wait is important. Sometimes it's all about not giving up. Give Him your despair. Yield your disappointment. Focus on the truth of His Word and trust God with every moment. Even in the midst of torment, do not give up!

Jesus, sometimes it's hard to keep believing, but I've decided that I have no other choice. I choose you! I choose to believe that you love me. Even though I haven't seen the answer to my prayer manifest, I won't stop believing. I will hold on to hope. I will touch you with my faith, love you, and praise you while I wait.

Cleansing Fire

"If your right eye seduces you to fall into sin, then go
blind in your right eye! For you're better off losing sight in
one eye than to have your whole body thrown into hell."

Matthew 5:29

Jesus used strong and colorful hyperbole to make a
very clear point—guarding ourselves from sin is serious
business. He loves us so much that He wants us to be free
of things that could hinder us from walking in our greatest
potential. Jesus never condemns us when we sin, but He
does expect us to turn from it and seek victory. He longs for
us to invite His searching gaze, especially into the deepest
areas we've yet to face. Our humanity will never push Him
away.

Trust the Lord to reveal habits, attitudes, and mind-sets
that hinder your relationship with Him. Keep your focus on
the Lord, not on your sins or shortcomings. Never resist His
cleansing fire. Never shy away from His fine-tuning. The
more time you spend with Him, the greater your desire to
be fully His.

*Jesus, cleanse me with the fire of your love so that nothing hin-
ders our communion. Examine my heart and reveal anything
that would distance me from you. I won't resist your searching
gaze—it's like fire in my bones. Transform me from the inside
out as I yield my soul to you.*

Spiritual Balance

"You are busy analyzing the Scriptures, frantically poring
over them in hopes of gaining eternal life. Everything you
read points to me, yet you still refuse to come to me so
I can give you the life you're looking for—eternal life!"

John 5:39-40

*D*iligently spending time in the Word is vital. It's the
foundation of everything we believe. However, it's
possible to study our Bible and have numerous Scriptures
memorized but still feel dead inside. That's because we must
encounter the Lord of the Scriptures in order for it to come
to life. The only way to do this is to approach the Word with
the help of the Holy Spirit. He will reveal to our hearts what
cannot be understood with our mind.

Truth must do more than touch our minds and give us
great theological answers. We can say all the right things, but
unless we're intimately acquainted with the Word Himself,
we're out of balance. Jesus has never been impressed with
how much Scripture we know, but by how much we know
Him. People can argue with our theology, but holy passion
that seeps from every pore has no rebuttal.

*Jesus, draw me into your presence. Teach me all there is to
know about you. Unveil my eyes to see truth and enflame my
heart with holy desire. Speak to me. Captivate me with love
so tangible and profound that those around me come face to
face with your presence in ways that defy logic.*

April

For Him Alone

"Of course you're unable to believe in me. For you live
for the praises of others and not for the praise
that comes from the only true God."

John 5:44

When we seek the praise of man and live to please others, we're living for lesser glory—trinkets of hope that wither away. There's only One whose approval gives meaning to our lives. Only One whose love becomes the stamp of approval upon our souls. When we're confident in His love for us, the opinions of others don't add or subtract to our worth.

We weren't created to wear masks that hide our true identity in order to fit in. It's stressful to pretend that we're something we're not. It's freeing to live for an audience of One. We flourish when we remember that we stand before our Father every day. He sees it all, even when no one else is watching. Don't let your desire for approval cloud your judgment. His validation of us is all that matters.

Jesus, let your love infuse me with confidence and contentment. Your opinion of me has given me courage to be myself. You call me your beloved, your chosen one who delights your heart, and I am greatly loved. I have no fear of rejection because you have accepted me. I live for you and you alone. I am yours.

In Times of Crisis

> But Jesus refused to listen to what they were told
> and said to the Jewish official, "Don't yield to fear.
> All you need to do is to keep on believing."
>
> *Mark 5:36*

What a powerful statement! Jairus had just been given the worst news imaginable. The world's final declaration had been made. His daughter had died. Nothing else could be done. Yet Jesus tells him to keep on believing and not to give in to fear. The conclusion—Jesus raised Jairus' daughter from the dead. What was impossible became possible.

Accepting fear means closing the door to possibilities of faith. Even when man's final declaration has been made and it feels like the gavel of judgment has sealed your fate, Jesus still has the last word. Despite the facts, do not give fear a place in your heart. Keep believing, even when fear is screaming in your face. Stand in His presence and find your peace. Nothing is too hard for Him. Absolutely nothing!

Jesus, I need the peace that passes understanding. I release every hopeless situation to you and ask you to breathe life into the chaos. Do what only you can do. You are the God of miracles—faithful, loving, and powerful. I declare your Lordship over _____ (name the problem). I believe in you. I trust you. I settle my heart in your presence. Take over.

Deliver Me

"Rescue us every time we face tribulation and set us free from evil. For you are the King who rules with power and glory forever. Amen."

Matthew 6:13

Who do we run to when we're facing temptation, adversity, and anguish? Seeking advice from godly counselors is wise. God has placed specific people in our lives that He knows we can trust so we can glean from them and find comfort and support. It's important to have people we can lean on in difficult times, but there's only One who can truly deliver.

In the dark night of the soul, when we feel alone and inconsolable, Jesus steps into the shadows and holds us. With glory and power, He overthrows every evil plan. His unfailing, endless love rescues us, time after time. He reaches into our pit and lifts us up to walk upon the waters of adversity with Him. He alone is the strength we need to overcome.

Jesus, you are my song, my joy, my life. When I feel like I can barely keep my head above the water, you rush to my side and rescue me. Teach me to run to you first—to seek you more than any other. And when I don't have the strength to breathe a single prayer, I'll simply close my eyes and know that you are here.

An Audience of One

"Examine your motives to make sure you're not showing off when you do your good deeds, only to be admired by others; otherwise, you will lose the reward of your heavenly Father."

Matthew 6:1

*G*od created you for greatness. Designed you with a desire for significance. Understanding your identity in His kingdom means believing you're significant. Embracing the importance of who you are creates a sense of responsibility to love others well, despite who's watching.

The sneaky ways of pride try to pervert our identity. Instead of doing good deeds simply because they're extensions of love, pride wants attention. It's not a sin to become great. It's sin when we do it with the wrong motives. What if no one ever saw the good we do? What if social media was swallowed up and our actions were only seen by the Lord? Let's live our lives embracing our identity as children of the King and live to please Him more than anyone else. Let's live for an audience of One.

Jesus, when no one else is watching, help me to remember that you alone see it all. Examine my heart and refine me with your holy fire so that my motives will be pure. Let my life be fully pleasing to you—a reflection of my love for you that's seen in all that I do and heard in all that I say.

Generosity

"But when you demonstrate generosity,
do it with pure motives and without drawing attention
to yourself. Give secretly and your Father,
who sees all you do, will reward you openly."

Matthew 6:3–4

Jesus is incessantly generous. He made it very clear that holy love gives without limitation. The cross was extravagant and costly—a gift so perfect and so pure in motive that it continues in its ability to set the entire world free. This is the generosity of Christ—all that we have and ever will have has come from Him.

Jesus' generosity gives us security. We understand how much we're loved, because He's proven it by His actions. He set a precedent for us to follow. Love isn't about getting; it's about giving. And giving. And giving—with no strings attached and for no other reason other than it's His nature. Therefore, as His children, it's our nature as well. Let's find ways to demonstrate radical generosity every day.

Jesus, your generosity raises the bar. You gave your life for the ones who despised you. What an example of unselfishness and humility. Help me to love like you—expecting nothing in return. Show me how to sow generously into the lives of those around me by paying attention to the needs I can meet. Freely have I received, and freely I will give.

103

Free to Be Yourself

"But whenever you pray, go into your innermost chamber
and be alone with Father God, praying to him in secret."

Matthew 6:6

There's nothing more beautiful than sharing the depths of your heart with the Lord and discovering His. That's what prayer is—a conversation that's more profound than words. There's no secret formula. No right or wrong way to pray. Even when you're dealing with heavy burdens and doubts and even if you're mad at God, He's there, waiting to walk you through it.

When you pray to Him in secret, you're tapping into a place of awareness that far surpasses human words. This "innermost chamber" is also a metaphor for praying from your innermost being—the storehouse where every deep emotion, desire, fear, and motive exists. The way you pray isn't as important as the condition of your heart. Take time today to talk through the things that are affecting you and expect His love, wisdom, and guidance in return.

Jesus, thank you for loving me regardless of how I feel or what I'm going through. Ignite my passion to know you more and to experience you more profoundly. Thank you for loving me just as I am. Help me to tap into the depths of your presence, where I'm free to be myself.

Our Father

> "Pray like this: 'Our Father, dwelling in the heavenly
> realms, may the glory of your name be the center
> on which our lives turn.'"
>
> *Matthew 6:9*

It's truly astounding to think that Jesus Himself taught us how to pray. In doing so, He didn't start with a list of ways to properly address God. He didn't tell us to fall on our knees, beat our chests, or even bow our heads. His number one priority was to direct our attention to God as our Father. To know Him as Jesus knew Him—filled with glory yet personal and loving, a strong foundation to build our lives on.

God's a perfect Father. If you had a poor example of a father, your heavenly Father wants to fill that void and give you a new perspective. Though His presence fills the heavenly realms, He longs to hold you close. He's beckoning you to know Him as both a glorious King and a loving Father.

✢

Jesus, thank you for introducing me to God as my Father. Heal any areas in my heart that have been wounded by improper father figures and fill me with excitement and trust. I embrace my role as a child of God and run into my Father's presence with open arms. Father, your love has become my foundation.

A Lifestyle of Communion

After this, Jesus went up into the high hills
to spend the whole night in prayer to God.

Luke 6:12

*G*od will never love us more than He does right now. We don't pray because we're trying to earn His approval. We spend time with the Father because nothing else satisfies the longing of our heart. We're drawn to this love. It's what we live for.

Jesus prioritized time with the Father. If it was important for Him, it must be important for us to do the same. We can live a lifestyle of communion with the Lord, but there's something beautiful, honoring, and powerful about setting time aside for nothing else besides seeking His face. This is the place where we lay aside every distraction and humble ourselves before our Maker. We settle our minds, listen for His voice, and experience the atmosphere of heaven that awakens our heart.

Jesus, thank you for teaching me the importance of prayer. Help me to be faithful and to set aside time to be with you. And when I come into your presence, settle my heart and mind so nothing will steal our time. You are my priority and from now on it will be seen in how I spend my time.

You've Been Chosen

At daybreak he called together all of his followers
and selected twelve from among them,
and he appointed them to be his apostles.

Luke 6:13

When Jesus chose His apostles, He didn't choose from the religious leaders of His day. He chose the least qualified and most unlikely candidates. Each had different personalities and came from diverse backgrounds. These would be the first of many who would be sent into the world to represent Him.

Jesus only did what He saw the Father do. In like fashion, the apostles learned what to do by watching what Jesus did. It was their relationship with Him, not their formal religious training, that qualified them. The people Jesus chooses today don't all look, act, or sound alike. We look in the mirror and know that our only qualification is Jesus within us, and that is enough.

Jesus, thank you for calling me to represent you, just as you chose your apostles many years ago. Teach me in the holy place of your presence as I seek your face and study your Word. Without you I'm nothing, but with you I have all that I need to see the world around me transformed.

Fasting

"When you fast, don't let it be obvious, but instead,
wash your face and groom yourself and realize that
your Father in the secret place is the one who
is watching all that you do in secret."

Matthew 6:17–18

Whether you're a seasoned faster or a newbie, it's easy to understand why fasting isn't at the top of our fun list. While the benefits of fasting are God-ordained, abstaining from something we enjoy isn't always easy. That's why it's important to fast with a heart set upon the Lord—we need His grace to get us through.

Fasting has a way of sensitizing us to the Lord. We say no to food or distractions in order to press more fully into His presence. We don't fast to earn His love or approval—we already have it. Instead, with longing to know Him in ways we've yet to discover, we slow down, turn away from commotion, and fasten our hearts to His. Fasting helps us become aware of His Spirit within and enriches our communication in ways far deeper than words.

✣

Jesus, I want to hear you more clearly. As I set myself to fasting and prayer, tune me into the frequency of your love. Within me are endless possibilities, which I discover when my heart is flowing in unison with yours. Thank you for the way fasting clears away the obscurities that cloud my vision.

You Are Filled with Glory

The entire crowd eagerly tried to come near Jesus
so they could touch him and be healed, because a
tangible supernatural power emanated from him,
healing all who came close to him.

Luke 6:19

It's not surprising to read that tangible power emanated from Jesus. The glory within Him illuminated the external darkness around Him. Physical sickness, spiritual disarray, and mental disorder—healed just by being near Him. Though He was fully man, Jesus knew His mandate and lived in a way that facilitated it.

The job of representing God to the world in all of His goodness, faithfulness, glory, and power has been passed down to us. In order to do that, we must know who we are. We must live in a way that guards the glory within. The same Spirit that raised Jesus from the dead lives in us, and the more we pay attention to that, the more we'll partner with it. Let's live in purity and wholehearted devotion so that we too will radiate with tangible, supernatural healing power.

✦

Jesus, I want to be everything you've called me to be. Help me to honor you by being the perfect partner you've called me to be. Let the anointing, glory, and power of your Spirit within me spill forth everywhere I go. Like you, I have a glorious destiny to live a life that reveals the Father's love.

Blessed

"Don't keep hoarding for yourselves earthly treasures
that can be stolen by thieves. Instead, stockpile heavenly
treasures for yourselves that cannot be stolen and will
never rust, decay, or lose their value."

Matthew 6:19–20

God wants us blessed in every area of our lives and that includes finances and the fulfillment of dreams. If it's important to us, it's important to Him. He imparts wisdom and creativity in order to propel us in the direction of our desires. However, earthly desires must never take the place of our relationship with Jesus, a heavenly focal point, or our integrity.

When a drive toward financial reward or self-indulgence becomes our prime focus, it leaves little room for humility and submission to Jesus. We'll find ourselves compromising holiness and relationship if desire for *things* takes priority over knowing Him. Setting goals and chasing our dreams is good, as long as it flows with the leading of His Spirit. But setting our hearts on Jesus and submitting each desire to Him is the surest way to a blessed life.

Jesus, thank you for caring about my finances and dreams. Give me wisdom and ideas for financial abundance but help me to keep my heart pliable in your hands. I commit my dreams to you and trust you to lead me. In all of my seeking, help me to always keep you first.

The True Treasure

"For your heart will always pursue what you value
as your treasure."

Matthew 6:21

His love is like a treasure overflowing with precious gems—each radiant, glorious, and alive. Nothing else satisfies like the abundance of His love. One blissful encounter with Him and we're ruined for anything less.

As we set out on this pilgrimage of discovery into His heart, we quickly find ourselves captivated. What once held our attention and anchored us to the trivial pursuits of men has become insignificant and meaningless. Our lives have become a habitation of His glory, and everything about us—the way we think, speak, and dream—is led by this new mind-set. We're driven by a passion so pure, it can only be prompted by Love Himself. He alone is the treasure we seek.

Jesus, everything you say to me is like discovering the jewels of a hidden, sacred treasure. I'm completely undone—nothing else will ever satisfy. Uncovering your cherished truths has become my lifelong obsession. All the riches and wealth in the world cannot compare to the glory of knowing you.

The Greatest Gift

Jesus replied, "Let me make this very clear, you came
looking for me because I fed you by a miracle, not
because you believe in me. I, the Son of Man, am ready
to give you what matters most, for God the Father has
destined me for this purpose."

John 6:26–27

The Lord wants us to come to Him with the desires of our hearts. He expects and encourages us to ask for what we want, because He loves us. Unfortunately, when we enter His presence only for what we can get, or to pour out complaints disguised as prayer, we've put ourselves before Him. Selfishness infiltrates devotion when prayer becomes an all-request hour instead of a time for sacred communion.

Jesus enjoys our company. His unselfish love is constantly giving. Loving. Tenderly reaching. In His presence is the answer to every prayer, the wisdom for every dilemma, and the joy that eradicates suffering. But when we constantly run to Him seeking things, we've forsaken the wonder of who He is—life's greatest gift. Let's be watchful over our own hearts and love Him simply because He's worthy.

Jesus, you are the delight of my life. I lay my cares at your feet and set my heart upon you. I want to be fully yours. For every part of my life to reflect this holy passion that burns within me. To know you and enjoy you, because you are the greatest gift.

Live Higher

"When someone curses you, bless that person in return.
When you are mistreated and harassed by others,
accept it as your mission to pray for them."

Luke 6:28

There's something freeing, ethereal, and totally contradictory to the ways of the world when we walk in forgiveness. When someone comes against us and we're able to step away from the pain and straight into the presence of Jesus where we receive grace to forgive, it's powerful!

The enemy wants to turn offense into hatred and bitterness so that our souls become crippled. But what if we viewed these attacks as opportunities to discover those who need prayer? Instead of taking it personally, we go to the Lord and ask Him to reveal their heart. Instead of focusing on ourselves and our hurt, we can turn it around. It's an incredible opportunity to take a bad situation and bring the presence of the Lord in the middle of it. We live in victory when we take what was meant to offend and cause division and use it as fuel for prayer!

Jesus, I want to live higher, above reproach. I want to see people the way you see them. When people lie, mistreat, and accuse me wrongly, lift me up, above offense, pain, and rejection. Give me your heart of mercy.

Grace

> "However you wish to be treated by others
> is how you should treat everyone else."
>
> *Luke 6:31*

Too often we unconsciously decide who deserves our tolerance and who doesn't based on how we feel about them. Let's be honest. We've all had people in our lives who unnerve us. We make split-second decisions about who they are and what they're like without getting to know them. We give grace to those who make us feel good but forget that God makes everyone in *His* image. That revelation alone should be a wake-up call for how we treat others.

We aren't called to highlight the areas that look nothing like Jesus. We're called to cheer others on, even in the midst of their greatest weakness. We've all behaved in ways that we're not proud of. Grateful for the grace Jesus gives in return. Volatile situations are often diffused by people who realize the power of kindness and understanding. Grace is life-changing, and we need to give more of it.

Jesus, thank you for the grace you show me, even on my worst days. When I'm going through a crisis of the soul, you don't cast judgment and push me away. Instead, you reach for me and draw me closer. Help me to show this same grace to others and be an imitator of your grace.

Faith Changes Everything

"So, which one of you by worrying
could add anything to your life?"

Matthew 6:27

It's almost funny how much time we spend worrying, thinking our mental gymnastics will change things, even though we know it never does. As if worrying gives us a smidgen of control. Of course, it doesn't. Jesus isn't looking for you to control the situation; He's inviting you to release it into His hands and trust Him.

Worry is fear. It causes panic, anxiety, and irrational thinking, but that's about all it can do. True Christian faith is established on this one foundation: being absolutely convinced of His love. Once that's been settled in our hearts, it's time to make a decision. Either we believe that He's a miracle-working God or we don't. There's no middle ground. Not only is He more than able to take care of us, He absolutely loves to. That's the truth that will settle our hearts in any circumstance if we truly believe it.

Jesus, forgive me for not trusting you and for taking the cares of life upon my shoulders, as if it's my responsibility to fix it all. As if I'm strong enough to carry what you've already lifted. Help me to let go of the things I cannot change and to simply exist in this moment with you.

Satisfied

"How filled you become when you are consumed with
hunger and desire, for you will be completely satisfied."

Luke 6:21

Within all of us is a yearning desire—a deep hunger to
know the One who is the Bread of Life. Once we
feast upon the substance of His love, nothing else will ever
satisfy. We become addicted to His love, drawn repeatedly
into the arms of Love Himself. Our lives are a perpetual mystery—filled with glory that's almost too much to bear, yet we
long for more.

Right now, the Father, Son, and Holy Spirit are with
you. You don't have to attend a special meeting in order to
encounter His love. You only need to stop long enough to
recognize His presence with you and in you. If you've never
experienced what it's like to encounter Him, or it's been a
while since you've felt His touch, let's pray together now.

*Jesus, I'm not satisfied with the memory of yesterday's encounter. I'm hungry for your presence, right now. Come with your
unmistakable glory and capture my heart fully. I want to experience the reality of your presence in ways I didn't know were
possible. Flood my dry ground with the glory of your tangible
love.*

True Riches

"But what sorrows await those of you who are
rich in this life only. For you have already received
all the comfort you'll ever get."

Luke 6:24

Jesus never said it was a sin to be rich. However, He did warn us that life is about much more than money. There's nothing wrong with wealth, but if the drive for money is greater than our willingness to lay it down, we're on a dangerous path.

God wants us to live under an open heaven of blessing. It's His desire that our needs are met in abundance, and He wants us to ask for what we need and want. When we seek the Lord and His ways first, our hearts cannot be tempted by counterfeit pleasures. Prosperity will come when our priorities are in order. We won't be lured by the riches of the world over the riches of the kingdom, because the abundance of His love has made us truly wealthy.

Jesus, let nothing consume my heart more than my desire for you. You know my needs, wants, and dreams. As I lay them before you today and focus on you, I know you'll take care of every one. Bless me with wisdom and wealth. Remind me that the true riches of your kingdom is life with you.

Forgive

> "But if you will listen, I say to you,
> love your enemies and do something wonderful
> for them in return for their hatred."
>
> *Luke 6:27*

If anyone has the right to teach us about loving our enemies, it's Jesus. He gave His life for the very people who crucified Him. One of the hallmark signs of a Christian is our ability to forgive as Jesus does. Letting go of pain and offense can be hard but holding on to it creates far more problems. Bitterness can wreak physical, mental, and spiritual havoc if we don't get rid of it.

Forgiveness starts with being honest with yourself. If there's pain, process it with the Lord and hand it over to Him. Perhaps you've believed a lie that's been magnified over time, making it bigger than it is. In order to heal, you must forgive the offender and release them from owing you anything. Forgiveness is a choice, but it's not magic. The lingering residue may take time to wash off, but it will, as you frequently spend time with the Lord.

Jesus, I forgive _____ (name the person). Show me where I've believed a lie about this situation. Help me understand what I need from you in order to fully release them and receive my healing. Show me how you see him/her and soften my heart.

Centered

"But love your enemies and continue to treat them well.
When you lend money, don't despair if you are never
paid back, for it is not lost. You will receive a rich reward
and you will be known as true children of the
Most High God, having his same nature."

Luke 6:35

Jesus gives the best financial advice. He cares about every aspect of our lives but knows exactly how to keep us centered so that we don't get sidetracked on the superficial things of this world.

Life is about more than tangible things. It's about the heart. Jesus isn't setting us up to be taken advantage of. He's telling us that when we bless someone, and they repay us with evil, not to worry. He's got our back. If our hearts are right and we choose to release the situation into His hands, He'll make sure we're repaid in ways we could never predict. More than money, His concern is that we aim to be like Him in every way. When we do this, especially in situations that cause us to humbly take a step back in order to embrace His nature, we're setting ourselves up for blessings that have no earthly comparison.

Jesus, I want to be known as a child of God. A lover. A person of integrity and honor. Someone who emanates compassion, joy, and incredible trust in you. To look and act like you is an honor far more valuable than money.

Loving Like Jesus Does

Jesus said, "Forsake the habit of criticizing
and judging others, and then you will not
be criticized and judged in return."

Luke 6:37

Today, let's work on our love-walk. If we're prone to noticing the faults of others, even if we don't vocalize it, we can change that. The Holy Spirit's amazing at seeing the good in people. Even when we mess up, He sees us through eyes of love and calls forth treasure inside. He's more than willing to help us on our journey of compassion and humility.

Let's ask Him to help us see people the way He does, even when they do something unbecoming. Let's look for something positive to say about people, no matter how badly they've behaved. When we hear stories of someone acting unloving or unwise, let's find a new way to respond other than criticizing. When someone's gossiping *to* us, let's imagine what we'd want someone to say if we were the one being gossiped *about*.

Jesus, I want to live a life above reproach. I want to be known as someone who always makes people feel good about themselves. I want to celebrate everyone I meet and see them the way you do. Help me to keep this in mind today and every day; give me grace to treat others the way you do.

The Perfect Gift

"But everyone my Father has given to me, they will come.
And all who come to me, I will embrace
and will never turn them away."

John 6:37

You are the gift God longs to give to His Son. Imagine—all of the beauty in the entire world belongs to Him, and yet He's chosen you over everything else. If only you could understand how desirous you are to the Lord. Nothing in all of creation moves His heart the way you do. Your worth is beyond measure because it's determined by His limitless love.

Sometimes we hear truth but don't allow it time to sink in and become reality. To let these holy truths alter our way of thinking. To invite them to shape the way we see ourselves and see the Lord. When we embrace His view of us and allow it to bypass our minds and penetrate our being, it changes every aspect of our lives.

Beloved, you have been chosen by God as the perfect gift for Jesus.

✠

Jesus, I come before you, humbled that you could possibly long for me more than I long for you. I'm not defined by the world, my past, or my mistakes, I am your bride. I've been beautified by love that flowed from a wooden cross, and I am eternally and entirely yours.

His Forever

"For the longing of my Father is that everyone who
embraces the Son and believes in him will experience
eternal life and I will raise them up in the last day!"

John 6:40

*Y*ou are the longing of the Father. Your life is not an accident. Before you were born, you were loved and known by Him. God loves you. He likes spending time with you and wants to do so for eternity, so He demolished every wall of separation. All you need to do is reach for the One who reaches for you.

What a beautiful Savior He is! Even now, when you're running in circles and forget who you are, He rushes to your side and reminds you. You're His beloved. Worth the price of love. His glory collided with the darkness that held you captive and offered you freedom. Eternity began the moment you said yes. Now you are His forever. He's lifted you from the ashes, and you've risen in the beauty only He could give. In Him you live, move, and have your being.

Jesus, there's a fire burning in my chest as I think about the price you paid to be with me forever. As I rest in your love, I'm reminded that I don't have to wait for heaven to experience your tangible touch. My life is hidden in you—may I never emerge.

Give Him Control

Jesus responded, "Stop your grumbling!"
John 6:43

The great I Am is in the midst of every trial you face. He's with you, tenderly pulling you close, so that He can infuse you with grace and power to overcome. His Word is substance to stand on and strength to sustain you. As you focus on the Lord, He'll faithfully lead you to the other side of conflict and give you victory.

When we lose perspective and turn our attention to the problem, we become discouraged and disillusioned. In the waiting, we complain while trying to figure things out in our own wisdom. Complaining is a symptom of feeling out of control. But control is better left in Jesus' hands, where He exchanges our burdens for victory. All He asks is that we relinquish the right to grumble and moan and release control to Him.

Jesus, forgive me for complaining. When I focus on the problem it never changes. You are the reality I will tuck myself into. Give me the grace to focus on the many things I have to be thankful for. As I worship you and lay every burden at your feet, I know you will faithfully come and set things in order.

Our Prevailing Passion

"So above all, constantly chase after the realm
of God's kingdom and the righteousness that proceeds
from him. Then all these less important things
will be given to you abundantly."

Matthew 6:33

You were not created for stress to dictate your thoughts. You were created for life in the kingdom of God—a life of divine perspective, where you see every situation from Jesus' viewpoint. When you live in the awareness of the Lord's presence, He'll draw you so close that the cares of this world no longer hold your attention.

Stress and anxiety are not your portion. That doesn't mean you won't face difficult or stressful situations. It does mean that in the chaos, you find God's presence and invite Him to walk you through the turmoil. Release every care into His hands every day. Though you need a breakthrough, don't allow it to become your ultimate goal. Jesus Himself must always remain your top priority. Seek Him first. Set all of your affection on Him without conditions. Keep the main thing the main thing.

Jesus, I'm running after you with all of my heart. Take every thought that's pulling my mind away from you and fill it with yourself. I want to know you and live with unveiled vision and deeper revelation. I believe breakthrough is my portion, but knowing you is my prevailing passion.

Today Is a Worry-Free Day

"Refuse to worry about tomorrow, but deal with each
challenge that comes your way, one day at a time.
Tomorrow will take care of itself."

Matthew 6:34

Take a deep breath. Right here, in this moment, Jesus is
with you. Release the past and let go of tomorrow's concerns. Today, at this very instant, He wants to bless you with
peace that surpasses understanding. He desires to answer
your prayers, but He first wants your undivided heart. It's in
His presence that we find fullness of joy.

Give yourself permission to get through today without
worrying. Turn your cellphone off, play your favorite worship
songs, and take time to be alone with Jesus. If you find that
problems, people, or situations keep popping up in your
mind, quickly hand them over to the Lord. For example, if
it's finances, simply say, "Jesus, I trust you with my finances."
Don't allow worry to send you into an hour-long cry of desperation. Our greatest prayers are the ones where childlike
faith takes over and frees us from anxiety. Faith makes today
a worry-free day!

✤

*Jesus, I choose to be happy, despite my concerns. I don't have
to fix everything or know exactly what tomorrow holds because
you are the Lord of my days. I place every care in your hands
and leave them with you. I declare today my worry-free day.*

Hungry?

Jesus said to them, "I am the Bread of Life.
Come every day to me and you will never be hungry.
Believe in me and you will never be thirsty."

John 6:35

Jesus offers true nutrition for spirit and soul. When we get bored and lose sight of Him, we experience cravings that can only be satisfied by His presence. Instead, we often reach for junk—a quick fix to appease our appetites. We easily waste time on social media or staring at our smartphones, none of which can truly nourish our souls. We're left feeling empty—searching for our identity, wondering why we don't hear God, and longing for something more.

God created us with a deep hunger for the Bread of Life—the encounters with Jesus that leave us undone and utterly astounded. When we turn our full attention to Him, we feel His nearness. When we put down our cellphones and quiet our souls, we hear His loving voice. Suddenly, nothing else matters—we experience the deepest, most satisfying "meal" of our lives.

✧

Jesus, forgive me for feasting on things that can't possibly satisfy this yearning in my soul. I want to experience the fullness of your love and the reality of your presence. As I yield my day to you, come and meet with me. I hunger for you. You truly are the Bread of Life.

What Are You Feasting On?

"For the overflow of what has been stored
in your heart will be seen by your fruit
and will be heard in your words."

Luke 6:45

One of the easiest ways to know what's going on inside your heart is by listening to what's coming from your mouth. You don't always need Jesus to tell you what areas you need to work on; you can discover that on your own if you'll pay attention to your conversations, prayers, and reactions.

The more we know the Lord, the more we want to feast on His presence. Holy encounters flow through our thoughts, words, and actions, releasing life-giving substance. It's simple to recognize when we're dry—we react in the flesh instead of responding with kindness, hope, and faith. There's no shame when we notice junk flowing out. It's a blessing to use our words as a measuring stick, by which we can judge the health of our spirit and soul. Instead of feeling guilty, we simply repent, refocus, and ask the Lord to restore our sense of direction.

Jesus, let rivers of living water flow from deep within me as I feast upon your love. When I get distracted, draw me by your grace. Instead of indulging in television, the internet, or other mundane things, I will nourish myself with more of you. You are the object of my desire.

They're Watching

Every time Herod heard John speak,
it disturbed his soul, but he was drawn to him
and enjoyed listening to his words.

Mark 6:20

When the anointing and glory of God flows through you, it causes people to notice you. They may not know why they feel comfortable opening up to you, a total stranger, or why they feel safe sitting near you, but they do. Even those who aren't sure about you are probably intrigued by the peace and joy you carry. They may never tell you—but they're watching.

Our lives are living examples of God's tender yet powerful love. When we pay attention to the people around us, we'll find copious opportunities to present the reality of Jesus. People are drawn to the answer that we carry, so we mustn't hide our light. As we listen to His Spirit, He will reveal exactly what and what not to say. Speak truth, expressed with love and never judgment.

Jesus, I want to present your tender mercy and powerful touch to the world around me. I want to listen with a heart of compassion and seek your desire for everyone I meet. Help me resist criticizing others, because only you truly know their heart and the things they've gone through. Let your Spirit flow through me to others.

May

To Know

"If you are really listening to the Father and learning
directly from him, you will come to me."
John 6:45

*S*tudying the Word, listening to anointed teaching, and reading eloquently penned depictions of the Lord mean very little, unless you discover Him for yourself. The voice of His Spirit speaks in many ways. It can be heard in the least likely places, such as movies and television shows. But hearing Him isn't enough.

In order to truly enjoy the life you've been designed to have, you must come close to the One who speaks. Let the voice that stirs your heart draw you to know Him for yourself. You don't have to listen from afar. You can run into the arms of your Savior right now. Encounter the One you hear about, read about, and sing about. Never be satisfied with anything less than Love Himself.

Jesus, your presence satisfies my deepest yearnings. To know you and to experience your love are my eternal quest. To offer myself to you unreservedly and without question is my greatest honor. Let my life overflow with your glory. Let my love bless you in return.

Obedience Paves the Way

"How many loaves of bread do you have?" he asked.
"Go and see." After they had looked around, they came
back and said, "Five—plus a couple of fish."

Mark 6:38

Jesus told His disciples to feed a crowd of thousands. They responded with a breakdown of exactly what they had in the natural: five loaves of bread and a couple of fish. Unalarmed by the scant menu, Jesus' instructions continued. He would feed the multitude. They did what He asked, and, in the end, there was more than enough. The will of God wasn't affected by lack.

Jesus loves to turn inadequacy into abundance. He often asks us to do things that we don't have provisions for. Our obedience and willingness paves the way for miracles. Being aware of our insufficiency, but choosing to obey with radical faith, becomes a magnet for miracles. When Jesus asks us to do something and then asks what we have to complete the task, it isn't to deter us. He does this so that when He comes through, we'll know exactly who deserves the glory.

Jesus, you are the all-sufficient One. I can do what you ask me to do, even when I can't see the way, because you wouldn't ask me to do something that was impossible. These radical lessons of faith have the power to change the world. All things are possible with you!

Trusted Love

> "If you, imperfect as you are, know how to lovingly
> take care of your children and give them what's best,
> how much more ready is your heavenly Father to give
> wonderful gifts to those who ask him?"
>
> *Matthew 7:11*

God is an amazing Father! He loves to bless us with the best gifts. He enjoys surprising us. Often, those surprises come by the way He answers our prayers. His ways are higher than ours, and the longer we walk with Him, the more we know how true that is. His wisdom and compassion are seen in all He does—in every answer, every choice He offers, and the paths He sets before us.

Seasons of waiting don't have to be trying. When we're thoroughly convinced of His love, we surrender doubt and frustration because His love is easily trusted. When we know He wants to give us the desires of our hearts, fear no longer plagues us. Faith's foundation is built upon love. When His affection is our focal point, it anchors us and keeps us stable. His love makes it easy to believe.

Jesus, your love for me is the best gift. It helps me put things in the right perspective, especially when I'm waiting for answers that are slow in coming. Though I cry out for one thing, I trust you to give me what I truly need. I lift my prayer to you and leave it in your hands.

Compassionate

When the Lord saw the grieving mother, his heart
broke for her. With great tenderness he said to her,
"Please don't cry." Then he stepped up to the coffin and
touched it. When the pallbearers came to a halt, Jesus said
to the corpse, "Young man, I say to you, arise and live!"

Luke 7:13–14

What a compassionate Savior He is. When you go through difficult times and feel as if no one understands, Jesus does. You're not alone. He's right there with you, moved with the same compassion that moved Him to raise this widow's son. He's drawn to you in your time of need, reaching out and drawing you close.

The next time you're sad and need comfort, let Him wrap His arms around you. Fully release yourself into the embrace of perfect love. Feel Him imparting strength as His tender voice streams into the depths of your being. Rest as He releases life and hope into every dark crevice. Give Him your gloomines, and in exchange, He'll fill you with joy in ways no one on earth can.

Jesus, saturate me with your love when my heart is overwhelmed with sorrow. Comfort me as I lean into your arms. Thank you for sticking close to me in my time of need and reminding me that you care. Together we can get through anything.

Superficial

"Stop judging based on the superficial. First you must
embrace the standards of mercy and truth."

John 7:24

Jesus isn't only merciful, He's merciful in a way that con-
founds the legalistic mind-set. He's not concerned about
the rules. He's focused on the heart. As a matter of fact,
when Jesus walked the earth He broke quite a lot of religious
rules. The people of His day had an image in their minds of
what the Messiah would look like and how He would act.
Because Jesus didn't fit that image, they judged Him.

Today, many of us still get hung up on appearances.
We judge people based on how they look, what they wear,
which denomination they belong to, or how they voted in
the last election. If it doesn't *seem* right to us, we decide
it must be wrong—and if it's wrong, we withhold love. We
think we're discerning, when really, we're only revealing our
lack of mercy and compassion. The world doesn't want us to
highlight their problems. It needs an example of the answer.
It needs us to demonstrate unbiased love.

*Jesus, forgive me for judging people when I don't really know
them. Enable me to see beyond appearances and straight to
the heart. Help me to get past my own inhibitions and show
them the same love and acceptance you've shown me.*

The Power of Gratitude

Then Jesus took the five loaves and two fish,
gazed into heaven, and gave thanks to God.
He broke the bread and the two fish and distributed
them to his disciples to serve the people—*and the food
was multiplied in front of their eyes!*

Mark 6:41

What an amazing example of the miraculous power of thanksgiving! With thousands of hungry people and only enough food to feed a handful, it would've been easy to send the multitudes away to get food somewhere else. But Jesus didn't focus on what He didn't have. Instead He praised God for what He did have. He blessed what wasn't enough as if it was. His thanksgiving created a miracle of provision.

Jesus knew lack was not God's will. This story is a beautiful example of the power of thanksgiving and the heart of God. When we're faced with lack, the One who has everything we need offers us an opportunity to see a miracle. When we stop looking at what we don't have and praise Him for what we do have, things change! A heart filled with gratefulness creates an atmosphere for the miraculous.

✦

Jesus, forgive me for focusing on what I don't have. It isn't your desire that I'd allow negativity to drag me into the pit of despair. I'm blessed in so many ways. Thank you for teaching me the power of thanksgiving. Help me to become a grateful person and to live with a grateful heart.

Effortless Surrender

Broken and weeping, she covered his feet with the tears
that fell from her face. She kept crying and drying his feet
with her long hair. Over and over she kissed Jesus' feet.
Then she opened her flask and anointed his feet with
her costly perfume as an act of worship.

Luke 7:38

Close your eyes and still your soul. Take a few moments
and turn your attention to the One who paid the greatest price to be with you for eternity. Jesus is with you, right
now. Allow yourself to release every care as His arms draw
you closer in holy embrace. As the reality of His presence
floods your being, lean into it. His love has no comparison.

This is the place of deep devotion. When we still our souls
and focus on the beauty of His unending, holy love, it's easy
to become overwhelmed with thankfulness. Like Mary, gratitude overwhelms our hearts, and we recognize that our lives
are not our own. When we know how much He loves us, we
effortlessly surrender all we are. We move from moments of
worship to a lifestyle of adoration—shattering everything that
would prevent us from being fully His.

Jesus, it's my honor to pour my life out at your feet. The mes-
sage of the cross has become my saving grace and powerful
foundation. Nothing matters more than being a true worship-
per who holds nothing back from following you. With tears of
surrender, I declare, "I am yours!"

He Knows You

When Simon saw what was happening,
he thought, "This man can't be a true prophet.
If he were really a prophet, he would know what kind
of sinful woman is touching him."

Luke 7:39

*Y*ou are not characterized by your past. Jesus has defined you. You are all that He says you are: unashamed, unafraid, powerful, and radiant. You are filled with His glory and created in His image. When Jesus looks at you, He sees a masterpiece. No one knows you better than He does.

Religion loves to focus on our shortcomings, but Jesus sees us through the eyes of love. He understands the transforming power of the cross better than anyone. This is the sacrifice that has determined our value. His victory made us beautiful. When we see ourselves the way He does, inhibitions fall away. Fully confident in His opinion of us, we worship extravagantly. Others may judge or criticize, but our focus is on Him alone. As we gaze upon His face, we cannot help but return His love.

Jesus, your love has transformed me. I'm powerful and pure—cleansed by your holy blood. As I kneel before you, glistening in the glow of your glory, I have total confidence in your love. It shapes me, defines me. I am who you say I am. May my worship move your heart the way your presence stirs mine.

Words of Hope

"How could you say to your friend, 'Let me show you
where you're wrong,' when you're guilty of even more?
You're being hypercritical and a hypocrite!"

Matthew 7:4–5

*H*ave you noticed that Jesus' correction always highlights our potential and stirs us to become the best
version of ourselves? Even in our biggest failures, He tenderly draws us into repentance and washes us clean. Jesus
never places a weight of shame on our shoulders. Instead He
places a crown of royalty upon our heads.

Love always wins over judgment. Like Jesus, let's cultivate an atmosphere of honor, mercy, and love. We've been
called to inspire and encourage, not judge or criticize—this is
what sets us apart. When we speak words of life, hope, and
compassion, we're building others up, just as Jesus does. The
overflow of our relationship with Him creates a desire to see
others walk in their identity. It stirs us to live with unrestrained
mercy, loving others the way He loves us.

*Jesus, teach me to love without restriction; to cultivate the gift
of mercy in my life and see others through your eyes. I want
my words to flow with encouragement and healing. When I'm
tempted to judge or criticize, help me to remember the extravagant mercy you've shown me.*

Tenacious Faith

"Ask, and the gift is yours. Seek, and you'll discover.
Knock, and the door will be opened for you. For every
persistent one will get what he asks for. Every persistent
seeker will discover what he longs for. And everyone who
knocks persistently will one day find an open door."

Matthew 7:7–8

Jesus is so encouraging! He never squashes our dreams
or discourages the desires of our hearts. He's optimistic about everything that concerns us. I absolutely love the
above verses. It not only reveals His heart, as He cheers us
on, but it gives us permission to have radical faith—the kind
that keeps going and never stops.

We come up against many barriers in life. Delay turns to
discouragement and we give up the dreams that once fueled
our souls. But Jesus never tells us to give up. He never tells
us we're too old, too poor, too dumb, or too unqualified.
He wants us to use those obstacles to build our muscles as
we push through them. What's stirring in your heart today?
If God hasn't given you a clear no, go for your dreams and
never give up!

*Jesus, I accept your invitation to courageously go after all that's
in my heart. I shake off discouragement and come boldly into
your presence where I'll find wisdom, favor, and skill. My eyes
are on you, and I trust your timing. I'll be faithful with all you've
placed in my hands.*

Making Room for Peace

There was such a swirl of activity around Jesus,
with so many people coming and going, that they were
unable to even eat a meal. So Jesus said to his disciples,
"Come, let's take a break and find a secluded
place where you can rest a while."

Mark 6:31

We all go through seasons of busyness. Being busy isn't a sin, but if your to-do list doesn't include time to relax, it's time to give it a Holy Ghost makeover. If Jesus thinks rest is important, then we should too.

Peace is a gift that we must make room for. In order to experience it, peace must not only be accepted, it must be protected. Though we can find His peace in the middle of chaos, it's also important to purposefully step away from the chaos and make time for rest every day. Rest helps put things in perspective. It invites peace, allows us to hear Jesus' voice easier, and connects us to His presence. When we learn to live a lifestyle of rest, anxiety is less prevalent. Though it may seem contrary to productivity, incorporating down-time into our daily lives actually causes us to work more effectively.

Jesus, teach me how to balance busyness and rest. Help me to live with an attitude of peace in order to hear you and experience you more clearly. I yield every pressing need that lies and says it's more important than time with you. Give me grace to make time for rest every day.

The Power of the Word

"Everyone who hears my teaching and applies
it to his life can be compared to a wise man who built
his house on an unshakable foundation."

Matthew 7:24

The Word of God has the power to transform our lives. It illuminates a path, which leads us into a future that's bright and exciting. It lays a foundation for us to stand on when the storms of life make us feel unbalanced and unsure. It has the strength to defeat the hordes of hell and the tenderness to heal every trauma.

When we meditate on the Word and spend time soaking in its truth, it rewires the way we think. It's alive—filling us with hope and drawing us into the depths of God's love. It's easy to recognize the lies that the enemy throws at us when we're living in the certainty of His Word. Never underestimate the importance of studying the Bible, regardless of the number of years you've read it. Its truth is eternal, and its depths are filled with treasures few dare to plunge.

Jesus, let your words and my being become entwined. Fill me with love for your truth. Let it blossom within me and become the fragrance that flows from my lips. Help me to embrace your Spirit and your truth equally. Lead me by your wisdom as I set my mind on you.

Solitude

So he dispersed the crowd, said good-bye to his disciples
then slipped away to pray on the mountain.

Mark 6:46

After Jesus did his first major public miracle, He went alone to pray. He'd just fed many thousands of people, and His public ministry was about to explode. Instead of sitting with His disciples and coming up with a strategy for managing His fame, He prepared His heart in the presence of the Father.

When success unfolds in our lives and busyness clamors for our undivided attention, time alone with the Father mustn't be neglected. These times of devotion and surrender equip us to go forth with wisdom and discernment. The anointing, strength, and grace we need to walk in our destiny is imparted in the secret place of prayer. When things are going good and you're busy, pouring your life out to others, don't forget to fill yourself back up in the presence of the Lord.

Jesus, you've taught me the importance of seeking your face in both times of difficulty and seasons of blessing. No matter how busy life gets, help me to never neglect my time alone with you. You are the strength of my life and the One I rely on to lead me each day.

Remember

> "She has been forgiven of all her many sins.
> This is why she has shown me such extravagant love.
> But those who assume they have very little to be
> forgiven will love me very little."
>
> *Luke 7:47*

The moment we bow in humility and surrender our lives to the Lord, everything changes. All of heaven rejoices and Jesus comes running to kiss our hearts with forgiveness. The gift of eternal life ushers us immediately into the family of God. Sin is stripped away and replaced with a garment of righteousness.

The Prince of heaven laid it all on the line for us, and it's important to remember what He's saved us from. It's the continual awareness of our great need for Him that leaves us undone, humbled, bowed low before His throne. At the same time, we stand as His children—confident and secure in His love. There is nothing cautious about the way He loves us. May we never take His love and forgiveness for granted.

Jesus, thank you for saving me and wiping away every trace of my sin. Your mercy astounds me. Your forgiveness knows no bounds. I bow before you in wonder, knowing I'm nothing without you. With all of my heart, I pray there will never be any part of me that isn't entirely yours.

Compassionate Jesus

Then he came closer and climbed into the boat with
them, and immediately the stormy wind became still.

Mark 6:51

All of us have been through trials that left us feeling like we've been stripped bare. At times our prayers are nothing more than weak whispers of, "I love you." Jesus doesn't reject us when the storms of life leave us exhausted. He doesn't shake His head in disappointment when our eyes of faith won't focus. Instead, with matchless compassion, He climbs into the boat to be with us.

When you're in the midst of the storm and can scarcely turn your heart to the Lord, but do so anyway, He sees. With tenderness He rushes to your side, wraps Himself around you, and becomes your strength. He creates hope out of hopelessness and stills the storm. With patience He breathes faith into your heart until you can see clearly once again. His love lifts you above the storm in a hurricane of grace. Victory becomes your song.

Jesus, all I can do is sit and wait for you in total dependence. I feel you here, breathing hope and igniting faith. I will not yield to despair. Instead, as you hold me in your arms, this storm will become a foundation for us to dance upon. With every breath, I will praise you.

Living Words

By the time Jesus finished speaking,
the crowds were dazed and overwhelmed by his
teaching, because his words carried such great authority,
quite unlike their religious scholars.

Matthew 7:28

Eloquent words backed by theological degrees are nothing without the anointing. But with the breath and glory of Jesus, even the simplest sentence carries the power to transform life. To truly wow the masses, we need less of us and more of Him. Jesus' words are spirit and life.

It's important that we don't rely on our wisdom, charisma, or persuasiveness when sharing the good news. Whether speaking to one person or from a pulpit, it's when we rely fully upon the Holy Spirit to turn words into substance that we witness their power. When Jesus spoke, His words were like thunderbolts to the hearts of those who heard. This is still His desire today—to stream through vessels like you and I, with the glory that streams from His heart.

✥

Jesus, touch my lips and anoint my words, so that they carry your presence. I trust you to give me the right words at the right time—words that emanate hope and glory to all who hear. Let the abundance of your glory swell and overflow through all I say.

Drowning in Love

"All you thirsty ones, come to me! Come to me and drink! Believe in me, so that rivers of living water will burst out from within you; flowing from your innermost being, just like the Scripture says!"

John 7:37–38

Nothing satisfies our thirsty souls like the extravagant love of Jesus. As we dive into His presence, He leads us into greater depths of wonder. His living waters quench our parched souls yet leave us longing for more. It's the mystery of this longing that compels us to draw close.

Never be satisfied with the touch of yesterday's encounter. Spend time with Him every day and mind-sets that are out of sync with His spirit will be brought into alignment. His presence is as vital to your spirit and soul as water is to your body. As it floods every fiber of your being, faith rises. Conversations sound more like Him and thoughts reflect His. Tune into the Holy Spirit within you and let His presence rise until His glory overflows into all you say and do.

Jesus, nothing affects my life as profoundly as your tangible glory. Crash upon me in waves of refreshment and draw me into the depths of your presence. Drown me in your love so every fiber of my being is saturated with you. Flood my soul until I drip with your holy love everywhere I go.

Wholehearted Devotion

Jesus replied, "You are frauds and hypocrites!
How accurately did Isaiah prophesy about you phonies
when he said: 'These people honor me with their
words while their hearts run far away from me!'"

Mark 7:6

Jesus sees it all. There's no escaping His loving gaze. The purpose of His correction is to strip away lies and exchange them for truth. In order to become all we can be, we must remain teachable, humble, and open to growth. We must be willing to face hard truths and then rise above them into glorious victory.

Jesus desires our devotion. It's in this place of surrender that we come face to face with His true nature and unconditional love. He's not moved by empty words that sound right; He wants our hearts. He wants to inhabit every part of us without restriction. Shutting out everything around us, forgetting how we look, sound, or appear, let's worship with sincerity and wholeheartedness. We may impress others with fancy words that sound holy, but He wants our heart.

✣

Jesus, you have my heart without reservation. I want to live every moment in authenticity and unashamed devotion to you. May my words, thoughts, and worship come into agreement and reflect my sincere love and heartfelt gratitude.

Undivided

So the crowd was divided over Jesus.

John 7:43

The world was divided then, and it remains that way today. That's why it's vital to know Jesus for yourself. Studying the Scriptures is important, but it must be accompanied by getting to know the Living Word. The Spirit and the Word work together, revealing truths that become a foundation for you to stand upon. When everything around you shakes and feels unstable, it's your relationship with the Lord, and the way you incorporate His Word, that keep you from falling.

Spend time with Him and allow Him to teach you. You don't need a theological degree to know the power of His love. When others are confused or try to argue, leave the debate behind and offer them an encounter they cannot deny. Pray for them and watch Jesus melt even the hardest of hearts. When you're convinced of His love, it's easy to share.

Jesus, give me an undivided heart that's anchored in you. Breathe upon every mention I make of you, infusing my words with your tangible anointing. Let the abundance of my heart swell and overflow with the evidence of your love.

A Resounding Yes!

Suddenly, a leper walked up to Jesus and threw himself
down before him in worship and said, "Lord, you have
the power to heal me ... if you really want to." Jesus
reached out his hand and touched the leper and said,
"Of course I want to heal you—be healed!"

Matthew 8:2–3

Jesus is not ashamed of us. Regardless how others feel
about us or how we feel about ourselves, He is not put
off by us, even in our worst state. Most of us probably haven't
experienced physical leprosy, but there are times when life
feels like it's tearing us to shreds, leaving us weary and alone.
We fall at His feet, knowing He has the power to heal but
wondering if He truly wants to.

The answer is always a resounding yes! In response to our
cry, He comes. Inside of His embrace is healing for our spirit,
soul, and body. When we feel spiritually dead, He breathes
life into our being. In Him we are alive! We are not untouch-
able, unworthy, and unimportant. Society may cast us aside,
but Jesus draws us close. His love is unlike any other. His love
has the power to heal.

*Jesus, you have not forgotten me. When I feel beaten down by
situations I can't control, you become my strength and hope.
When sickness tries to steal my health, you heal me. When I
feel like a failure, you celebrate me. When others reject me,
you accept me and call me beautiful.*

149

Fix Your Gaze

Then Jesus said to the woman,
"Your faith in me has given you life. Now you
may leave and walk in the ways of peace."

Luke 7:50

Never underestimate the power of faith. When everything's going wrong and nothing makes sense, we can choose to believe. As we fix our eyes on Jesus and cry out for His point of view, He lifts the veil of darkened illusions and illuminates us with Himself. We don't ignore trials. Instead, we find Jesus in the midst of them. We refuse to allow our emotions to lead us, and we decline the enemy's opinion.

Faith is the anchor that keeps us from drifting into fear. It doesn't mean the storm doesn't cause the boat to rock, but despite the rocking, faith gives us sea legs and keeps us balanced. Breakthrough moments come when we decide to remain aware of God's presence, even when circumstances are screaming for our attention.

Jesus, let my faith in you breathe strength into the places I've become weary. I won't give up. I will not stop believing! I will not dwell on things that contradict the reality of your kingdom. I will keep your face ever before me. You are the truth that leads to breakthrough.

Wonderful Jesus

The people were absolutely beside themselves and
astonished beyond measure. And they began to declare,
"Everything he does is wonderful!"

Mark 7:37

Turn your eyes to the One who encapsulates beauty. Everything He does is wonderful. Creation declares His splendor. Our beings flow in harmony with the Creator who designed us. All that He touches is transformed. Life streams from His presence, making all things new.

Each day we have the opportunity to live in awe and wonder of our omnipotent Lord. It's impossible to become complacent or bored when we look into the face of the One whose eyes are flames of fire. When we remember that imperfect people who harbor imperfect thoughts are the place He's chosen to reside, it's hard to doubt His redeeming love. We were created to behold the One who taught the stars to dance. It's easy to believe that He's a good Father when we keep our eyes on Him and the magnificent things He does.

Jesus, nothing seems impossible when I stare at the proof of your miracle-working power. It's easy to believe when I'm not distracted by the lesser things of this world. May my soul resonate with wonder at the sound of your voice. May fascination tether me to your glory and constantly remind me of your love.

Celebrating Women

His twelve disciples traveled with him and also a number
of women who had been healed of many illnesses under
his ministry and set free from demonic power. ...
Many other women who supported Jesus' ministry from
their own personal finances also traveled with him.

Luke 8:1–3

Jesus came to set the captives free. Bondage and condemnation go against His very nature. Everyone that the Father brought to Jesus was set free. This includes women. Never once do we see them referred to by Him as second-class citizens. The One who created men and women in His image gives everyone the right to flourish in their identity.

Throughout the Gospels we read that Jesus liberated women from the cultural suppression of His day. He taught, protected, and validated them. When leaders pushed them aside, Jesus accepted them. He was never ashamed of women; as a matter of fact, we read in the above Scripture that women were some of His disciples. The army of God and the family of God are one and the same, and Jesus never separates the two based on gender.

Jesus, I praise you for loving and empowering women. May women in the church experience freedom from bondage and step into their calling with no restrictions to limit your anointing. May confidence in your love lift us high above the repression of religious confusion.

Glorious One

Then Jesus said, "I am light to the world and those
who embrace me will experience life-giving light,
and they will never walk in darkness."

John 8:12

Jesus has come to illuminate every dark crevice of our souls. Once we invite Him in, nothing's off limits. His love never withdraws from a willing heart. He's not intimidated by sin, anger, doubts, or pain. Jesus, our radiant hope, will shine His truth into every mind-set that's been tainted and blurred. We never need to live a single moment in darkness.

The Most Glorious One knows how to brighten every day. His presence flows with life. Victory begins with our decision to embrace Him instead of focusing on the darkness trying to drown us. He is the joy that chases away gloomy clouds. Let the light of His love spark hope and faith within you.

Jesus, illuminate my life. Let every dark place radiate with you. Brighten my path, lead me with wisdom, and let every thought and action reflect the glory of your Spirit within me. I want every part of me to experience the truth of who you are.

He's Not Afraid of Your Mess

So Jesus stood up and looked at them and said, "Let's have the man who has never had a sinful desire throw the first stone at her." And then he bent over again and wrote some more words in the dust.

John 8:7–8

Jesus isn't afraid to stoop down in the dirt with us. He's not afraid that we'll contaminate Him with our humanity. He isn't ashamed of our propensity to sin. In fact, it's the reason He came to save us. Humbling Himself and bowing low to meet us in our mess is something He's very good at.

Nothing about us, regardless of what we've done, repels Him. Unfortunately, even though Jesus doesn't focus on our transgressions, we often do. We become critical of ourselves and feel like we've failed when we don't do everything just right. Many have an internal war raging inside, overanalyzing everything that's wrong and cutting themselves no slack. Jesus is much more merciful than we are. He's not only merciful. He's also able to give us the grace we need to overcome every weight of sin.

Jesus, even when I try to do everything right, I still mess up. Save me from myself—from wrong mind-sets and impure motives that disconnect me from you. Embrace me once again. Consume me with your love so that every fiber of my being looks like you. Give me vision to see myself the way you do.

Empowered by Grace

"Dear woman, where are your accusers?
Is there no one here to condemn you?" Looking around,
she replied, "I see no one, Lord." Jesus said,
"Then I certainly don't condemn you either.
Go, and from now on, be free from a life of sin."

John 8:10–11

This is the story of a woman caught in the act of adultery and thrust before a crowd where Jesus was teaching. The Pharisees, wanting to test Him, asked what should be done to her. Would He side with their perception of the law and have her stoned or expose Himself as a fraud, ignorant of God's truth? Instead, Jesus confronted them with the all-encompassing need for mercy.

After the religious leaders walked away, the woman stood face to face with her Savior. Though her sin was exposed, Jesus wrapped her in forgiveness. Mercy freed her from punishment. Grace would enable her to live free from sin.

Jesus always empowers. Points us in the direction of victory and leads by grace. Let's remember this when we're tempted to condemn someone. It's easy to extend mercy when we remember how much we need it ourselves.

Jesus, thank you for your unfailing mercy. You see every sin and unrighteous motivation, and yet you love me as if I've never done anything wrong. Let me see others through the lens of compassion and empower them to run with you.

The Freedom of Love

> For the Pharisees, like all other Jews, will not eat without
> first performing a ritual of pouring water over their
> cupped hands to keep the tradition of the elders.
>
> *Mark 7:3*

I wonder how many things we do based on tradition, religion, or culture that have absolutely no bearing on our relationship with the Lord. I imagine Him watching our fruitless efforts to appear holy and shaking His head. Even if we do everything right, yell the loudest "Amen!", dress like the pilgrims of old, and go to church every Sunday, the *why* behind our *do* is what matters. Do we want a person's approval more than God's? Or do we believe we're earning God's love? If so, we don't understand His heart.

You can't make God love you. Even if you completely ignored Him, He'd love you just the same. It's time to become consumed with this love that has no rules, no pressure, and no condemnation. He loves us—because He does! What we do is simply an outflow of this love-connection. It's time to leave the rules behind and discover the freedom of love.

Jesus, I want everything I do and say to flow from the posture of love. Make your Word come alive and teach me what's right or wrong for me, personally. I want to know and serve you, far more than the religious systems of man. I want to know what pleases you.

MAY 28

Outrageous Mercy

Jesus said, "Then I certainly don't condemn you either.
Go, and from now on, be free from a life of sin."

John 8:11

God's grace always seems to startle the religious. His mercy astounds us all. We don't need to hide from His searching gaze. We never have to fear His correction. This great love sees every sin and chooses us regardless.

What a beautiful example of effective discipline. Jesus acknowledges our sin, but never connects our identity to it. Instead, He points us in the right direction and reminds us who we're called to be. Jesus doesn't distance Himself from us when we sin. He isn't harsh and never belittles us. He wraps us in His everlasting arms, wipes away the past, and offers outrageous freedom and strength. What a perfect example of discipline that actually empowers us to become better.

Jesus, I honor you for your great mercy. I am not defined by my sins and failures. I am a new creation in you! I want to learn from you and extend this same mercy and grace to others. Teach me your ways as we journey through life together.

Unclouded Vision

"Because this revelation lamp now shines within you,
nothing will be hidden from you—it will all be revealed.
Every secret of the kingdom will be unveiled and out in
the open, made known by the revelation-light."

Luke 8:17

One of the most profound revelations is of the love and
mercy of Jesus. He knows us, every hidden aspect of
our hearts, and still loves us without exception. As we grow in
His likeness, we too must embrace this unconditional love for
others. Saturating ourselves in the light of His glory penetrates
our attitudes and viewpoints. Gazing into His countenance
causes our vision to change. Our focus adjusts and suddenly
we see the world the way He does.

When others see sin, we see the potential for righteousness. When confronted with limitations, we get excited about
miraculous possibilities. Sickness stirs us to pray for healing.
The lost appear as sleeping hearts, ready to be awakened.
Those who struggle in their faith are unveiled to us as gar-
dens ready to bloom with beauty. Everything changes when
we see with His eyes.

*Jesus, give me eyes to see the way you do. Teach me how to
interpret every situation so I can pray and act in a way that
invites truth and breakthrough. Anoint my eyes with healing
salve so my vision will be clear. Let me see things as they truly
are. Give me the revelation of your love.*

No Room for Doubt

"For I absolutely know who I am, where I've come from,
and where I'm going."

John 8:14

It isn't prideful to be secure in your identity when it's established in Jesus. It's His will that you soar with confidence in His unconditional love that defines your life. When the world tries to mold you in its image, you simply shrug it off and tuck yourself into His grace. You're a living expression of Jesus on this earth, and you don't need to prove it. It effortlessly flows because you believe.

The One who was, is, and is to come lives inside of you. His life flows through your veins and you're bound to Him with cords of eternal love. You are a vessel of purity and devotion—wholly beautiful to Him. You are powerful, smart, worthy, and anointed. You're everything Jesus says you are, even on your worst day. When Jesus looks into your eyes He sees every detail of your life and calls you perfect.

Jesus, pour out your grace so that I'll never doubt who I am. Your love transforms me, gives me purpose, and fills me with courage. You've made me your holy dwelling place. I am your child—cherished by the God of all creation and chosen before time began.

Discover

"So pay careful attention to your hearts as you hear my teaching, for to those who have open hearts, even more revelation will be given to them until it overflows."

Luke 8:18

Recognizing the Lord's voice as He speaks through anointed teaching, music, or time spent alone with Him is relatively easy. Our hearts, stirred by the tangible presence of God, swell with emotion that cannot be denied. Though we may not intellectually grasp what the Lord's saying, His glory unlocks our soul and infuses us with life. It draws us with indescribable longing to discover truth.

Don't walk away from moments of encounter, when He's addressing certain issues or teaching you something, without allowing yourself time to process with the Lord. Grab a pen and paper, get quiet, and ask Him to expound on what you're sensing. When you desire truth, He's faithful to give it. Wisdom, revelation, correction, and healing flow as we pay attention to His Spirit when He stirs our heart.

Jesus, when I feel your Spirit tugging at my heart, I won't ignore you. Open my understanding and connect me to your revelation truth. I long for you to teach and refine me. Clear away wrong thinking and unite me to the wisdom that will change my life.

June

Together

"Then what I say about who I am is true, for I am not
alone in my testimony—my Father is the other witness,
and we testify together of the truth."

John 8:18

*Y*ou are not alone. Jesus is with you, cheering you on, every step of the way. You don't need anyone to confirm what's in your heart or to validate your desires when you have the agreement of the Father, Son, and Holy Spirit. Trust the truth that abides within you—it testifies of His will for your life.

Never doubt your position in Christ. Together, you will conquer every opposition. Trials will only cause your roots to go deeper when you remember that you and Jesus are a majority. You're a well of testimony—draw from the waters within and let them wash your soul. He is with you, in you, and will never forsake you. Remember your history with God and be bold. Let your faith explode as you run hand in hand with the One who leads you to your destiny.

Jesus, I want my thoughts to agree with your thoughts and my words to only declare what's pure and trustworthy. When lies disturb my faith, point me to your Word and wash me in your truth. May I daily experience the power of walking in unity with you so that together we release heaven on earth.

You Are Righteous

"Evil originates from inside a person.
Coming out of a human heart are evil schemes,
sexual immorality, theft, murder ..."

Mark 7:21

Sin is no longer a part of your nature. Evil desires no longer define you. Established in Jesus' righteousness, He has graced you with a new identity. You're a holy vessel, filled with the Spirit of God. You're dead to sin, and your life is hidden inside the One who calls you beautiful. His love has redeemed you and set you free.

With the power of the Holy Spirit inside of us, we're able to overcome every temptation. When we keep our eyes fixed on who we are, we live free from sin. Righteousness is now a part of our identity, and when we focus on that, it empowers us to live with pure desires. When we do sin, Jesus doesn't condemn or belittle us. Instead He reaches out with nail-scarred hands and draws us close.

Jesus, you have become my righteousness. Every day I am transforming more and more into your glorious image. I am defined by the price of perfect love; holy because your Spirit lives inside me. I dedicate myself to you as I learn to walk in the ways of righteousness.

Courageous

Then Jesus said to them, "Why are you fearful?
Have you lost your faith in me?"

Luke 8:25

Fear is one of the most debilitating forces on earth. It locks us into rehearsing the enemy's plans instead of freeing us to believe God's best. It pressures us into acknowledging the giants blocking our promised land, rather than roaring with faith and rushing in to claim what's ours. We weren't created to suffer under fear's oppressive regime, which is why it feels so dreadful when we do. We were created to believe. To overcome fear and rise in victory, but the decision is ours.

Faith is a choice. It's more than digging our heels in and refusing to give up. It's unmovable and unstoppable because it's sustained by the belief that Jesus loves us and wants what's best for us. Faith is tenacious, taking risks and refusing defeat. It gets up time and time again, running after what's been promised and courageously believing in the face of opposition.

※

Jesus, demolish every fear with your powerful love. Fill me with your perfect love and fear will find no place to settle. I choose to believe and will not relent until I'm all that you created me to be. I am courageous and strong because you're with me.

Unexpected

As soon as Jesus landed, he was confronted
by the Pharisees, who argued with Jesus and tested him.
They demanded that he give them
a miraculous sign from heaven.

Mark 8:11

The Pharisees asked for a sign even though they had already seen many miracles by the hands of Jesus. Instead of it enthralling their hearts, it hardened them and blinded their eyes to truth. They wanted Him to behave in a way that they could somehow anticipate; and nothing about Jesus was as they expected.

It's important we don't fall into the same trap. Jesus seldom comes on the scene the way we assume He will. Trial after trial, He demonstrates His faithfulness, yet the next time adversity knocks, we forget what He's shown us. We want Him to answer us in a way we can anticipate, and when He doesn't, we yield to fear and rely on what we understand. We want Him to behave in a way that eases our nerves, but He wants us to believe despite what we see.

Jesus, forgive me for leaning on my understanding when I'm facing difficult situations. Your ways are perfect, and your timing is infallible. I yield every fear to your holy love. Even though it may not look like I expect it to, you always come through for me.

Fearless

But Jesus reprimanded them. "Why are you gripped
with fear? Where is your faith?" Then he stood up and
rebuked the storm and said, "Be still!" And instantly it
became perfectly calm.

Matthew 8:26

At this very moment, Jesus is with you. Every storm you face, He faces with you. He's your strength, your hope, and the miracle you need. His voice alone sparks courage—still your soul and listen. When you believe He's with you, you can conquer any opposition that stands in your way. Facts won't faze you when you submit every thought to His majesty and trust His unfailing Word.

You weren't created to live in the torment of dread—you have the mind of Christ. You're an overcomer, and Jesus is your fierce protector. Cast every unruly imagining aside. When the talons of fear lash at your soul, His glory rises within and ignites your faith. Trust Him. Shake off the doubt. Stir yourself to praise. With a single word, Jesus will calm the storm. Don't give up!

Jesus, you're the peace that dispels every fear. I know you're with me—let me feel your arms of strength around me, and I will declare that I am fearless and brave. I yield my thoughts to you. Come and quell the raging storm within and kindle my faith. My heart comes alive when I feel you near.

June 6

You Delight His Heart

"I am his messenger and he is always with me,
for I only do that which delights his heart."
John 8:29

What an incredible statement! Jesus, as a man, declared with total confidence that He only did the things that delighted the heart of the Father. This must be our declaration as well. We can't focus on the times we've failed. We mustn't judge ourselves based on our humanity. Jesus sees our hearts. He looks at us through the eyes of mercy and love. His grace enables us to live with hearts that desire one thing—to please Him.

We're captivated. Lovesick. Our imperfection draws us ever closer as we recognize our great need for Him. We long to be the brides He says we are. We desire to live in a way that honors Him and reflects His extravagant love and undeserved mercy. When we truly believe in His saving grace, we declare with total confidence and dependence upon Him: "I only do the things that delight His heart!"

Jesus, nothing's too hard for you! You saved me so outrageously, set me free, and fill me with your glory. I know you see my desire to live before you in purity and holy zeal. Come, lead me today and every day so all that I do reflects my desire to live before you always.

The Person of Truth

"For if you embrace the truth,
it will release more freedom into your lives."

John 8:32

Everything about Jesus is good. He's the truth that enables us to overcome every lie. But truth must be embraced and not just mentally acknowledged. Many study the Scriptures but lack revelation. They know what the Bible says but never experience the freedom it offers.

Embracing the truth means we embrace the transforming power of that truth. We know who He is because He's revealed Himself to us through His Word. If our beliefs contradict His truth, we'll have a hard time experiencing the kind of life we were created for.

Pay attention to what you're thinking, and when your thoughts don't match His, find the truth that exposes and replaces the lie. Embracing truth means no lie can force you into questioning His good intentions for you. Knowing what He says about your situation and getting to know His heart behind all He says will release you into the freedom you've always desired.

⟡

Jesus, I'm not satisfied with glimpses of truth or occasional impartations of revelation. I want more. I want to live in freedom because of how acquainted I am with you, the person of truth. I'm pressing in to know you more and to experience a lifestyle of freedom.

Your Breakthrough Has Been Released

Just then Jesus turned around and looked at her
and said, "My daughter, be encouraged. Your faith
has healed you." And instantly she was healed!

Matthew 9:22

The promises of God are manifested in His heart prior to them transpiring on the earth. They're every bit as powerful and certain before our eyes behold them as they are when they're safely held in the arms of faith. We tend to judge His promises by what we see with our natural eyes, forgetting that faith calls it done the moment it agrees with His Word.

Before the woman in this story physically received her healing, she received it by faith. Jesus responded to her by saying that her faith *had* (past tense) healed her. He declared that she'd been healed *before* she experienced it. He stated the truth before it was a fact and then it manifested.

Your breakthrough is alive in the heart of God. Don't surrender your faith as you wait for your promises to manifest.

Jesus, thank you for encouraging me today. I feel you gently breathing upon my faith, reminding me not to give up. You love me, and your Word is trustworthy and sure. I choose to believe that I will have the desires of my heart.

Don't Give Up!

Jesus put his hands over the man's eyes a second time
and made him look up. The man opened his eyes
wide and he could see everything perfectly.
His eyesight was completely restored!

Mark 8:25

What an amazing story! Jesus prayed for a man who wasn't instantly healed. We don't read that Jesus threw His hands in the air and questioned God's desire to heal. He didn't get frustrated or show signs of discouragement. He laid His hands on the man again and the man was healed.

How often do we pray for something, or someone, believing at first that it's His will to intervene, but when we don't see results, we stop? We reason why our prayers aren't being answered instead of persisting in faith and patience. Discouragement and doubt drive our attention away from the confidence we originally had, and with mental assertion, we try to determine the problem. Maybe there's no problem at all! Perhaps we simply need to reach with faith, as many times as it takes, and not give up or try to understand.

Jesus, your timing is perfect, and I ask that you'd help me to trust it implicitly. Give me grace to persist when things aren't happening as fast as I'd like. Thank you for giving us this story as an example of how to handle delay. I yield frustration and doubt to you. Strengthen my resolve.

Confident and Powerful

Jesus cast the demon out of him, and immediately
the man began to speak *plainly* ... But the Pharisees
kept saying, "The chief of demons is helping
him drive out demons."

Matthew 9:33–34

Abundant life surges through your being, waiting to be released. Everywhere you go, His glory spills out. The darkest shadows cannot resist the light within you because you are a child of God.

The glory within you is meant to be shared, but that doesn't mean it will be understood. Freedom is a gift everyone needs but many reject. When people don't understand the power of God, they often despise it. Your very existence is a threat to the enemy's kingdom. Refuse to be angry when they misinterpret, and don't allow their ignorance to push you away. Give them a taste of what it's like to be a true representation of Jesus. Love well. Carry yourself with integrity. In confidence and humility give them a taste of His tender mercy and glorious power.

Jesus, let my life be an example of tenderness and power. I want to reflect the truth of your kingdom everywhere I go. Let the reality of your presence flow through my life. When I'm rejected or despised, help me avoid arguing or feeling offended and humbly release the brightness of your love.

Living Examples

Jesus walked throughout the region with the joyful
message of God's kingdom realm. He taught in their
meeting houses, and wherever he went he demonstrated
God's power by healing every kind of disease and illness.

Matthew 9:35

Discovering the truth about God's kingdom rejoices the heart and makes us happy! The gospel is more than words: it's living substance that brings life to everything in its path. When we understand the power of the Living Word inside of us, we'll honor it by trusting it to manifest *through* us.

It's not enough to tell people that Jesus loves them. They need to experience it. We mustn't tell the world of His unmerited love and then turn our backs when they act in a way that reveals their great need. The spiritually, emotionally, and physically sick need a Savior who doesn't just say He loves them; they need the reality of His healing touch. The power to heal the sick resides within every believer. Do more than offer the world lifeless words that reveal your knowledge; let His power flow through your hands and give them a taste of heaven.

Jesus, everywhere I go I want to release the joy of your kingdom. Stir the fires of holy compassion and let my life exemplify your love. Help me to represent you well by giving the world an encounter with you that heals everyone I meet.

We Are the Answer

He turned to his disciples and said, "... As you go, plead
with the Owner of the Harvest to thrust out many more
reapers to harvest his grain!" ... Jesus commissioned
these twelve to go out into the ripened harvest fields ...

Matthew 9:37–38, 10:5

The Lord often instructs us to pray for something in order
to connect our heart to His. Jesus told His disciples to
pray that the Father would send people to tend the harvest.
Little did they know, they would become the answer to their
prayers.

Prayer stirs our compassion and enables us to see the
problems around us through His eyes. Anyone can complain
and point out the injustices that are so evident, but few will
seek to discover the heart of the Lord and do something
about it. Even then, actions must bring Jesus into the center of the problem and not make things worse. We are the
answer to many of the prayers we pray. The light of the world
lives inside of us, ready to be displayed in love, compassion,
power, and wisdom.

*Jesus, I seek to honor you with every prayer and every action.
Free me from a mind-set of selfishness and ease. Light a fire
of holy zeal within me that cannot be quenched. I won't turn
away from the needs I see but will bow in intercession and rise
to light the world around me with your glory.*

Altogether Lovely

And Jesus' appearance was dramatically altered,
for he was transfigured before their very eyes!
Mark 9:2

*J*esus is the same yesterday, today, and forever, but the way He chooses to manifest in our life is creative and diverse. The gentle Shepherd who leads us to rest beside still waters is the same mighty God who splits the sea to save us from our enemy. He is the righteous King who rules over life itself, and He's the humble Savior who bowed low in suffering. The lion who roars with strength that cannot be denied is also the gentle and soothing lamb nuzzled close to our side.

The journey of acquainting ourselves with His presence is one of intrigue and excitement. As we intentionally look for Him in every situation, we find that life with Him is adventurous, exciting, and safe. He is faithful to reveal Himself exactly the way we need Him to.

Jesus, you walk with me in the cool of day and the storms at night. Your glory leaves me undone yet longing for more. All I know and have yet to discover brings light to my soul as it draws me to you. Surprise me with the beauty of your holiness and the splendor of your majesty. Everything about you is lovely.

Beautiful Union

> Then Jesus spat on the ground and made some clay with
> his saliva. Then he anointed the blind man's eyes with the
> clay. ... So he went and washed his face and as he came
> back, he could see for the first time in his life!
>
> *John 9:6–7*

The merging of deity and humanity is illustrated here by the mingling of spit and clay. Saliva comes from the mouth—a picture of the spoken Word. Clay is a symbol of man because our human vessels are jars of clay. Bring the two together and healing, life, and freedom will flow. Jesus loves to pour perfection into our imperfection, making us equally perfect.

He doesn't separate Himself from our humanity. He isn't embarrassed to call us His own. Our imperfections don't repel Him; they draw Him close. The blind man in this story is such a tender reminder of this. Blindness was considered a curse. He'd likely heard people spit at him as he walked by, but Jesus would turn a symbol of disgust and rejection into a sign of acceptance. This was the day of his healing—the day Jesus demonstrated what a beautiful union with God looks like.

Jesus, the treasures you've hidden for me to find in your Word never cease to amaze me. Thank you for never pulling away from me, especially when I'm veiled by sin or the frailty of my flesh. Empower me with your love, for I am yours—the place where dust and deity unite.

The Encompassing Love of Christ

Later, Jesus went to Matthew's home to share a meal
with him. Many other tax collectors and outcasts of
society were invited to eat with Jesus and his disciples.

Matthew 9:10

Jesus didn't spend His time hanging out with the religious rulers of His day. He wasn't looking for acceptance within the church, and He wasn't concerned about making a name for Himself. His energy wasn't spent striving for a big ministry in order to fulfill His mission on the earth. Instead, He embraced humility, demonstrated power, and exemplified compassion everywhere He went. He didn't strive to prove anything. He simply embraced every moment.

Jesus knew who He was and what He needed to do. With the approval of His Father, He did it. He didn't work to maintain an image. He simply paid attention to the people around Him and poured wisdom and glory into everyone who came across His path.

Jesus, your love is all-inclusive—no one is left out. What a beautiful demonstration of humility you showed us when you became a man and illustrated outrageous love. Help me to demonstrate this love to the world around me and to look beyond race, gender, educational or financial status, and political differences to see the treasure inside.

Who Is He to You?

Jesus asked them, "But who do you believe that I am?"
Luke 9:20

Over two thousand years ago, Jesus asked a profound question that's still relevant today. Whether you're a minister of the gospel, can quote Scripture from memory, or have been a Christian for many years, the question still remains: Who is Jesus to you? There isn't a right or wrong answer. It's a personal and heart-searching question that must be answered honestly.

Knowing Jesus is more than a confession of faith. It's a connection that pierces the heart and seeps into our entire being. Though the relationship is sometimes challenged and shaken by storms, faith remains—and it's activated by love. When Jesus is the center of our life, everything revolves around that relationship. It isn't an effort—the reality of it simply fuels every aspect of our life. He's not only Redeemer—He's Lord, Counselor, and Best Friend.

✦

Jesus, come and shine the spotlight of truth upon my heart. If there's any area of my life where I'm not fully convinced of your love, show me. Make yourself real to me in ways I never knew were possible. I want a relationship with you that sets my heart ablaze and keeps my faith alive.

The Joy of Surrender

Jesus said to all of his followers, "If you truly desire to be
my disciple, you must disown your life completely, embrace
my 'cross' as your own, and surrender to my ways. For if you
choose self-sacrifice, giving up your lives for my glory, you will
embark on a discovery of more and more of true life."

Luke 9:23

Embracing the cross means living in total abandon
to the One who gave His all for us. Sometimes total
surrender is scary. Distracted by the cost of following Him
whole-heartedly, we may forget that everything the Lord
requires ultimately blesses us in the end. We must see past
the crucifixion to the resurrection.

As we embark upon this discovery for more and more
of life, we realize that true life comes when we surrender all
and die to self. Not a physical death, but death to obsessing
over things that never gave us life to begin with. We find freedom as we realize how much more we need Him than the
promises we've been waiting for. Surrendering to His ways
may sound like a painful sacrifice, but it's really a magnificent exchange—our plans, methods, and need for control in
exchange for His ability flowing through us.

*Jesus, it's my delight to offer myself to you without restraint.
It's my honor to give you the reins of my life and allow you
to take control. Nothing is more important than laying every
distraction at the foot of the cross in order to fix my eyes on
the wonder of your love.*

Mercy and Compassion

Then he added, "Now you should go and study
the meaning of the verse: I want you to show mercy,
not just offer me a sacrifice. For I have come to invite the
outcasts of society and sinners, not those who think
they are already on the right path."

Matthew 9:13

Christianity isn't only a confession of faith and surrender to Jesus; it's about knowing Him. The more we know Him, the more we understand His heart. Jesus had no problem spending time with those we call outcasts. He was moved with compassion because He knew He had the answer they needed. He didn't look down on anyone. He ate with sinners and taught anyone who would listen.

Jesus calls us to do the same. The proof of His love must be demonstrated through us. We are filled with life that's meant to be shared. If we offer the sacrifice of a yielded life but lack mercy and compassion toward others, we're missing a vital element of Christianity. Christ in us is the hope of glory—not just for us, but for everyone we encounter.

Jesus, teach me to pay attention to those around me as I go about my day. Interrupt my plans and bring people across my path who need a touch from heaven. Give me the words to say and help me genuinely convey your love to all who will listen. Overflow my soul so that I cannot contain the glory that is meant to be shared.

Most Holy Pursuit

"Even if you gained all the wealth and power of this
world, everything it could offer you, yet lost your soul
in the process, what good is that?"

Luke 9:25

Life is such a delicate balance between spirit, soul, and body. We have dreams, goals, and ideas that make our heart soar. We desire the natural rewards that come from earthly wealth. We want to be healthy, fit, and attractive. None of these things are wrong. As a matter of fact, God wants us to have the desires of our heart, as long as they don't oppose His will for our lives. He wants us to be happy, successful, and prosperous.

Being wealthy and powerful isn't a sin. God is a perfect example. He's omnipotent and owns every piece of earth and sky. The problem is when we lose sight of Jesus in the process. Neglecting our relationship with Him in order to gain fame and fortune opens us up to temptation, which, if we're not careful, will lure us away from God. Above everything else, Jesus must remain our first and most holy pursuit.

Jesus, I want to be prosperous in spirit, soul, and body. Though I want to see my dreams come to pass and enjoy wealth, you are my true and ultimate desire. Help me to keep you first, even if it means sacrificing my plans in order to stay connected to your heart.

Weary

When he saw the vast crowds of people, Jesus' heart
was deeply moved with compassion, because they
seemed weary and helpless, like wandering
sheep without a shepherd.

Matthew 9:36

When you're weary and broken, Jesus is there. He knows everything you need, even before you ask. He's a God who remembers everything—every prayer, each tear, and every time you've declared His praise in the face of hopelessness and opposition. When your soul is bowed low and your shouts of love have turned to whispers, you still delight His heart.

Jesus is merciful and compassionate. When you have nothing left to give but the yes in your heart, it's enough. He's drawn to the fragrance of complete surrender and utter abandon. Your weakness is a magnet for His strength. Every breath is an opportunity for His love and strength to infuse every cell. Never give up. In your desperation, He'll come.

Jesus, I come before your presence and wait. Let waves of glory crash upon my soul as you wash me in your love. Though delay has made me weary, you will make me strong. I need more than answers; I need the light of your face. As I pause in the tension of this moment, you will come. You will fan the flame within my heart.

His Ways Are Higher

Jesus opened his heart and spoke freely with his
disciples, explaining all these things to them. Then Peter
the Rock took him aside and rebuked him.

Mark 8:32

Jesus loves to share His heart with His friends. The God of
all glory, power, and wisdom longs to impart revelation,
if we'd only set ourselves on a journey of discovery. When
we set distractions aside and listen for His voice, He unveils
mysteries. For many who feel as if they don't hear Him, it's
usually a matter of faith—believing you can hear Him. Sometimes, it's simply a matter of not setting time aside to listen.

Spiritual truths often contradict rational thinking. Much
of the kingdom opposes natural understanding. At times we
may think we've missed Him entirely—what we hear sounds
too outrageous to be true. That's what happened to Peter.
He tried to understand spiritual truths with his natural mind
and thought he'd help Jesus with a better plan—one that
made sense. When we set ourselves to hear from heaven, we
must listen and trust without conditions.

⚜

*Jesus, reveal your secrets to me as I set myself aside to listen.
Teach me and illuminate my heart and mind so that they flow
in harmony with your Holy Spirit. Bring me into agreement
with your truth. Your ways are higher than mine—perfect and
complete without exception.*

Everything Changes in His Presence

As he prayed, his face began to glow until it was
a blinding glory streaming from him. His entire body
was illuminated with a radiant glory.

Luke 9:29

When Jesus was transfigured in front of Peter, James, and John, He was illuminated with glory from the inside out. We tend to look at this Scripture with awe and wonder, as we should, but we forget one important element—Jesus came to the earth as a man. He demonstrated a relationship with the Father so glorious that it could be seen. He exemplified a life of prayer so intense that it not only influenced everything He did, but it also altered His appearance.

That's what the glory of God does within us. Though we've yet to experience radiant glory shining from our face, it's most definitely flowing inside of us. His Spirit is alive within every believer, altering the way we think, speak, act, and even the way we look. If Jesus, as a man, radiated with visible glory, perhaps one day it will be seen shining through us. Everything changes in the presence of God.

Jesus, go straight into the darkest crevice of my soul and illuminate it with your presence so that not even a shadow of sin exists. Let your glory flow from each word, every movement of my soul, and the very flicker of my eye. Transform me in your presence until I glow with your likeness.

Ponder

Peter, James, and John were speechless and awestruck.
But they didn't say a word to anyone about
what they had seen.

Luke 9:36

Peter, James, and John had just encountered the glory of God in a new and miraculous way. Not only did they see God's glory shining through Jesus, but they also witnessed Him talking with Moses and Elijah, who had come from heaven. On top of that, a cloud of glory enveloped them, and they heard the voice of God instruct them to pay attention to what Jesus said. Talk about a heavenly encounter! Yet they kept it to themselves.

I wonder what our first response would be once we scraped ourselves up from the ground after an encounter like that. Would we have tried to capture the remnants of fog for a photo op, jumped on social media to inform the world of our heavenly connection, or called our closest friends? Let's take time to ponder our interactions with heaven before disconnecting from the experience. Some encounters are too precious to be shared.

✣

Jesus, though sharing our lives on social media has become the norm, I want to honor our times of holy connection. Forgive me for rushing to share. From now on, I'll ponder these precious moments and hold them close to my heart until the proper time has come.

Made Holy

Jesus told them, "If you would acknowledge your
blindness, then your sin would be removed. But now
that you claim to see, your sin remains with you!"

John 9:41

The gift of salvation is free, but it requires one thing—
that we acknowledge our need for a Savior. When we
humble ourselves and invite Jesus into our lives, He not only
wraps us in His righteousness, He also saturates every part of
us with His divine nature. Our old attributes are swallowed
up by His glory, and everything about us that's contrary to
holiness is made holy.

We owe it all to Jesus. Freedom from sin is a lifestyle that
involves our continued dependence on His Spirit. Remaining humble, in recognition of our great need for Him, keeps
us pliable in His hands. Living before His presence and not
ignoring Him when He points out areas that need refining
ushers us into a lifestyle of ongoing transformation.

*Jesus, thank you for your tender mercy. It's your kindness that
leads me to repentance. I owe everything to you. Even on my
best days, I know that it's all because of you. Illuminate my
paths with your radiant splendor and give me grace to remain
humble so I will never lose my way.*

Loving the Unlovely

"Lord, if you wanted to, you could command fire to fall down
from heaven just like Elijah did and destroy all these wicked
people." Jesus rebuked them sharply, saying, "Don't you realize
what comes from your hearts when you say that? For the Son of
Man did not come to destroy life, but to bring life to the earth."

Luke 9:54–55

*J*esus came to the earth to save men, not destroy them.
In His mercy, He revealed the heart of the Father in a
way the disciples didn't understand. The example of Elijah
calling down fire to destroy wicked people contradicted
Jesus' message of mercy and compassion. He wanted them
to demonstrate the Father's heart.

As His children, we're called to embrace the message of
mercy. Though we see the moral decay of society, rampant
sin, and failure to differentiate between right and wrong, it
isn't our job to condemn. We're called to bring life, to exhort,
edify, and encourage. The most vile and horrendous sins may
be done through the hands of the world's next great evan-
gelist. Love draws men to the Father—not condemnation.
Anyone can judge, criticize, and chastise. It takes someone
willing to love like Jesus does to revive a hardened heart.

*Jesus, I want to see past the sin and into the heart of the sinner.
You've extended grace and mercy to me more times than I can
count. Now it's my turn to do the same. Give me wisdom and
teach me how to release light into darkness in a way that softens
even the hardest heart.*

Raise Me Up

As the boy lay there, looking like a corpse,
everyone thought he was dead. But Jesus stooped down,
gently took his hand, and raised him up to his feet,
and he stood there completely set free!

Mark 9:26

Jesus' love always leads from death to life. Just when the situation looks and feels hopeless, He bends low and raises us up to set us free—gentleness and power flowing in perfect synchrony.

It may look to you and everyone else that your hopes, dreams, or maybe a relationship or a career have died, but Jesus always has the last word. He knows exactly how to pick up the broken pieces and breathe life back into them. If you find yourself in a situation like this, first hold the lifeless situation loosely and offer it to the Lord. Sometimes, we hold things so tightly, we aren't aware that the Lord has something better. Be sure that what you so desperately desire isn't second best. If you have a clear word that this is His will, lay the remains before Him and let praise fill the atmosphere. As you wait, rest. Believe. See with the eyes of faith and expect your deliverer to raise you up!

Jesus, as I release all of my frustrations and questions to you, flood me with the knowledge of your will. I'll do my part to follow your lead, putting faith into actions or stepping back and letting go. I trust you.

Significance

"If you tenderly care for this little child on my behalf,
you are tenderly caring for me. And if you care for me,
you are honoring my Father who sent me.
For the one who is least important in your eyes
is actually the most important one of all."

Luke 9:48

If we truly believed that our significance isn't measured by our social status, titles, or positions, but by the way we care for others, it would inspire us to live with greater humility. When the desire to be recognized by man is our driving force, we're self-serving—chasing after titles and stature instead of seeking to honor the Father by serving others in secret.

The character of Jesus is formed within us when we don't do things to gain prestige because our hearts are moved with compassion. Jesus didn't flaunt His divine status in order to be admired by men. It's quite the contrary—He humbled Himself to the point of death, honoring the Father until the very end. As we follow His example and do the right things for the right reasons, we have the attention of heaven.

Jesus, I want to live a life of humility and compassion. One that honors the Father and emulates you. You were the greatest servant of all, caring for those who society didn't esteem highly. Children, women, the poor, the demon-possessed, sinners, and the sick were all treated with respect and dignity.

He's a Good God

A thief has only one thing in mind—he wants to steal,
slaughter, and destroy. But I came to give you
everything in abundance, more than you expect—
life in its fullness until you overflow!

John 10:10

We have a good Father who loves to bless His children. Everything about Him points to fruitfulness, increase, and abundance. Nature attests to His desire to create beauty and power and place them in our hands. Salvation highlights a giving, compassionate God, full of love, tenderness, and blessing. His character confronts the ways of evil and He delivers us from its snare.

What do you expect when you pray? Do you believe He delights in giving you the desires of your heart? Or has the enemy confused your view of God? There's only one who steals, slaughters, and destroys, and it isn't our magnificent Lord. He doesn't afflict us with sickness or destruction to teach us a lesson. If an earthly father did that he'd be considered an unfit parent. It's ludicrous to think God would hurt those He loves. It's time to expect His goodness to manifest in your life. Shake off doubt and discouragement and dare to believe again!

✤

Lord, there's no one as perfect as you. You're the confidence of the entire planet and the One who saved my soul. Forgive me for believing the lies of the enemy and yielding to doubt. You are a good Father, and it's your delight to bless me.

When You Doubt

"If you are able to believe, all things
are possible to the believer."

Mark 9:23

When we're wrestling with doubt and unbelief, there's no use pretending that we're not. Besides the fact that the Lord sees through every façade, we're only hurting ourselves when we're not honest about our struggles of faith. The enemy loves to tempt us to doubt, and once we've succumbed to the temptation, he throws guilt and shame on top of us. But Jesus pulls us close and whispers a word that breathes life into our soul: "Believe."

When the impurities of doubt rise to the surface, don't ignore them. Letting doubts fester without laying them at the feet of Jesus leads to trouble. Be honest with the Lord and ask Him to help you make Him real to you again and protect you from the onslaught of the enemy. Then do your part. Feed your spirit by spending time in the Word, listening to anointed teaching, and spending time listening to the One who never condemns you in your weakness.

Jesus, shine the spotlight of your loving compassion on me and strengthen me. I commit myself to you and refuse to give into the lies of the enemy. Speak to me. Refresh me. Remind me of your love. Make yourself real to me again.

Authentic Encounter

"Freely you have received the power of the kingdom,
so freely release it to others."

Matthew 10:8

Authentic encounter initiates authentic Christianity. Our transformation isn't the result of mental agreement. It's the power of the kingdom lighting upon our hearts. It's these brushes with the heavenly realm and the sovereignty of Christ that truly changes us.

In the same way, Jesus asks us to release this reality to others. It isn't a burden to let what naturally happens in us flow from us. When we live in authenticity, there really is little effort involved in dispensing the kingdom within. There's no pressure to convince people since we're only releasing what's become real—we pour out from our experience, not our knowledge. Living this way means we're able to offer substance instead of theory. The power of our authenticity is revealed when we trust in the reality of His kingdom *within* us, because it's been made undeniably real *to* us.

Jesus, you've made yourself so beautifully real to me. Now I want to release this tangible substance everywhere I go so others will encounter your love and embrace their identity. I want to live with authenticity, offering the reality of your presence that draws all men to you.

July

Equipped for Battle

Jesus replied, "While you were ministering, I watched Satan topple ... Now you understand that I have imparted to you all my authority to trample over his kingdom. However, your real source of joy isn't merely that these spirits submit to your authority, but that your names are written in the journals of heaven."

Luke 10:18–20

Jesus has such an amazing way of teaching us. He imparts the entirety of His authority over the enemy to us. Then pulls our attention back to what matters most—the source of true joy.

When we understand our position in His kingdom, we merely tell the enemy to flee and he does. We stand in true authority as a confident bride, wielding our weapons of war with unshakable confidence. From the position of bold love, we remain victorious. Our stance in battle is one of rest—not craning our necks to see what the enemy is up to but relaxing peacefully in Jesus' arms. The glory of His presence shields us, and His kiss strengthens us for battle.

Jesus, in your presence I am steadfast and immovable. Your Spirit within me has declared me victorious! I'm a conqueror, and you're my Champion. I love that I can stand against the enemy with confident trust that you've got my back. Of course the enemy's scared—I look a lot like you!

Victorious

"You will trample upon every demon before
you and overcome every power Satan possesses.
Absolutely nothing will be able to harm you
as you walk in this authority."

Luke 10:19

Never underestimate the power you have. The same Spirit that rose Jesus from the dead lives inside of you. Jesus, your Champion, has equipped you for battle and deemed you victorious. You do not fight the enemy alone.

A life kissed with holy intimacy prepares you for battle. It's from the place of union that true champions emerge. Worship and praise become your greatest form of warfare because they flow from a heart that trusts God. You face your adversary with confidence and authority, not because you scream louder but because faith in the One who loves you has captured your heart. Nothing gives you more confidence as you stand against the enemy than the reality of Jesus in your life. Your devotion is a mighty weapon against the enemy.

Jesus, your presence gives me confidence. Your love makes me brave. As I rest in your presence, safe in your arms, my spirit roars with triumph. Even when the enemy steals or hurts me, I know you are with me, in me, and together we will never be defeated. You are my strength and guaranteed victory.

Joy

Then Jesus, overflowing with the Holy Spirit's anointing
of joy, exclaimed, "Father, thank you, for you are Lord
Supreme over heaven and earth!"

Luke 10:21

Nothing changes our perspective more than when we let go of inhibition and lies and allow ourselves the freedom to rejoice. Joy is the Lord's invitation to triumphant faith. It rises in opposition to everything the enemy throws at us by keeping us free from the entanglements of doubt and fear. Joy feels good because we were created for it.

If you're having trouble finding something to laugh about, do it intentionally. If God laughs at His enemies, you should too (see Psalm 2:4)! Laughter is healing to the body (Proverbs 17:22). It's your prescription for mental and physical wellness. Joy, gladness, and rejoicing are found over 840 times in the Bible for a reason. If you haven't laughed in a while, today's devotion is especially for you! Go find something funny to watch and laugh out loud. It's time to release your inhibitions. Joy is the remedy you've been looking for!

⚜

Jesus, thank you for reminding me of the importance of joy and laughter. May the secrets of joy and the ability to laugh in your presence be released to me fully. Today I choose to joyously celebrate your goodness! I'm going to find every reason to laugh out loud.

Don't Hide

The religious scholar answered, "It states, 'You must love
the Lord God with all your heart, all your passion,
all your energy, and your every thought. And you must
love your neighbor as well as you love yourself.'"

Luke 10:27

Learning to love is so much easier when we're only focused on Jesus and ourselves. It's not very hard to love Him when He's given everything and continues to lavish us with unconditional love. But unless we take the love that stirs within our hearts and pour it out into the world around us, we're not fulfilling love's ultimate design.

Honor, love, respect, and encouragement should be the platform we project our lives from. Whether we agree with people or strongly oppose their views, we mustn't forget that Jesus died for everyone. Words of truth, spoken in a timely fashion with a heart of compassion and understanding, should be backed up with actions that offer substance to all we say. Don't be afraid of those who you disagree with or who live differently from you. You are the light of the world. Be a friend and don't hide!

Jesus, I want to represent you well and carry the beauty of your love to the world around me. Let my love be unconditional, my laughter contagious, and my heart full of compassion. Help me to look for the good in everyone I meet and be known for the way I encourage others.

Faithful

"I do believe, Lord; help my little faith!"
Mark 9:24

*Y*ou can't force yourself to believe. Faith comes when you fill yourself with truth and refuse to entertain lies or natural facts. But often, when we've experienced a traumatic event, such as emotional or physical trauma, we need Jesus to heal those areas and reignite the fires of faith.

If doubt feels like it has a vice around your mind, it's time to invite Jesus to be the Lord of every thought. Prostrate yourself before the Lord and ask Him to manifest His love again. If you've partnered with unbelief and entertained thoughts that oppose God's Word, it's important to ask the Lord for forgiveness, to forgive yourself, and forgive anyone who has wronged you. The presence of God can heal years of pain in a moment. Reacquaint yourself with His love—this alone has the power to transform doubt into mountain-moving faith.

Jesus, meet with me. Wash my soul with pure love. Heal every wound and each contaminated thought that's been poisoned by unbelief. Forgive me for doubting when you've proven your faithfulness many times. I invite the flames of holy love to incinerate every lie and fuel my faith afresh.

Prioritize

The Lord answered her, "Martha, my beloved Martha.
Why are you upset and troubled, pulled away by all these
many distractions? Are they really that important?"

Luke 10:41

*L*ife is filled with distractions that compete for our attention. At times it's all we can do to stay on top of our many responsibilities. Busyness will not only dictate our time but our frame of mind. That's when stress sets in.

Stress causes physical and mental sickness. But there's a positive side to stress—it's an indicator that we're out of balance and need more time with Jesus. Stress reminds us of our need for His grace and strength, but most of all for increased intimacy with Him. No matter how busy we get, Jesus must remain our top priority. When you're on edge, find time to spend in His presence. Let the house be dirty, cancel an appointment, stay up late, or get up early—do whatever you have to in order to be alone with Him.

Jesus, forgive me for allowing the outward demands to affect my inward reality. Give me grace to change my daily habits so that I don't allow myself to fall into the enemy's trap. When I seek you before everything else, my life is brighter and less stressful. Help me to respond to love's gentle pull and never to forsake time with you.

Centering Our Prayer

So Jesus taught them this prayer:
"Our heavenly Father, may the glory of your name
be the center on which our life turns."

Luke 11:2

The very first thing Jesus teaches us to do in prayer is to turn our attention to the Father. He doesn't give us instructions for cleansing spirit and soul, nor does He remind us how little we deserve His affection. Instead, He welcomes us into the family and reminds us how glorious our heavenly Father is.

When we purposefully take our eyes off ourselves and allow our entire focus to settle on Him, we gain perspective. The Creator of the universe, the One who made it all, loves us. And every provision for our success has been made. When we remember that all we need is found in Him, we're able to release every care and fully surrender to this holy union. Our relationship with Father, Son, and Holy Spirit becomes the center from which all other aspects of our lives flow in perfect harmony.

✦

Father, let my attention flow to you as naturally as taking a breath. Lead me by your perfect wisdom, directing every step, every relationship, and each decision. Be my center—the truth that anchors my life. I want everything I do to flow from this posture of complete confidence in your love. How amazing it is to be your child!

The Power of Persistence

"Every persistent seeker will discover what he needs.
And everyone who knocks persistently
will one day find an open door."

Luke 11:10

*J*esus loves when we dream with Him. The desires of our heart matter. He created us to have hopes, dreams, and goals that stir our soul. He wants us to be successful and happy. He's created us to be fruitful and live an exuberant life, but He wants our motivation for external joys to be secondary to our relationship with Him.

When your love for Jesus and the persistent way you pursue Him supersedes everything else, you've got the attention of the King. He becomes your number one cheerleader, encouraging you to do your part. Let your heart soar as you walk out your dreams—study, prepare, practice, and declare the Word. Go after what's in your heart and don't let obstacles stand in your way. Pour into your dreams with prayer and focused determination. As you set your heart on Him and work hard, He'll bless your persistence.

✣

Jesus, lead me by your wisdom. Bless me with creative ideas and the understanding and favor I need to walk them out. When one door closes, I'll be right there, knocking on another. With faith in you and hard work, nothing will stop me from pursuing my dreams.

Childlike Faith

"Yes, Father, your plan delights your heart, as you've chosen this way to extend your kingdom—by giving it to those who have become like trusting children."

Matthew 11:26

There's nothing like the sound of a child's laughter. Pure, uninhibited, and contagious, the gleeful joy of a child touches our hearts because it's not tainted by fear or influenced by disappointment. For the young one who has no reason to wonder if they'll be taken care of or if they'll be made fun of, they fully trust—and that trust frees them to fully enjoy life.

This is how Jesus wants us to be—absolutely trusting of our Father's love. That doesn't mean we don't go through difficult times, but it does mean we've discovered His unwavering faithfulness in the midst of trouble. Becoming childlike frees us to enjoy the process of faith, because it's fueled by love and discovery. Let's learn to smile more, laugh without restraint, and act like we truly believe Jesus loves us and will take care of everything.

✢

Jesus, restore to me the joy of my salvation. I want to live carefree—led by your Spirit, experiencing the freedom of wholehearted trust. I want to laugh with total abandon, even in shadows of darkness. With childlike faith, I'll enjoy life to the fullest with you.

The Father's Love

"No one fully and intimately knows the Son except
the Father. And no one fully and intimately knows the
Father except the Son. But the Son is able to unveil
the Father to anyone he chooses."

Matthew 11:27

Jesus wants to unveil our hearts to the Father's love. Our view of the Father profoundly affects our life. When we experience His goodness, it shapes our understanding in a healthy way. Conversely, if we're caught up in a legalistic understanding of what He requires or believe He'll withhold blessings if we don't behave a certain way, our perception of His unmerited love is tainted.

The Father's love has the power to build an unshakable foundation in our lives. It's more than religious rhetoric or mindful awareness. Knowing Him comes from encountering the reality of His nearness and the undeniable faithfulness of His Word as it's revealed to our hearts. So, let's cry out for greater understanding. Let's yearn for true encounters and deeply impacted hearts and get to know the Father the way Jesus does.

Jesus, unveil my heart. I want to know the Father the way you do. I want His smile to be the first thing I sense when I wake and His whisper to saturate every thought as I fall asleep. I long for encounters with His tangible presence and to know Him the way you do.

Secrets

He took the twelve aside privately and told them
what was going to happen.

Mark 10:32

Jesus trusts those He's closest to. As His beloved, you are one of those people. He wants to share the hidden treasures of His kingdom and entrust you with the secrets of His heart. He longs to meet with you every day to share stories, times of laughter, and the things that have His attention. He is both your Lord and your Friend.

Too often prayer is a one-sided conversation. We spend most of our prayer time talking instead of listening. Today, let's nurture our personal communion with Him by finding out what's on His heart and diving into the mysteries He longs to share.

If you're feeling like it's hard to hear Him, all you have to do is ask Jesus to touch your spiritual ears and then be faithful to pay attention. He knows exactly how to fine-tune your hearing.

⬥

Jesus, let's meet in our secret garden. Hold me close and whisper secrets that only your beloved may hear. Pour out fresh revelation upon my heart and unlock the secrets I've yet to hear. May your truths become my delight and the anchor of my soul.

Come to Me

"So everyone, come to me! Are you weary,
carrying a heavy burden? Then come to me.
I will refresh your life, for I am your oasis."

Matthew 11:28

Jesus promised us peace, and everyone wants it. When we first gave our lives to Jesus, many of us experienced peace for the first time. Eventually, the cares of life overshadowed our serenity, and we found ourselves distracted by burdens we weren't designed to carry. In an effort to find that peace again, we look for things to *do*—vacations, prayer meetings, conferences, hobbies, exercise—the list is endless. We want peace, and we'll go all out to find it.

Jesus says that the way to peace is simple—go to Him. Release control and learn *His* ways. How does He see our situation? Until we learn to let go of our need to understand, we won't find true rest. Let's stop trying to figure everything out and give Him our need to understand. As we trust Him and surrender fully, we'll find the peace we crave.

Jesus, teach me your ways so I'll find rest and refreshment for my soul. I set my mind on your goodness, provision, and faithfulness. Let your love anchor my soul and give me the rest and peace that passes understanding.

Excited Giving

"Yes, Father, your plan delights your heart, as you've
chosen this way to extend your kingdom—by giving it
to those who have become like trusting children."

Matthew 11:26

Our heavenly Father has such amazing plans for our
lives, it even makes *Him* excited! Think about what it
feels like when you've bought your child (or someone you
care about) something you know they're going to love. You
can hardly contain yourself as you await their reaction. I
imagine God being the same way as He anticipates our looks
of joy when we see His kingdom manifest in our lives.

This is the loving Father who Jesus introduced us to. He
wants us to understand the Father's heart and intentions the
same way He did—a Father we can trust without reservation.
A Father whose love is so real that we never fear He'll stop
taking care of us. Let's embrace our position as children of
God and surrender our need to control what we cannot see.
Let's walk in simple childlike faith, fully at rest and unafraid of
what tomorrow brings.

*Jesus, thank you for introducing me to a Father who loves me
more than I could ever fathom. All I need is available to me
now because He's already granted me the kingdom. Help me
to rest in you at all times and to constantly expect the goodness of God to follow me forever.*

When You're Sad

Then tears streamed down Jesus' face.

John 11:35

The humanity of Jesus means that He experienced the same emotions we do. His sovereignty means that He not only empathizes with our suffering but He can perfectly comfort and strengthen us in it as well.

Everyone goes through times of sorrow, and Jesus never once condemns us for it. Emotions help us understand ourselves and the things that move us. They keep us real, relatable, and honest. While it's important not to dwell on negative emotions, it's healthy to feel. To cry. To be moved. And most importantly, to invite Him into those feelings and process them with us. Emotions can be fickle, but they're also a doorway to deep encounters with the Lord. He gave us emotions for a reason. To ignore them is to push away an opportunity for Him to meet us in profound ways. Embrace what you're feeling with the purity and love of Jesus.

Jesus, sometimes my emotions are so profound that I don't know how to process them. Come, walk me through this. Saturate every emotion with your glory. Breathe hope. Comfort me so I can release my pain and see things from your perspective.

Let Jesus Lead

"Learn my ways and you'll discover that I'm gentle,
humble, easy to please. You will find refreshment
and rest in me. For all that I require of you will
be pleasant and easy to bear."

Matthew 11:29–30

The responsibilities placed on us by others, and our tendency to over commit, can often result in burnout. Jesus' way of doing things always imparts grace for the task.

It's important to keep our spirits in tune with His heart. When we take time to listen for His instructions, He'll lead us with wisdom. It's when we say yes to everything and everyone, without checking with Jesus first, that we become exhausted and stressed. Even things started in obedience to Him must be walked out with continued sensitivity to His Spirit. If we find ourselves anxious, overwhelmed, and frustrated, we need to reexamine our priorities and get His perspective. Set time aside every day to enjoy His presence. When we're flowing in His anointing and grace, things that normally suck our time and energy get done quicker and with greater ease.

Jesus, I commit my day to you. Lead me by your Spirit and help me resist ignoring your gentle warnings when I'm overextending myself. Forgive me for letting my priorities get out of line. I don't want schedules to dictate my life; I need you to guide me.

Revealing Truth

Jacob and John, sons of Zebedee, approached Jesus
and said, "Teacher, will you do a favor for us?" "What is it
you're wanting me to do?" he asked. "We want to sit next
to you when you come into your glory," they said,
"one at your right hand and the other at your left."

Mark 10:35–37

*J*esus had just finished telling his disciples how He would
die. He told them ahead of time about the holiest, most
unselfish act mankind would ever witness. Their response
wasn't one of curiosity or compassion; they selfishly asked
for more.

The mystery of the cross is difficult to understand. It strips
away the mask of pious religion, unveiling what hides in our
hearts. As we spend time before His throne and worship in His
holy presence, areas of selfishness and unholy ambition are
revealed. It's to our advantage that His purity reveals our impurities. Unless we know what's lurking in the cavern of our souls,
we won't know how to get free. To experience the thrill of resurrection life, we must always begin at the cross. It's in death to
selfishness that we discover the delight of life with Him.

*Jesus, as I gaze upon your face, restore my soul. Illuminate the
shadows of selfish ambition that darken my heart. I surrender every thought and desire that contradict the ways of glory
you've called me to. You've created me in your image. Now
I will grow in your likeness and honor you with every desire.*

Purity

"Everything hidden and covered up
will soon be exposed."

Luke 12:2

One of the beautiful joys of the kingdom is that our hearts long for purity. As those who've fallen in love with the Lover of our souls, we've learned to invite the fires of His holy passion. Instead of hiding, we prostrate ourselves before Him. Longing to be cleansed by love. Wanting nothing to hinder us in our divine relationship.

Loving Jesus will always lead to a revelation of our own condition. Recognizing our weaknesses isn't a call for guilt and condemnation. Instead, it's an invitation for true repentance—where we come face to face with our great need for mercy. Jesus doesn't uncover areas of darkness to harm us; rather, he does it to answer our cry for more of Him. To protect us from the enemy and teach us how to live in total freedom.

Jesus, let the fire of your love burn away anything that doesn't resemble you. Have me fully. I want to be beautiful and radiant in the deepest part of my being—even the places that I haven't wanted to face. Together we will conquer every area of sin and, by your grace, I will live in purity.

Heavenly Family

"Look closely, for this is my true family.
When you obey my heavenly Father,
that makes you a part of my true family."

Matthew 12:49–50

The way we grew up has great impact on our lives today. Our family dynamics influences the way we view the world. We learned respect, love, honor, faithfulness, or their negative counterparts, by the way we were raised. We expect certain family members to react or behave in a certain way because we're familiar with their personalities.

Now, as members of the family of God, we're invited to a new and outrageously inviting way of viewing life. Every unhealthy lens that childhood placed over our perception of reality is wiped clean as we see with clarity how much He loves us. As children in the family of God, we're growing into His image—the healthy ways we were raised being reinforced, and the negative ways being healed. We're learning about His personality, realizing that His goodness and faithfulness can be expected in every situation.

✣

Jesus, with outstretched arms you have welcomed me into your family. Heal every unhealthy way I've seen the world. Infuse me with overwhelming confidence in your love and seal me with a holy kiss. Teach me how to love well, expect your goodness to be revealed often, and to be a true reflection of our Father.

Extravagant Love

> Miriam picked up an alabaster jar filled with nearly
> a liter of extremely rare and costly perfume—the purest
> extract of nard, and she anointed Jesus' feet.
> Then she wiped them dry with her long hair.
>
> *John 12:3*

One of the most outrageous Scriptures in the Bible is also a tender and poignant account of unrestrained devotion. A former prostitute, so overcome with gratitude, risks further criticism and unashamedly lavishes Jesus with her best gift. This rare and expensive perfume was most likely purchased with funds from her former occupation. As she pours it out upon Jesus, she's breaking her connection to her former life. This was a symbol of total and complete surrender. She gave her all, perhaps not knowing how she'd support herself from now on, but she didn't care. Jesus had loved her in ways no man ever did.

This is where you may find yourself today—kneeling before the Lord in reverent wonder. Undone. Struck silent. Amazed at who you've become because of Him. Surrender everything. Break every connection to your past. Offer your hopes, dreams, and even your pain. Lavish your love upon Him. Hold nothing back.

❖

Jesus, you've become my everything. Your extravagant love has completely changed me, and I want nothing more to pour my life out in your honor. To become a fragrant offering of holy devotion. I'm yours—totally and completely, forever.

Leaders

"Those recognized as rulers of the people and those who are in top leadership positions rule oppressively over their subjects, but this is not the example you are to follow. You are to lead by a different model. If you want to be the greatest one, then live as one called to serve others."

Mark 10:42

Leaders have a very important job of cultivating an environment of honor—which is a two-way street. Too often we see leaders oppressing their flock, demanding submission, and threatening exclusion to those unwilling to yield. Instead of bending low in compassionate ministry to their followers, they demand to be served. That is not the example Jesus left us with.

It's a painful reality that sometimes those who should be guiding you unjustly persecute you. They force religious rules instead of fostering holy passion. How you respond determines a lot, not only about your future but also about how fast you will heal from their abuse. If you've suffered at the hands of unhealthy leaders, pray for them and receive healing for yourself as well.

✦

Jesus, thank you for the leaders who have mentored me and poured into my life. Bless them and draw them closer to you. For those who have wounded me and treated me unjustly, I forgive them. I lay offense at your feet and ask for your mercy to cleanse their impure motives. Heal my heart and bring leaders into my life who love like you do.

Our Friend

"What about the seemingly minor issues of your life?
Do they matter to God? Of course they do! So you never
need to worry, for you are more valuable to God
than anything else in this world."

Luke 12:7

The One who created the heavens and the earth, the mountains and the blades of grass, the crashing waves and the grains of sand, cares about all things great and small. From the beat of our heart to the pores in our skin, every finite detail of our body was perfected by His hand. So why would we ever think that the issues of our life, even seemingly insignificant ones, wouldn't matter to Him?

Jesus isn't only our Lord and Savior. He's our Friend. We can talk to Him about anything, confident that He's not only listening but also sincerely interested. Unlike other friends, He knows the answer to every problem. He'll show us exactly how to pray and when to let go. One moment in His presence can satisfy our greatest needs and most trivial desires.

Jesus, thank you for being my very best friend. For holding me when I'm weary and knowing exactly what I need to make it through the day. Your grace is astounding. Your patience is inspiring. Your compassion and attention to detail never ceases to amaze me.

It's Time to Be Free

Everyone was shouting, "Lord, be our Savior!
Blessed is the one who comes to us sent from
Jehovah-God, the King of Israel!"

John 12:13

Let a cry of freedom rise from within! Shout if you must! Shake off every restriction, every lie that's held you back, and remind yourself exactly who Jesus is. Your Savior could have stopped when He gave His all for you. He could have suffered, died, and rose from the grave and decided eternal life was a great enough gift for you to look forward to. But He didn't stop there.

Our Savior is the same yesterday, today, and forever. His generosity and faithfulness never end. He offers you abundant life every day. His Spirit within you empowers you. His Word is truth to guide you. He's also given you a choice—you can choose to agree with heaviness, fear, confusion, and disappointment, or you can decide every day to ignite your faith afresh. Freedom is yours to embrace.

Jesus, I'm not going to sit around and focus on what's wrong. I refuse to let my circumstances dictate my state of mind. You've already proven your love and faithfulness many times, so why should I doubt now? Breakthrough is mine, and while I wait, I'll celebrate your goodness! You love me, and this is the truth I'm focusing on.

Relentless

Those in the crowd were indignant and scolded him
for making so much of a disturbance, but he kept
shouting with all his might, "Son of David,
have mercy on me now and heal me!"

Mark 10:48

aith is tenacious. When we really understand who Jesus is and how much He loves us and wants us to be whole, we'll cry out for His touch and not be denied. Dignity takes a back seat when we chase after what is rightfully ours.

Don't be afraid to relentlessly pursue what the Word says is yours. Ignore those who try to confuse you by telling you that certain biblical promises aren't for today. His desire for you is filled with life, joy, and blessing. When you're fully convinced that He is a good God, it will change your prayer life. Faith will explode from within and peace will settle every doubt. Rise up with confidence and claim your healing, your deliverance, and your breakthrough.

Jesus, you are faithful to every promise you've made. In confidence I stand, boldly reaching for your healing touch upon every area of my life that's out of sync with your Word. I believe I'll experience the quickening of your Spirit, like a wind of refreshment upon my faith. Because I believe in your love, I know I'll have all that's rightfully mine.

JULY 24

Waiting

Now Jesus' disciples didn't fully understand the
importance of what was taking place, but after he was
raised and exalted into glory, they understood.

John 12:16

Time serves as a teacher, instructing us through our greatest lessons. Day by day, through varying seasons and trials, we mature. We grow to understand the advantages of allowing Jesus to lead, even when we don't understand the path He's taking.

Let's be honest, waiting's hard. Life doesn't always make sense. Jesus doesn't always do what we want Him to. But in times of seeming denial, we're given a divine opportunity to present Him with our truest, most authentic love. We bow low and offer Him our heart. We surrender the right to understand. We refuse to quit, deny doubt a place in our heart, and adamantly reject every lie. It isn't until much later that we'll realize how much we've learned and how faithful He is.

If this describes you today, be encouraged. This is your chance to be known as a radiant lover. He'll show Himself strong on your behalf!

⁜

Jesus, draw me close. I know you're teaching me about your faithful nature, but sometimes the waiting's hard. Weariness tries to plague me, but I choose to be a radiant lover who honors and worships you, even in the hardest of times. Come, make your strength my own.

Unstoppable

> But the Pharisees were disturbed by this and said
> to each other, "We won't be able to stop this.
> The whole world is going to run after him!"
>
> *John 12:19*

*J*esus is unstoppable! He's also controversial and misunderstood. His actions, as He works behind the scenes establishing His will upon the earth, are absolute and irrepressible. Though they were filled with fear and a need to control, the Pharisees unknowingly declared the truth. There would be no way to stop what God had set in motion.

This is the case for your life as well. Despite what others say and regardless of the negativity you're surrounded with, or perhaps filled with, what the Lord sets in place cannot be overturned. Stop giving credence to the viewpoints of those who aren't led by His Spirit. Don't worry if it seems the entire world is against His will. His plans will stand, and as long as you're running alongside Him, nothing can stop you either!

Jesus, no one can convince me that your love isn't powerful enough to set the world ablaze. Every plan you've set in motion in my life and my country will never be quelled. Nothing's going to stop me from running with you and seeing your intentions become reality.

Anxiety

Jesus taught his disciples, saying, "Listen to me. Never let anxiety enter your hearts." ... So don't ever be afraid, dearest friends! Your loving Father joyously gives you his kingdom realm with all its promises!"

Luke 12:22, 32

Jesus knows us well. He knows that at some point we're going to encounter problems that shake us to the core. Experiencing an initial reaction of fear is normal. It's what we do after that initial reaction that determines our state of mind over the next few moments, days, or longer.

Jesus was tempted in the same ways we are (Hebrews 4:15), so we can conclude He experienced fear. He overcame it and gave us keys to do the same: "Never let anxiety enter your hearts." Then He points us to the love of our heavenly Father.

Our hearts, the very core of our belief system, must be filled with a true experience of His love. When this love goes deeper than mental agreement, it has the power to repel fear. Fear and love cannot fill the same space. When we're filled with anxiety and fear, we need a fresh impartation of His love.

Jesus, I resign myself fully to the power of your love. Though fear may attack my mind, I won't allow it a place in my heart. Fill every crevice of my being with your perfect love. I release every anxiety and give you full control of my life.

A Compass to Our Soul

"For what has been stored up in your hearts
will be heard in the overflow of your words!"
Matthew 12:34

If we ever want to know what's happening inside of us, we only need to listen to what we say. When we're filled with His Word—truth that has deeply rooted itself in our hearts—it will pour out in every situation. Words are like a compass to our soul. Most honest when we're with our closest friends and in times of prayer.

We've all been there. Listened to those voices of fear that crept into our ears and quickly escaped through our mouths. Lost focus of truth, even if for a moment, and gave into doubt. Felt out of control and anxiously grasped for control. And in all of these things, it's easy to tell how we feel by what we say under pressure. The good news is that these reactions aren't who we are. They're just as temporary as the slippery slope we occasionally fall upon. So, don't be discouraged, but pay attention. Learn to recognize when it's time to detox your soul.

✧

Jesus, help me stay filled with your Word and remain focused on what's true. Nudge me and help me resist ignoring what's happening inside of me, especially when I need to de-stress. Surround me with your presence and unite me to your heart so our words will be one.

Heavenly Benefits

"And if you truly follow me as my disciple, the Father
will shower his favor upon your life."

John 12:26

When you believe you're one of God's favorites, you look for His kindness to manifest in your life every day. From the moment you wake up, you feel the smile of God shining on you. Even while you sleep, you anticipate His goodness.

The benefits of living a submitted life as Jesus' disciple far outweigh the cost. He'll overwhelm you with favor everywhere you go. People who never noticed you before will suddenly be drawn to the Jesus inside you. When you pull from His favor on your life, doors that were previously closed open wide. Little things like catching incredible sales or receiving unexpected gifts become commonplace. And big things like debts *mysteriously* being paid off or advancement in the workplace and other ventures are just some of the perks of living a life consumed with His kindness.

Jesus, you could've stopped at eternal salvation, but you didn't. The many ways you pour your love, kindness, and unexpected blessings upon me leave me undone. How generous you are. How surprising your hospitality! Your presence is my ultimate desire, but I'm thankful for the way you shower me with favor.

The Priority of His Presence

"Each and every day he will supply your needs as you
seek his kingdom passionately, above all else."
Luke 12:31

Jesus never told us to be consumed by our needs.
Though He does tell us to ask for what we need, He
doesn't want our minds preoccupied with anything other
than the kingdom of heaven. He wants to be our provider.
To be our peace. To faithfully take care of us so we can enjoy
the blessing of heaven and partner with Him in releasing His
kingdom on the earth.

Jesus knows exactly what we need, but when we're overwhelmed by what we can't understand, it hinders our ability
to hear Him clearly. When His presence becomes our priority, we flow in streams of grace, where His hand continuously
and effortlessly guides us in the right direction. When we
seek Him first and simply enjoy Him, we find everything else
falls into place.

*Jesus, you're more than able to take care of my needs. You
can provide for my needs in ways I can't even imagine. So, I
release every care, every burden, and anything that's consum-
ing my thoughts. I choose to seek you first and to enjoy the
pleasures of heaven above all ese. Your love puts things in the
right perspective.*

When It's Hard to Believe

Even with the overwhelming evidence of all the many
signs and wonders that Jesus had performed in front
of them, his critics still refused to believe.

John 12:37

What do you do when unbelief comes as a result of disappointments, failures, and setbacks? How do you keep your heart from growing cold and allowing doubt to erect walls covered with vines of bitterness? Here's the answer: you lay every pain at the feet of Jesus and cry out in faith for His glory to come and heal you. Then you wait.

Every day, as you wait before His presence, the frequency of love will recalibrate every fiber of your being. The traumas in your soul will heal. When you remain open, time will allow Jesus to give you a new history. He'll fill the pages of your story with so many new blessings that you'll be able to look back with confidence and remember who He is to you, when fear and unbelief knock at your door. Keep your heart open to Him. Faith and trust will bloom again.

Jesus, I don't want to be like those who harden their hearts and refuse to believe, forgetting your goodness. I want you to be honored upon the altar of my heart, always. Come, heal the trauma of the past and rewrite my history.

Defined by Love

So he threw off his beggars' cloak,
jumped up, and made his way to Jesus.

Mark 10:50

The account of blind Bar-Timai's healing is astounding. He not only reached out with outrageous faith, believing Jesus could heal him, but he also cast aside his worldly identification to embrace a new identity. The beggars' cloak had defined him for too long. Society had labeled him and set restrictions he no longer would accept. Instead of clinging to self-pity and believing God had abandoned him, he jumped up and chased after a miracle. After what most likely had been many years, Bar-Timai was about to be free.

If you've been waiting for your breakthrough for what seems like a prolonged amount of time, don't give up. Don't wrap yourself tighter in the cloak that has defined you. Throw it aside even before you see the manifestation of your answer and begin to walk toward the life you've been believing for.

✣

Jesus, I'm not going to focus on my weaknesses or problems. I cast off doubt, weariness, and fear and come to you, believing you're ready to release my answer. Heal unhealthy mind-sets that connect more with a painful past than with a vibrant future. It doesn't matter how long I've waited; I choose to believe. I am defined by love.

August

Hearts Ablaze

"I have come to set the earth on fire.
And how I long for every heart to be already
ablaze with this fiery passion for God!"
Luke 12:49

*L*et your heart be awakened today. The love of Jesus is like a furnace of fiery passion, ready to ignite our hearts with life and melody. It consumes us, inviting us to dance within its flames of glory, which alter our very makeup. Nothing has the ability to eternally change us like the love of Jesus. When we make Him the King of our hearts, He'll rule with passion that's stronger than death.

Let's beautify ourselves with His love—honoring the Lord with purity and zeal. When we become known as radical lovers of Jesus, humility, integrity, and relevance will attract others to Him. Our lives will become a spark that sets others on fire. Love sets us free from fear, infusing us with courage and compassion that cannot be contained.

⊹

Jesus, set my heart on fire with holy desire for you. Satisfy me with the glory of your love that mysteriously leaves me longing for more. With each beat of my heart, may I discover you in surprising ways. When you return, may you find the earth filled with passionate, zealous lovers of your presence.

Discernment

"You are such experts at forecasting the weather,
but you are totally unwilling to understand the spiritual
significance of the time you're living in."

Luke 12:56

The Pharisees looked at the face of the sky to forecast the weather. They did the same thing as they scanned the faces of men—concluding they understood someone based on what they saw. They put more effort into discerning outward circumstances than they did peering into inward realities.

How often do we do the same? Judge a person, situation, or world event by what we see in the natural, instead of seeking insight from the Lord about what's happening spiritually. Jesus wants us to look from His perspective. To see the bigger picture by tuning into the atmosphere of heaven. To look and see past what's evident in the natural and gaze into things that can only be spiritually discerned. Then, and only then, will we know how to partner with heaven and pray.

Jesus, give me eyes to see and a heart that cries out for true discernment. Forgive me for judging situations based on popular opinion or a lazy attitude. Lead me by your Spirit to seek the truth that comes from you alone and teach me how to pray for the things only you fully understand.

Decisions

> Yet there were many Jewish leaders who believed
> in Jesus, but because they feared the Pharisees they kept
> it secret, so they wouldn't be ostracized by the assembly
> of the Jews. For they loved the glory that men could give
> them rather than the glory that came from God!
>
> *John 12:42–43*

*E*very believer will experience a time where they must choose between honoring God and pleasing man. The fear of human rejection is a real and common problem. If we yield to that pressure, we'll miss out on some of the greatest opportunities to discover who we really are. We'll forsake some of our most exciting adventures with Jesus.

Some of the things the Lord nudges us to do won't make us very popular with our peers, and at times, our leaders. Though we don't strive to be controversial or dishonoring, our submission to Jesus as Lord must be the governing factor that guides our decisions. His will doesn't violate His Word, but at times it contradicts mind-sets. That doesn't mean we take an attitude toward those who don't agree with our decisions, but it does mean that we protect our relationship with Jesus first and live to honor Him in all things.

Jesus, it isn't a sacrifice to live in a way that honors you. It's my joy! I forsake the fear of rejection, knowing I'm not only loved by you but accepted. I choose to make you the King of my decisions and my life.

AUGUST 4

What Do You Need?

Jesus said to him,
"What do you want me to do for you?"

Mark 10:51

Have you ever felt like your life is so hectic that your mind swirls with about ten different thoughts at once? Your heart needs something and you know your spirit and soul are out of sync, but you're not even sure what exactly you need to feel better. You find yourself crying out to the Lord in prayer, but even your prayers feel lifeless and dull. Then suddenly Jesus tenderly interrupts you mid-cry and asks, "What do you want me to do for you?"

Sometimes we have a list of prayers a mile long, and other times we haven't stopped long enough to figure out precisely what we want. Slow down. Take a deep breath and take some time to get to the root of things. Whining that everything's out of control isn't going to change anything. Be intentional and specific with your prayers and then believe that He's ready to answer. Give yourself time to unwind in His presence.

✢

Jesus, thank you for reminding me to slow down and pay attention to what I need. I'm going to sit in your presence and be still so that you and I can figure it out together. You are the Good Shepherd who leads me into all truth.

Motivated by Love

"And I know that the Father's commands
result in eternal life, and that's why I speak
the very words I've heard him speak."

John 12:50

All that the Father has commanded us to do leads to an abundant life now and eternal life to come. Loving God, others, and living lives of holiness and purity—these things aren't burdensome to the person who's been totally raptured by the love and glory of the Lord. We aren't given commandments to restrict us but to free us and launch us into a life of blessing.

Grace has covered what legalism required. We aren't told to live righteously so He'll accept us. We don't earn our way into heaven or into His heart. Because of Jesus, we're already fully loved and accepted. His grace doesn't give us license to live with no regard to our actions; instead, it draws us close. It creates desire to protect our relationship with Him and put it before everything else.

⁜

Jesus, no amount of obedience can ever make me righteous—only your blood can do that. You don't yoke me with religious duty but with the yoke of holy union. Now, everything I do or don't do happens because I love you. Your love is all the motivation I need to live a life of purity and holiness.

Wash Me

But when Jesus got to Simon Peter, he objected and said,
"I can't let you wash my dirty feet—you're my Lord!"

John 13:6

There is no one like our Lord. No one else whose streams of tenderness have the ability to wash us. Scrub away the painful remnants of our earthly life and make us new. What other king would stoop down to wash dirty feet? Yet Jesus doesn't stop there—He washes every inch of us, inside and out. Fills our lungs with holy breath and floods our being with inexplicable glory.

Jesus stands before us with a towel wrapped around His waist and serves—unceasingly. He bows low and extends mercy that flows like liquid love from the cross He bore. We lean into His presence and find ourselves face to face with holiness, but instead of turning our heads in shame, we're bathed in the light of His glory. Saturated with the oil of the Spirit until every cell drips with the fragrance of His love.

Jesus, wash me. Let me stand before your presence with no trace of worldly debris. May our spirits flow in perfect harmony. May your desires be mine, your thoughts be my own, and your holiness be my holiness. Consume me with flames of glory until every part of me is yours.

Truth

"That's why I teach the people using parables,
because they think they're looking for truth, yet because
their hearts are unteachable, they never discover it.
Although they will listen to me, they never fully
perceive the message I speak."

Matthew 13:13

Truth isn't found by mental perception but by heart penetration. It can be heard a thousand times, but unless our hearts are willing to embrace what our minds cannot grasp, it won't truly make a difference in our lives.

Jesus is truth. That means truth isn't a dead formula but a living substance. It can penetrate places that doubt and confusion have infiltrated, when we reach for it. Reach for Him. Everything that flows from Jesus is true. Powerful. Too magnificent for us to understand fully with our limited ability. It draws us from a deeper place—where spirit and soul are woven together by streams of glory. Truth makes us feel alive inside. Hopeful, even when circumstances, symptoms, and lies are screaming in our face. This is where we live from. His truth always sets us free.

Jesus, speak to me. I open my heart to you. Help me to remain tender and pliable, able to accept things that make no sense to my mind. Let your truth penetrate the deepest, most hidden places of doubt. Illuminate me with the wisdom and understanding of your Spirit that rises above facts and keeps me centered in you.

Pride

"Do you really think that they were more guilty than all of the others in Jerusalem? No, they weren't. But unless you repent, you will all eternally perish, just as they did."

Luke 13:4–5

One of the areas where the enemy has deceived many Christians is in the area of pride. This attitude of superiority that falsely elevates us above others is a dangerous condition of the heart. Pride is a sneaky and deadly sin. It causes us to notice the wrongs of others and keeps us from loving with a pure heart. It judges and often silently criticizes, blinding us from our own sins and faults.

In order to break free from pride, we must guard our hearts and protect our walk. We must go after compassion and humility with zeal. When we see others walking in error, it's our job to pray. To cry out to see them the way Jesus does and then cry out for purity in our own hearts. To remain humble, teachable, and to remember how much mercy we need in our own lives.

Jesus, I want nothing to do with pride. I repent for thinking I'm better than others. I humble myself in your presence and ask you to examine my heart and set me free. I'd be nothing if it wasn't for your mercy. I break off a critical spirit and ask you to help me see others the way you do.

He Makes Us Whole

All at once, the man's eyes opened and he could
see again, and he began at once to follow Jesus,
walking down the road with him.

Mark 10:52

One touch of His presence, one encounter with His love, and you'll never be the same. Jesus has come to make you whole in spirit, soul, and body. Every aspect of your life is important to Him and nothing's off limits. He sees the areas that need His touch even before you do, so don't be afraid to ask. Jesus not only healed Bar-Timai's blindness, but He also set his spirit free to follow Him and released peace into his soul.

When you cry out for His touch, Jesus draws you close, so that nothing will hinder your walk with Him. Every shadow of darkness that tries to obscure your path is illuminated by His glory. When you invite Him into your life, His presence saturates every part of your being—spirit, soul, and body. And you are offered the chance to live from the place of victory every day.

✤

Jesus, all that I need is found in you. The reality of your faithfulness is unfolding before me. The days of unbelief, which clouded my vision, have ended. Touch me. Set me free and make me whole so that nothing hinders me from following you.

You Are Free

Then he said, "Dear woman, you are free.
I release you forever from this crippling spirit."
Instantly she stood straight and tall and overflowed
with glorious praise to God!

Luke 13:12–13

Whether it's physical, spiritual, or mental, we weren't created to live under the weight of heaviness and despondency. Regardless of what life or the enemy throws at us, it's up to us to embrace freedom. Right there, smack-dab in some of our most crippling trials, we can invite the Healer to set us free and celebrate by faith what He's promised.

Jesus has already declared your breakthrough. What you do while you wait is up to you. If you've been stuck in heaviness, shake it off! Sometimes you have to force your body to do what it doesn't want to do. Dance! Shout your praise! Declare His faithfulness! Praise Him for His goodness! The truth will set you free.

✢

Jesus, I'm not going to allow my situation to dictate how I feel. I refuse to sit around and have a pity-party. I shake off heaviness and put on a garment of praise! You're worthy, faithful, and you care about me. Nothing's too hard for you. You've already declared my breakthrough ... and that's the truth that sets me free.

Processing Truth

"The seed sown on gravel represents the person who gladly hears the kingdom message, but his experience remains shallow. ... he quickly falls away, for the truth didn't sink deeply into his heart."

Matthew 13:20–21

Stop. Listen. Do more than let time pass and moments of His glory slip away. Be present with His presence. Linger with Him in the wonders of divine love. You'll never have another adventure like this one. Every encounter with holy passion is unique. Stand in silence. Ponder. Journal. Reflect.

Life gets busy. It's easy to forget to pause and process the beautiful truths revealed to your heart. But shallow glimpses aren't enough to sustain you. It's vital to your well-being and future victory to tuck every golden nugget of revelation and encounter, safely in your heart. Talk to the Lord about everything. Write down what He says and refer back to it often. Let the Word sink deeply into your heart—especially the Scriptures that seem to come alive exactly when you need them.

Jesus, I'm not satisfied with glimpses of glory. I'm certainly not fulfilled when I rush from my devotional time, only to forget everything you've said. Give me grace and help me remember to slow down and allow your truths to sink in. Teach me and bless me with understanding that I'll carry for a lifetime.

The Truth

> The disciple that Jesus dearly loved was at the right of
> him at the table and was leaning his head on Jesus.
>
> *John 13:23*

Standing in a world whose lens of truth is smeared, it's tempting to allow confusion to blur our vision. But right here, in the midst of polluted identity, children of God see themselves through the eyes of love. Love makes us bold. It envelops us with confidence so we can fearlessly declare exactly who we are.

We are worthy because Jesus has given us value that can only be compared to the price of sacred blood. We're beautiful because mercy has awakened us with a holy kiss; it has become the mirror of truth for our soul. The wonder and privilege of leaning into His arms is ours to enjoy every day. We're the ones Jesus dearly loves. Those He shares secrets with. Died for. Rose for. Calls to. Defines.

Jesus, when I feel you near, I remember who I am. Stay close. I can't imagine life without you. Won't imagine it. I'm different because of you. Your love has rearranged me in ways I didn't know were possible. I am yours—one of your favorites. This is the truth that has set me free.

You are Enough

"Then the godly ones will shine like the brightness
of the sun in their Father's kingdom realm."

Matthew 13:43

You are radiant. Illuminated by a love so pure, every crevice of your being is saturated with glory. Not a shadow of darkness exists within you—it's impossible for light and darkness to coexist. Jesus' love has transformed you. You are enough because all that He is, He is inside of you.

You don't have to look outside of yourself for the answers you need. Right there, in the struggle for clarity, peace already exists perfectly within. Tap into the hope that's abundantly available at all times. Draw from the well of profound wisdom, gloriously stirring within. Inhale. Exhale. Every breath is teeming with His life. Agree with it. Let it flood your soul, so you can release it everywhere you go. Look in the mirror and see the brilliance of the Son shining through your eyes. The glory of His Spirit abides within *you*, radiant one!

Jesus, I can sense you now—the anointing of your Spirit flowing through my veins and illuminating my entire being. Some have said that you wouldn't give your glory to another, but I'm not another. I'm your child, fearfully and gloriously made in your image and shining as bright as the sun!

Dearly Loved

Then the dearly loved disciple leaned into
Jesus' chest and whispered,
"Master, who is it?"

John 13:25

When we understand how dearly loved we are, life changes. Love propels us beyond ourselves, stirring courage and faith. Fearless, we gaze into the eyes of the Savior and feel no need to hide. Stirred by holy zeal, we run into the arms of the One who holds us for eternity.

Jesus longs to spend time with you. He wants you to feel at home in His presence. You can lean against His chest and, with confidence, ask the questions no one else is willing to ask. You believe He'll answer you because Jesus isn't only your Lord; He's your friend, and friends share secrets. Today, lean into Jesus and listen for His whispers of captivating love, as He unveils your heart to know Him more.

Jesus, as your love blossoms in my heart, I'm infused with holy boldness. Speak to me and share your heart. I want to know you more than any other person has ever known you before. Your love is a treasure of friendship worth more than anything this world has to offer.

Perfect Timing

"Blessings rest on this kingdom he ushers in right now—
the kingdom of our father David! Bring us the victory
in the highest realms of heaven!"

Mark 11:10

*J*esus loves to release victory into our lives. He's committed to bringing every promise to pass. Once we've settled the matter of *if* and truly believe He is who He says He is, our focus tends to shift to the *when*. In order to live a life of peace, we must trust the process. We have to surrender to His timetable, especially when it makes no sense to us.

In the above Scripture, people recognized who Jesus was and, because of that, expected Him to usher in immediate victory. They had no idea that before the breakthrough, there would be a season of waiting. Resurrection power would release the peace they desired, but first there would be a sacrifice. This is the way of the kingdom—through surrender of our will, and confidence that rests in Him, we receive our victory.

Jesus, thank you for revealing your plan for my victory. Help me wait patiently and trust you without reservation. I release every care and surrender to your perfect will. Unite my heart and mind so I can move in full cooperation with your Spirit— never ahead and never behind.

Unveiled

"And very soon God will unveil the glory
of the Son of Man."

John 13:32

Every day we're invited to partake of His presence—inexplicable and overwhelming glimpses of the One who holds the stars in His hands. Dazzling brilliance overwhelms our hearts with love and awe. We behold Him with love divine. See Him with the eyes of our hearts.

But there's more. There will always be more. Until the day we behold the glory of our Beloved with unmuddied vision, we'll always reach. Yearn. Train our eyes to see what's obscured by sacred glory just beyond the veil. A veil that was torn by the tips of three bloody nails just so we can be near Him. Though we wait, we know. We see, even if it's not clearly. And we enjoy the moments that lead up to that glorious day, when Love Himself will free us from all restrictions.

Jesus, I look forward to the day that we'll dance together in unbroken fellowship—your arms entwined with mine, never to be separated again. For now, I want to know you more than anyone ever has. To drink of the pleasures of your love and repeatedly allow myself to be overcome by those eyes that blaze with fire.

You Are His Treasure

"A person discovered that there was hidden treasure
in a field. Upon finding it, he hid it again. Because of
uncovering such treasure, he was overjoyed and sold
all that he possessed to buy the entire field just so
he could have the treasure."

Matthew 13:44

You are the treasure Jesus paid everything for. You are the one shining like gold in the midst of a dark and fallen world. If only you could understand how valued you are. How loved. How desired. Before mountains and hills were brought forth, He chose you for Himself.

Now He hides you in His love. Cherishes this relationship He paid for with His blood. What an incredible thought—that we are His delight. How astounding that the One who fills us with joy says that we are the joy that was set before Him (Hebrews 12:2). And this is what we must remember—that we are His beloved. That He's absolutely enthralled by our beauty. That the most magnificent One—the Creator of all that exists—is totally committed to us and will never leave us.

Jesus, when I wake each morning, let me experience the wonder of your smile. Throughout the day, may I remain aware of the breathtaking awe of living in continual communion with you. Hide me in your presence. Have me fully and let my life bring you joy, always.

The Work of the Spirit

> "How can I describe the kingdom of God?
> Let me give you this illustration: It is like something as
> small as yeast that a woman kneads into a large amount
> of dough. It works unseen until it permeates the
> entire batch and rises high."
>
> *Luke 13:20–21*

Carefully and consistently, Jesus pours the oil of His Spirit upon our hearts and massages it until all of the kinks are worked out. The Spirit and the Word are alive, working together to infuse our every cell with life, grace, and healing. At times, we're unaware of the metamorphosis happening within, and other times the work is so deep and intentional, it requires our full cooperation.

The love of Jesus is real. He's more involved in our lives than we often realize. Although ours is a relationship lived in the unseen realm of the spirit, the fruit is evident—seen by our amazing transformation. Everything about us is becoming more like Jesus every day as we yield to His powerful yet often hidden work in our lives.

Jesus, I love how involved you are in my life. It amazes me how much you care. Help me keep my heart soft and pliable in your hands so you can mold me into the person you've called me to be. Transform me continually and help me to remain heavenly minded.

Burning Hearts

"Heaven's kingdom realm is also like a jewel merchant
in search of rare pearls. When he discovered one very
precious and exquisite pearl, he immediately gave up
all he had in exchange for it."

Matthew 13:45–46

*E*ncountering the love of Jesus is like discovering a hidden, sacred treasure, more precious than the rarest of jewels. Just one touch and our hearts melt with desire to know Him as He really is. We have come to a place of insatiable hunger for His presence. We are those with burning hearts—willing to pay any price for a moment in His glory.

It will take all of eternity to fully unpack the abundance of His beauty—a joy that has no comparison. And now, as we yield our lives to Him and forsake all other loves, we know that it's worth it in more ways than we can possibly comprehend. We have fallen in love with the Lover of our soul, and one moment in His splendor leaves us utterly undone yet longing for more.

Jesus, flood my being with the treasures of your love. Consume me. Reveal every selfish motive and catch the thoughts that try to take your place. I'm undone by these limited encounters, trinkets of splendor that are nothing compared to the glory yet to be revealed. Cover me with your priceless love and let nothing steal my holy affection.

Love Causes Us to Believe

"This is the reason I urge you to boldly believe for
whatever you ask for in prayer—believe that you
have received it and it will be yours."

Mark 11:24

L ife is meant to be heaven on earth. Jesus wants us to
experience the same joy and freedom now as we will
the day we enter our heavenly home. Though He did tell us
we'd experience trials here, He also encouraged us to live
with mountain-moving faith in the midst of them. The kind
of faith that believes Jesus wants us to be happy and blessed.

Faith isn't a magical key. There's no formula to successful
prayer. The longer we walk with Him, the more we experience His faithfulness and the more we trust Him. That's the
way it works—His love makes us bold in faith. This is where
relationship with Him becomes the foundation for answered
prayer—the more we know Him, the easier it is to believe. If
doubt has crept in, it could be a result of not prioritizing our
time with Jesus.

*Jesus, knowing you doesn't only help me believe; it reminds
me that you actually care about the things that are on my
heart. I'm bold, not just because I know you want to bless me
but because I know you love me.*

Greater Insights

He responded, "Every scholar of the Scriptures,
who is instructed in the ways of heaven's kingdom realm,
is like a wealthy home owner with his house filled
with treasures both new and old."

Matthew 13:52

As we grow in Christ, we're constantly learning, growing, and transforming. Revelation enlightens our spirits as He takes us from glory to glory. Our zealous hearts love the adventure of journeying with Him and discovering new truth.

Every encounter with the unveiling of truth seems to set us free in new and extreme ways. It can be easy to run hard after fresh revelation and neglect the foundational wisdom that touched our hearts initially. In order to remain stable and grounded in Him, we need both new and old insights. Comprehension of what He taught us in years gone by must be applied as we forge ahead for greater understanding. We mustn't turn the page and forget what we learned. Jesus is the same yesterday, today, and forever; we need the truths that are eternal, in order for our story to be complete.

Jesus, life with you is such a beautiful discovery. I'm filled with anticipation of all I'll find as you lead me through heavenly halls filled with untold treasures of truth. But I know that my life is built on a strong foundation that will never crumble, so I will esteem every revelation, both old and new.

Transformation

"Isn't he just the wood-worker's son?"
Matthew 13:55

Transformation is a beautiful thing. A surprising thing. Especially for those who knew us before this heavenly metamorphosis. How we can literally see life and ourselves through new lenses, not just once but continually, is miraculous. And though those who watch us change may be shocked, no one's more surprised, or more pleased, than we are. It's true—we're nothing without Jesus. With Him we're the very image of His glory revealed.

We'll never cease to be amazed by the way a moment in His presence can alter us at the very core. And heal us from years of pain and heart-breaking trauma in an instant. As we grow and become more and more like our heavenly Father, and less and less like a reflection of a dreary world, we'll stand out from a bewildered crowd. But this is what draws others to Him—seeing a life genuinely transformed by the mercy of God.

Jesus, your grace and mercy never cease to amaze me. I look in the mirror and scarcely recognize the person I've become. I look like you. Every day, as I spend time with you, I'm washed in your healing waters. Becoming a radiant bride. A testimony of your love for the world to see.

He Sees You

"And take note of this: There are some who are
despised and viewed as the least important now,
but will one day be placed at the head of the line.
And there are others who are viewed as 'elite' today
who will become least important then."

Luke 13:30

You are not overlooked. Humility, shyness, and servanthood have not placed you in the back of an eternal room of invisibility. Weakness, poverty, and rejection have not sealed your fate. You are not defined by these temporary labels. You are defined by the One who knows your heart. Who sees what others don't see and smiles with pleasure.

Never believe the lie that you are not enough. That you are forgotten or alone. Jesus is with you. Celebrates you when the world forgets. Has blessed you with facets of His character that no one else has. Though at times it may feel like only the elite receive red-carpet treatment, you are destined to walk streets of gold.

Jesus, you see me when it feels like no one else does. You hold me, dance with me, and lead me to places of prestige I never thought I could have. You are the door of opportunity. The favor that pours out eternal blessings, more stunning than anything this world could offer.

Surrendering to Truth

There was nothing they could say—
all were silenced.

Luke 14:6

When Jesus corrects us, there's no arguing. Truth births life inside of us that cannot be ignored. It touches us in the most profound way. We're left with no rebuttal. Faced with our inaccurate way of understanding things, we are left with two choices: bow low and surrender to His majesty or angrily and pridefully dismiss it.

Jesus never forces truth down anyone's throat. He responds to souls that yearn for purity. Pours the oil of holiness upon our soft and pliable hearts and lovingly draws us to Himself. As we yield our all to Him, He lifts the heavy weights of deception. Frees us from sins that seek to separate us from walking in unbroken fellowship. There's nothing more healing or freeing than prostrating ourselves before His holiness and allowing the power of His truth to wash us clean.

Jesus, silence the lies that I've accepted as truth. I want no part of deception and don't want to rely on my own understanding. I want to embrace holy truth with all that I am. To have nothing in me that doesn't reflect your purity, holiness, and character. Breathe life into me and cleanse me with truth.

Wonder

"This was the Lord's plan—and he is wonderful
for our eyes to behold!"

Mark 12:11

We were created to live in wonder. From the brilliant sunset to the stars that dance on the edge of His fingertips, He's given us all things richly to enjoy. The snow that sparkles as it reflects His glory and the birds that sing His praise are mere glimpses of His goodness. Nothing compares to the beauty of knowing Him and realizing that the King of Glory calls us His own. To see with our hearts the beauty of the One who holds us.

Today, pay attention to the beauty that surrounds you and acknowledge the majesty of the One alive within you. His love can be found in the most obscure places—from the flower that breaks through the dry ground to the soft breeze against your skin. It's heard in the laughter of a child and seen looking back at you when you look in the mirror.

Jesus, all of the glory that I see around me and encounter when I lay my head upon your chest is too wonderful for words. I cannot convey what burns within my heart, so I will sit in silence. Content in the wonder.

Eternity Now

"And when everything is ready, I will come back and take you to myself so that you will be where I am. And you already know the way to the place where I'm going."

John 14:3–4

The kindness of the Lord is astounding! He didn't leave us unclear about His intentions. He wants us to know how incredibly loved and desired we are. All that He did was to create a way for us to be with the Father, Son, and Holy Spirit forever. If we ever have a day when we're feeling rejected, unappreciated, or unloved, we only need to remember how incredibly desired and celebrated we are by Jesus.

Jesus said that we already know the way into His presence, because we know Him—*The Way*. We literally step into eternity now, because we step into Him. We live, move, and have our being in Him. It's possible to walk with Him each day, experiencing the bliss of heaven right here on earth. When we really believe that we exist in Him and His Spirit lives in us, Jesus becomes our eternal reality—now.

Jesus, thank you for making a way into the Father's presence. For loving me so much that I can taste your goodness and love, at all times. Saturate me with the awareness of your glory every day. I want to be where you are forever, starting now.

Our Provider

"We acknowledge you as our Provider
of all we need each day."
Matthew 6:11

Jesus wants every area of our lives to overflow with blessing. As our Provider, His plans are designed to prosper us and give us a future filled with hope. Lack isn't our portion, and poverty is a curse we mustn't accept.

He is our source of endless blessing. As we seek Him first and tune our hearts into righteousness, He's promised to shower us with more than we need (Matthew 6:33). When we believe that Jesus has secured a beautiful inheritance for us, we'll confidently ask for it. We'll receive wisdom and power to create wealth, because we're actively pursuing His guidance. As we behold Him, every part of us is transformed. Everything that pertains to life and wholeness—including provision, flows from His presence.

Shake off despair and come to know Jesus as your Good Shepherd, who faithfully leads and provides. He will bless you and open doors that no one else can. All He asks is that you believe.

Jesus, I submit myself to you fully. You've created me to live a glorious life, free from stress and anxiety. I declare that my soul is prosperous, my health is vibrant, and my needs are met in abundance, because my heart is set on you.

Jesus Is ...

Jesus explained, "I am the Way,
I am the Truth, and I am the Life."

John 14:6

With the many ways it's possible to know Jesus, it's vital that you know Him as *I Am*. For every trial, He not only holds the answer, but He is the answer. Jesus is your true and present reality. As you reach out to Him, His palpable presence becomes more real than what you see.

When shadows of uncertainty fall upon your path and the road to your promises seems to be littered with despair, He not only makes a way, He becomes the way. As He walks, you walk, because you're in Him. Though doubt screams in your face and tells you that you'll never have your breakthrough, Jesus becomes the truth that quells every lie. When you feel as if your life has been sucked dry, executed by hopelessness or failure, you discover that He's not only your source of life; He quite literally is your life.

Jesus, I want to be continually aware of all you are in me and all that I am as I abide in you. You do much more than hold the answers that I need; you have become the answer I need. Thank you for becoming my reality—the truth that fuels my life with breakthrough and joy!

Loving Well

"You are to love the Lord Yahweh, your God, with every
passion of your heart, with all the energy of your being,
with every thought that is within you, and with all your
strength. This is the great and supreme commandment.
And the second is this: 'You must love your neighbor in
the same way you love yourself.' You will never find
a greater commandment than these."

Mark 12:30–31

If we were to describe the Father, Son, and Holy Spirit in
one word, it would be *love*. All that He is and does has
love at the core. As His offspring, love is the foundation of who
we are. Our union with the Godhead is rooted in love. Our
strength, vibrancy, and identity come to life as we yield every
passion of our hearts and consumptions of our mind to Him.

As we become consumed with Him, we become more
relevant to the world around us. We learn to tap into His
heart for people, regardless of their ethnicity, social status, or
political differences. We're those who care about our com-
munities, neighbors, the hurting, and the forgotten, because
He does. When we love the way He does, we give the world
a true interpretation of Christianity and the One.

⁜

*Jesus, I want every thought, word, and action to be fueled
with holy passion for you. With my heart fixed upon you, may
your desires become mine. I want to become obsessed with
the things of your kingdom—loving you and knowing you so
intimately that I learn to love others just as well.*

Never Forget

Jesus replied, "Philip, I've been with you all this time
and you still don't know who I am?"

John 14:9

It takes time to know Jesus, not because He withholds Himself from us but because His goodness is so overwhelming that we can't take it all in in one sitting. Ours is a beautiful journey of discovery—a chance to seek revelation and still be okay with the mysteries yet to be revealed. As we live and move and have our beings in Him, He's alive within us, surging through our veins and making Himself known in ways that mean more to our heart than to our minds. Yelling over the pounding chaos, "I've got you! We'll get through this together!"

There is a tension in faith. A sort of death to what makes sense to our understanding and a resurrection of life so deep that it's hard to understand. It's like taking a deep breath and inhaling the substance of peace, remembering that the Prince of Peace is always good. Always on our side. Always for us.

Jesus, I want to know you and encounter you so profoundly that trials have no ability to steal my awareness of you. As I lean into this divine relationship, open my eyes, reveal yourself to me. Touch my soul. Never let me forget.

The Glory of a Wasted Life

"What a total waste! It could have been sold for
a great sum, and the money could have benefited
the poor." So they scolded her harshly.

Mark 14:4–5

The world will never understand this passion that stirs within us. To them, our energy would be better spent seeking worldly wisdom and aligning our thoughts with theirs. Many say we're wasting our lives and our talents by following Spirit-breathed desires. They evaluate our worth based on what we do, but God declares our value based on who we are.

For those who have forsaken the acceptable to run after the indescribable, we know no other way. We no longer strive for temporary pleasures but allow our lives to flow from the overflow of His Spirit in us. We wear no mask to appease those who are watching. The world may scorn, but what they have yet to understand we have encountered—here, in the secret chambers of His love.

Jesus, the glory of your love has ruined me for anything else. I want my devotion to you to rise as a pleasing offering. Not one drop of love is ever wasted on you. I lay my life at your feet and pour myself out to discover the glory you've hidden for me to find.

September

Dare to Believe

> "And that is how the Son will show what the Father
> is really like and bring glory to him. Ask me anything
> in my name, and I will do it for you!"
>
> *John 14:13–14*

*J*esus wants us to know the goodness of the Father. Experiencing what He's really like not only blesses us, but it brings Him glory. As we acquaint ourselves with the kindness of God, we get to know Him the way Jesus does. By answering our prayers, He's glorified. Ask anything in His name and Jesus said He'd do it!

Anything? Well, we know that when we make a request in someone's name, it's because that person has already given us permission. Unless our prayer contradicts the Word or the Lord has specifically shown us that what we're asking for isn't His will, we've got His permission. The bigger question is, do we really believe it? It's time we reject rationality and dare to believe! Too often we limit our breakthrough because we don't believe it will really happen. It's time to shake off the disappointments of unanswered prayer and reach out with fresh faith.

Lord, forgive me for doubting that you'd do anything in the world in me. I don't want unbelief to limit my life. Ignite my faith afresh. Breathe hope and excitement into every area that I've yielded to discouragement. Nothing is too hard for you!

A Humble Heart

"Remember this: everyone with a lofty opinion
of who he is and who seeks to raise himself up will be
humbled before all. And everyone with a modest opinion
of who he is and chooses to humble himself
will be raised up before all."

Luke 14:11

*J*esus wants His personality to shine through those who are known by His name. He wants us to leave thumb-prints of His tenderness and humility everywhere we go. All that He is, we were created to be. Understanding our identity as royalty in His kingdom means recognizing our great need for Him. It leaves no room for pride.

Jesus was the greatest servant of all. The Son of God came to earth to lay down His life for others. The King of kings chose the humble posture of love when He died on the cross for the very people who put Him there. Nothing about Him is harsh, and He doesn't rule with a heavy hand. It is our greatest honor to walk the path of perfect strength, exemplified with humility, just like our Lord.

Jesus, let the revelation of your mercy pierce my soul and keep me in remembrance of my great need for you. I will never be good enough, holy enough, or memorize enough Scriptures to deserve what you've offered me. Reveal areas of pride that would hinder me from being a true reflection of who you are.

Obedient in Love

> "Loving me empowers you
> to obey my commands."
>
> *John 14:15*

Jesus doesn't threaten us with punishment. He doesn't require obedience without the empowering of His love to fuel it. Following His commandments happens when we know the tenderness of the One who has given them to us.

His love is the power and source of all we do—even in obedience. Even the love we love Him with is a gift from heaven. When we love, we don't strive to prove it. It happens naturally. There's no forcing ourselves to obey when we've experienced His love. Yes, there are times we must stand against temptation and make wise decisions, but love has become our greatest motivator. When we live in the awareness of love, we don't want to turn away.

Jesus, give me grace to remain mindful of your love for me so I'll never become indifferent. To keep my heart pliable in your hands. Thank you for showing me what perfect love looks like. I want to live my life honoring you in everything I do and say, simply because I love you.

Taste and See

"So the master told him, 'All right. Go out again,
and this time bring them all back with you. Persuade the
beggars on the streets, the outcasts, even the homeless.
Urgently insist that they come in and enjoy the
feast so that my house will be full.'"

Luke 14:23

The Lord is so much fun! He wants to be surrounded with those He loves—and He loves everyone. He isn't put off by the outcasts or those who carry the scent of a filthy world. To Him, everyone is beautiful. Everyone is desirable. Everyone is wanted.

With urgency in His voice, He's calling the world close, and He wants us to do the same. We've been equipped to carry the Lord's presence in a way that truly represents His heart for all mankind. Jesus doesn't have favorites, and He doesn't play religious games that require people to look or act a certain way before they're welcome to sit at His table. Instead, He prepares a feast so everyone can taste and see that He's good. Then, He loads us up with samples to share with the world.

Jesus, I want to be just like you! To see people the way you do and be as excited to talk to a total stranger as I am my best friend. I want to offer the world a taste of your presence in all I do and say so they'll know how amazing you are.

The Joy of Honoring Him

"She has done all that she could to honor me."

Mark 14:8

What an incredible statement Jesus made to Mary! Now imagine Jesus saying it to you. He's standing in front of you, holding your hands, and looking into your eyes. He's smiling at you, overjoyed with what He sees. "Thank you for honoring me with your life, your choices, and your heart," He says. How does that feel? It should warm your heart, because this is the way He thinks about you.

Nothing you've ever done to honor Him has gone unnoticed. When you guarded your heart against defilement or cried out in repentance because you failed, He was right beside you, cheering you on. Every time you surrendered your will for His, He leaned closer and kissed your soul with peace. Your desire to live with humility and purpose, reaching past the shadows of lowly thinking, has touched His heart.

✤

Jesus, I want to be known as a person who seeks to honor you in all things. You're worthy of my heartfelt devotion and full surrender. Starting now, and throughout eternity, I want the joy of living before you in purity and holiness, unafraid of how I look to anyone but you.

Holy Spirit's Friendship

"And I will ask the Father and he will give you another
Savior, the Holy Spirit of Truth, who will be to you a
friend just like me—and he will never leave you."

John 14:16

*Y*ou are never alone. The One who always was and
ever will be, is with you, in you, and all around you. He
knows all there is to know about you and offers you more
than acceptance—He offers you friendship.

Life with the Holy Spirit is a journey of discovery—about
Him and about ourselves. He loves to challenge us in the
best possible ways. He not only reveals areas that hinder us
from experiencing an amazing life, but He also makes it easy
to partner with Him to overcome those areas. Like a true best
friend, He loves to highlight our strengths, encourage us in
our dreams, and point us in the right direction. Conversations
with Him, if we'll take the time to listen, always result in freedom, hope, and joy.

✤

*Father, thank you for answering Jesus' prayer so I can enjoy life
with your Holy Spirit. Lead me into my divine purpose, where
my deepest desires are not only known but celebrated. Holy
Spirit, teach me how to stay tuned in to your wisdom and to
glean from my friendship with you—a friendship unlike any I've
ever known.*

The God of Second Chances

"Come and join me," Jesus replied. So Peter stepped out
onto the water and began to walk toward Jesus. But when he
realized how high the waves were, he became frightened and
started to sink. "Save me, Lord!" he cried out.

Matthew 14:29–30

Have you ever prayed for something that you really
wanted and once you received it, felt like you were
sinking under the weight of it? We can probably all relate to
Peter to some degree. What we thought would be exciting
and adventurous becomes scary and intimidating when we
take our eyes off Jesus.

Storms rage, contending for attention. Roaring winds fight
to extinguish the sound of Jesus' voice as He leads us into the
great unknown. Stepping out of the boat and taking a risk is
commendable, but I've often wondered what would've happened if Peter had asked Jesus for a second chance. Too many
dreams are sacrificed when radical faith meets seeming failure. Instead of giving up, let's remember that our Redeemer
loves to redeem both souls and dreams. He truly is the God
of second chances.

*Jesus, you've called me out into the waters of the unknown—
the place where faith and action give birth to beautiful dreams.
I yield my fear of failure, knowing you'll rescue me if I sink. By
your grace, I'll see the desires of my heart come to pass. I'll
keep my eyes on you and never give up.*

Consumed

"Whoever passionately loves me will be passionately loved by my Father. And I will passionately love you in return and will manifest my life within you."

John 14:21

The devotion that burns within you draws the attention of Jesus. He hears every word of worship, reflects upon each movement of longing, and joins you in joyous celebration. As you pour out your heart in loving abandon, He answers with waves of tangible glory much too profound for words.

You'll never be able to love Him more than He loves you. Even the love you love Him with is a gift. He's the Lord of all mystery, the One who stepped out of eternity in order to lead you along the path of resurrection life. While you were still cloaked in sin, Jesus revealed your worth. Lean in. Abandon yourself to a lifestyle of passionate pursuit and watch as He unveils the work of His Spirit within you.

Jesus, I want to know you more than anyone ever has. I'm not satisfied with glimpses of glory. I want to be consumed with holy passion that leaves me longing for more of you. As I pursue you, align my heart and infuse me with purity and courage. Let me see you as you are and hear the sound of love.

You Are Powerful

"And I will ask the Father and he will give you another
Savior, the Holy Spirit of Truth, who will be to you a
friend just like me—and he will never leave you. ...
you will know him intimately, because he will make
his home in you and will live inside you."

John 14:16–17

You are filled with the strength of God Himself. Nothing about you is weak and powerless. No enemy can stand against you when you tap into the greatest source of power the world has ever known. The very life source that raised Jesus from the dead now lives inside of you (Romans 8:11). Imagine that! Every fiber of your being is saturated with the same glory that saturated Jesus.

Though you can't see Him, the Holy Spirit is with you. Defending. Comforting. Helping you in every situation, every second of the day. Because of the Holy Spirit, you're never alone. Take time to build a friendship with Him and get to know Him, as Jesus does. He longs to lead you, to warn you of danger, offer you wisdom, and show you how to pray. Everything you need to live successfully has been granted to you.

Holy Spirit, I want to know you more. Thank you for making your home in me and for filling me with the same life that Jesus had when He walked this earth. I want to feel you, hear you, and experience the reality of you in my life more than ever before.

The Joy of Choosing Him

"When you follow me as my disciple, you must
put aside your father, your mother, your wife, your sisters,
your brothers—yes, you will even seem as though
you hate your own life."

Luke 14:26

othing must consume our hearts more than Jesus. Every other relationship must be secondary to our connection with Him. The spark of life is found in Him, making all other loves fall short. He alone holds the love and fulfillment we crave. When He unveiled our hearts and introduced us to the Trinity, we truly came alive.

This is first-love passion—a flame of desire that must be constantly tended so it doesn't grow dim. Friendship with Him actually empowers us to be better friends, spouses, and family to those we care about. It enables us to love ourselves. It teaches us how to recognize His voice over the clamor of every other. Some call choosing Jesus over and over again a discipline, but lovesick believers consider it a joy!

Jesus, I love your company. To think that you long for mine as well leaves me utterly undone. No one cares for me like you do. I want to know you more and become acquainted with what moves your heart. You are my dearest and closest friend, and it is my joy to choose you over all others.

Contagious Zeal

*"Salt is good for seasoning. But if salt were to lose
its flavor, how could it ever be restored?"*

Luke 14:34

Never lose your zeal for Jesus. Fan the flames of holy passion by regularly setting time aside to be alone with Him. Listen for His voice and bask in His glorious presence regularly. Your encounters with Jesus provide the substance that leads others into encounters of their own. When your heart is full, it's hard not to splash others with the overflow of your internal reality.

Our relationship with Jesus must be so vibrant that it flows from us with ease. As the salt of the earth, we must be able to point others to Him, share His love, and season the earth with the taste of heaven, especially in the darkest times. All we need is passion for Jesus and the courage and compassion to touch the world around us with the joy and freedom that comes from living with Him.

Jesus, may my words, thoughts, and actions be filled with kingdom truth and seasoned with grace. As I saturate myself in your presence, may my life resonate with hope and draw others to you. I want my heart to be true—filled with unquenchable passion that becomes an epidemic that cannot be cured.

Empowered by Love

Jesus replied, "Loving me empowers you
to obey my word."
John 14:23

Our relationship with Jesus is the most empowering force on the planet. Nothing else transforms us the way His love does. When we understand how He sees us, it completely changes us, refines our desires, and causes us to live differently. Once we embrace the truth of who we are, we don't strive to obey Him; it flows effortlessly from a heart that's ravished by love.

The knowledge that we are perfectly loved, accepted, and forgiven draws us to Him like a magnet. The discovery of His heart, His nature, and His presence stirs our desire to know Him more. Our life becomes a love song, where holy passion for His ways drowns out every other voice. It's impossible to saturate ourselves in the depth of His love and not be overtaken with the desire to please Him.

Jesus, your love is tender and outrageous. It comforts me in my weakness and ignites my zeal to live every moment from a place of holy communion. I want nothing to hinder me from being fully yours. Refine me in your presence and consume me with desire to live for you always.

The Gift of Peace

"I leave the gift of peace with you—my peace.
Not the kind of fragile peace given by the world,
but my perfect peace."

John 14:27

Peace. Everyone wants it but few find it, because it cannot be accessed by the mind but with the heart. It contradicts circumstances and fact. Its foundation—an invisible rock of faith. Peace is risky because it means releasing the ability to control what we cannot shape with our own strength. It abandons the right to worry and free-falls into the arms of the One it cannot see.

Anxiety and fear make us feel as if we're doing something to make things better. It's the enemy's way of giving us false confidence that we're controlling unmanageable situations. True peace isn't obtained by fixing everything that feels chaotic. It is gifted to us in exchange for our total trust in the One who is completely trustworthy. May you find sweet release from every worry as you surrender every care at the feet of Jesus.

✧

Jesus, unshackle me from the noisy distractions that play inside my head. I relinquish the right to worry and surrender my need to fix everything. Fill me with peace that's beyond my understanding. Forgive me for trying to analyze every finite detail of life instead of trusting you with the sheer abandon of a child.

The One Within

> So they brought him all their sick, begging him to
> let them touch the fringe of his robe. And everyone
> who touched it was instantly healed!
>
> *Matthew 14:36*

What an incredible image of dynamic power! The glory of God exuding from Jesus was so strong that merely touching the clothing He was wrapped in brought instant healing. Now Jesus wraps Himself with us. We are like that outer garment—emanating with healing virtue. We are the vessel He's chosen to abide in. The ones He trusts to disperse His glory and healing.

It's such a mystery—the way we're in Christ, yet He's in us. How we can be held by the One who holds us from the inside. How the healing we need for our tattered hearts is already pulsating within. And the answer for those around us is inside us, longing to be freed. As Christians, we base our lives on these truths. But if we really believe it, it's time to live it. To release it. To live with a constant awareness of the One inside and see the power of God stream from us.

Jesus, the substance of your love has made us one. Sensitize me so that I become aware of this continual and holy union. The power of your resurrection surges through every part of me, and I am yours—completely. I bow before you, undone by the glory and power of the One within me.

To Be One

"So you must remain in life-union with me, for I remain
in life-union with you. For as a branch severed from the
vine will not bear fruit, so your life will be fruitless
unless you live your life intimately joined to mine."

John 15:4

B y grace we've been brought into union with Christ.
Perfect oneness. Unlimited blessing. Unceasing power.
We've done nothing to earn it—this unimaginable gift of
mercy called salvation that's available to all yet personally
suited to each. All He asks is that we enjoy it. Soak it up and
remain in it. Live with relentless passion stirring within us;
never forsaking it. Not just for our sake but for His.

As we cultivate this delicate and delightful relationship,
we learn to abide in peace. To see things through His eyes.
To rest. Find joy. Weep with passion that makes our hearts
feel truly alive. To allow ourselves to ebb and flow in perfect
harmony with Him. Bear fruit that remains for eternity. We
are one with Him.

✢

*Jesus, you are the beauty that lives inside me. The light that
illuminates every darkened shadow of my soul. I choose to
remain in you. To stay in this place of satisfying wonder and
ultimate pleasure so that I'll never be out of sync with you.*

Happily Steadied

"As you live in union with me as your source,
fruitfulness will stream from within you—but when
you live separated from me you are powerless."

John 15:5

Everything changes when we discover the joys of living in unbroken fellowship with Jesus. All of life proceeds from this one truth—our union with Him streams into every facet. Jesus cares about it all—family, relationships, business, finances, health, and spirituality—the list is as vast as He is. He doesn't remove Himself from anything that matters to us. As we live in union with Him, our desires beat in perfect rhythm with His.

The more we tune into His presence—the living experience of His nearness, the less we strive to make things happen. Grace is poured out so abundantly that we find ourselves stepping into favor, abundance, healing, and other blessings with little effort. Life streams out of a solidity and confidence inside of us that we never knew before. There's power. Strength. Deep-seated peace. Joy. All because we live in union with Him.

Jesus, how can I describe the fruitfulness of life with you? I'm undone by your ability to replace anxiety with peace. Grateful for healing. Surprised by the glory. Unafraid of what the future holds. Happily steadied by the safety of your arms.

Be Encouraged

"And I will send you the Divine Encourager from the
very presence of my Father. He will come to you,
the Spirit of Truth, emanating from the Father,
and he will speak to you about me."

John 15:26

Jesus knew that we'd need encouragement. He loves us so much that He gave His best. When doubt clouds our vision and chokes our faith, His Spirit gently fans the flames of hope and gives sight to our eyes. He reminds us of the One who holds nothing back from us and holds things for us until we're ready for them.

Pain is inevitable. Brokenness afflicts us with puzzling perplexity. At times our hearts feel stiff, and we wonder if Jesus is still there. He is our comfort in a place that suddenly feels empty. And all of these reasons are why He stays and why He gave us the Holy Spirit. His joy becomes ours. The softness of His hands massages our hearts and brings us back to life. We need Him. Expectantly long for the miracle of hope that He always brings. *Is* bringing right now.

Jesus, even now I can feel the breath of heaven reviving me, lifting me up and strengthening me with surprising wonder. Only you can do this—completely strip away the heaviness that felt like it would be there forever. I can breathe again. You're here, and you'll never leave.

The Lost Will Be Rescued

"So the shepherd left the ninety-nine lambs out in
the open field and searched in the wilderness for that
one lost lamb. He didn't stop until he finally found it.
With exuberant joy he raised it up and placed it on his
shoulders, carrying it back with cheerful delight!"

Luke 15:4–5

Other than the cross, nothing demonstrates the love of Christ more than the way He relentlessly pursues those who reject Him. It's almost hard to relate to such an extravagant, steadfast love, especially toward those who turn their backs on us.

The cross is such a beautiful image of outrageous love. Jesus placed on His shoulders the burden and joy of holy redemption. That passion is eternal—nothing stops Him from searching for the ones He loves. Today, He still carries lost lambs on His shoulders as He rescues them from the enemy's snare. Jesus will never force anyone to walk in fellowship with Him, but He most certainly knows how to woo the hearts He created. If you know someone who has turned away from the Lord, let's pray together.

Jesus, we call __ (say the person's name) back into your family. We declare that every lie is being illuminated by the light of truth. Make yourself undeniably real to them again. Breathe gently upon the embers of their heart and reignite the flames of holy passion. Everywhere they go, let them be reminded of your love. Do what only you can do.

Blissfully Content

"I love each of you with the same love
that the Father loves me. You must continually
let my love nourish your hearts."

John 15:9

You've been given an invitation to experience holy love—not just once in a while, or in a special meeting, but continually. Jesus wants you to live in the place where the tangible reality of His love is a regular part of your life. He wants you to recognize the swell of affection that rises within and lets you know He's present.

Jesus' holy passion for you isn't an earthly, natural love. Encounters of this living flame impart life and sustenance to the very depths of your being. Yielding to it burns away every stale and lingering thought of discouragement. Embracing it creates an atmosphere for the miraculous. Like fire in your veins, it cannot be ignored. His love is His goodness, mercy, kindness, and power, revealed to you with unceasing certainty.

Jesus, drown me in your glory. Rapture me with your love. I feel it so profoundly, rising within me and fusing me into oneness with you. Let this glorious kindness overtake every thought, setting me free in ways I've never known. You're here now and I'm blissfully content.

Self-Focus

"These people honor me only with their words,
for their hearts are so very distant from me."

Matthew 15:8

*L*et's never let this be said of us. When we worship, let's be so consumed with His presence that every other thought simply doesn't exist. When we speak of Him, may our words pour forth from hearts overflowing with sincere devotion. As we go about our day, even the most miniscule tasks are filled with the knowledge that He's our everything.

If life has become dry and you can't get the muck of the world off of you, consider where your thoughts have settled. Lift your eyes to Him. Let every prayer request wait until another day. Give yourself permission to enjoy the Lord, without praying about your needs. Don't allow problems to thrust your attention on yourself. Self-focus keeps us weary and dry. Today, put worship music on and stay in that posture until you're so consumed with His presence, nothing else matters.

Jesus, I want to stay in constant communion with you. The foundation of my relationship with you isn't based on what you do for me but on who you are. I want my heart to remain close to you—fixated on your glory, always. May my words always reflect sincere devotion. I love you.

Enjoying Each Other

"When you pray, there is no need to repeat empty
phrases, praying like those who don't know God, for they
expect God to hear them because of their many words."

Matthew 6:7

There's nothing more beautiful and sacred than our relationship with the Lord. Each sigh of our heart, every declaration of love, and every cry for help—Jesus hears every one. Even the way we look at Him thrills His heart. Not one word goes unnoticed.

Jesus isn't impressed with prayers that sound eloquent. How could we possibly think we'd impress the One who created language itself? We can recite the most beautiful prayers, but unless we know the One we're praying to, our words are void of substance. Jesus is looking for our hearts in whatever way conveys them best. He wants to enjoy time with us, even if that means sitting in silence with our hearts entwined with His.

Jesus, I don't care how I sound. I just need you. Come, meet with me. Tell me what's on your heart. I simply want to step into the reality of your love and offer you my heart. I have no other motivation than to honor you, to love you well, and to live face to face in unending communion.

Women

> "When she finally found it, she gathered all her friends
> and neighbors for a celebration, telling them, 'Come and
> celebrate with me! I had lost my precious silver coin,
> but now I've found it.' That's the way God responds
> every time one lost sinner repents and turns to him."
>
> *Luke 15:9–10*

One of the most overlooked references to the importance of women is found in this Scripture. The woman in this parable is a metaphor for God. Jesus had no problem comparing the Father with a woman, or with a woman's role in the kingdom. After all, God Himself created men and women in His image. We see women judges, queens, prophetesses, and leaders all the way back to the Old Testament.

Jesus loved to stir up the religious who were more concerned about their understanding of the law than God's heart. Today, many are still stirred by the value He's placed on women and the obvious anointing they carry. The truth is that while many in the church restrict a woman's title, nothing can stop women from fulfilling the call on their lives.

Jesus, thank you for placing such a high value on women. We pray for women everywhere to rise up in their identity and be free from oppression. We declare that they are powerful and have a voice that must be heard within the church. Jesus, let your cherished ones arise and shine!

Authentic, Happy People

"My purpose for telling you these things is
so that the joy that I experience will fill your hearts
with overflowing gladness!"

John 15:11

Jesus wants your life to be happy and your joy to be full. He wants you to be so aware of His goodness that it's obvious by the smile on your face and the wisdom you carry. He wants you to be so in tune with His kindness that it rises from you like a sweet-smelling fragrance everywhere you go.

When we stay tuned in to the presence of God, our hearts overflow with gladness, even in the middle of life's messes. We're not afraid to talk about our problems because we know He wants to use them to demonstrate His faithfulness to those watching. Let's be known as people who laugh in the face of adversity. People who aren't characterized by the mask we wear but by our genuine trust in Him. In the church and outside of its four walls, it's time Christians are recognized as authentic and happy people.

Jesus, I want to represent you well. To be known as someone who carries wisdom, peace, and joy. Help me to look at every trial as an opportunity to testify of your goodness when breakthrough comes. May I be genuine with everyone I meet—a source of encouragement and joy.

The Joy of Heaven

"That's the way God responds every time one
lost sinner repents and turns to him. He says to all his
angels, 'Let's have a joyous celebration, for that
one who was lost I have found!'"

Luke 15:10

Heaven is excited about you! The day you turned to Jesus, the Father smiled at His angels and all of heaven rejoiced. Think about that—*you* are the joy of heaven. The joy that was set before Jesus on the cross. The one whose life attracts the attention of His heavenly kingdom.

Imagine for a moment what it must look like to see the Father of glory smiling, dancing, and celebrating with the angels. I dare say that we've never seen joy like we'll see in heaven. We are the Lord's great delight. Even if we turn away from Him, His eyes remain fixed on us, anticipating our return. The cross isn't good for a one-time use. It's eternal in its saving grace. Its glorious power flows into the deepest darkest lies and sets us free. Able to save us to the uttermost, turning our hearts to the One who loves us greatly.

Jesus, the sound of your laughter is like a lightning bolt to my soul. To think that I can put a smile on your face is incredible! Thank you for saving me. Though heaven rejoices over me, you are the joy of my heart. The love that keeps me from falling.

Known by Love

*"So this is my command: Love each other deeply,
as much as I have loved you."*

John 15:12

Love has awakened our hearts. Love that fulfills every longing and demolishes every fear. Love that's alive and has a name—Jesus. He draws us with relentless passion and kisses our darkness with mercy. His love is outrageous—it never stops, and we've done nothing to earn it. His presence is a safe haven—drawing us away from religion, into the chamber of the King.

Our lives are no longer our own. To truly be transformed by this love means we're stirred to not only soak it up but to pour it out. Love becomes the driving force behind all we do and say. Let's be known by our radical love and how relentlessly we honor each other. Hearts that are truly ignited with holy passion don't just talk about love, they demonstrate it.

Jesus, let me live in the awareness of your overwhelming love forever. To taste and see that you are good. To be so wrecked by the beauty and power of your love that I cannot help but share it. Let me be known by love, not just for you but for the way I care about others.

When You're Tempted

"Keep alert and pray that you'll be spared from
this time of testing. For your spirit is eager enough,
but your humanity is feeble."

Mark 14:38

Jesus gave us two powerful bits of advice for times of testing and temptation. Being a man who experienced temptation Himself, He knew exactly what we needed in order to overcome. Remember, Jesus didn't breeze through temptation because He was God. He came as a man in order to show us what we could do with God's help.

When you're going through a particularly rough season of temptation, doubt, fear, sickness, etc., it's vital that you feed your spirit. First, Jesus said, "Keep alert." That means, pay attention when the enemy is luring you into sin, confusion, doubt, etc. Second, He said to pray. The moment you notice you're being tempted, run to the Lord. Turn off the distractions of TV, the internet, and cellphones and spend time in His presence. Strengthen yourself in the Lord by feeding your spirit, and you'll find you've made it through times of testing with His grace.

✢

Jesus, thank you for loving me when my faith is weak. I surrender my life to you afresh and ask that you fill me with strength and grace. I want nothing in me to contradict the holiness of walking with you. Wrap me in your presence as I choose to overcome.

Agape

"So this is my command: Love each other deeply,
as much as I have loved you. For the greatest love
of all is a love that sacrifices all."

John 15:12–13

Jesus loves extravagantly, and the more we spend time with Him, the more we want to be like Him. As we grow and become secure in our identity, our perspective changes. We begin to see others through His eyes. We sense His love for our friends and family in a way we never have before. Suddenly, compassion overpowers criticism, and we're able to love purely and without agenda.

Jesus never turns us away, even in our messes. He encourages, loves, corrects with empowering hope, and believes the best. When we remember how outrageously He loves us, and how He gave His life to prove it, it frees us to love with the same carefree abandon. We're not afraid of getting hurt because the love we pour out is constantly being poured right back in by Jesus. We're one family engrafted into one vine. Love and mercy have become our life source—the very seal upon our hearts.

Jesus, your mercy and love have set me free; now help me to love others as graciously as you love me. May I not look for what I get out of relationships but for what I can give. I want to love like you do, displaying your heart with outrageous zeal and compassion.

SEPTEMBER 28

Listen to Yourself

"But what comes out of your mouth reveals
the core of your heart."

Matthew 15:18

If we ever want to know what's stirring in our heart, all we have to do is listen to what's coming out of our mouth. What we say, especially during times of stress or when we feel comfortable enough to open up to someone, reveals our truest beliefs. Our words unveil our fears and doubts. Anger and tears are more than moments of venting; they point to areas that need the healing touch of Jesus and the truth of His Word. Even sarcasm can indicate a place of wounding.

Don't mask your true feelings. Listen to your heart and tend to your soul. Being honest about what's going on inside of you and taking steps to find freedom is vital. Invite Jesus into every area of your life and hold nothing back. He's able to strip away what doesn't agree with truth when you don't hide from your areas of frailty, unbelief, and pain.

Jesus, shine your spotlight into the deepest wells of my soul. Help me to pay attention to the places that need the cleansing fire of your love. I want every area of my life to radiate with truth and wholeness. Heal me. Speak to me. Saturate every fiber of my being with your truth.

Jesus Is Fun!

"And this great love is demonstrated when a person
sacrifices his life for his friends."

John 15:13

Right now, Jesus calls you friend. Our beautiful Lord and magnificent King has chosen you to enjoy the miracle of holy friendship. He loves you more than anyone else ever could. He enjoys spending time with you, talking about your day, laughing, and sharing secrets. He *gets you*, understanding your personality more than your closest friend.

Jesus isn't some far-off friend who only notices you when you're praying. He's relevant—able to relate to the various situations you face because He chose to experience them Himself when he walked the earth. Even when you disappoint yourself, He's by your side, encouraging you and brightening the atmosphere with His smile. He's fun, playful, and wants you to enjoy life as much as He does. He's certainly not boring, and if you'll invite Him, He'll introduce you to the joys of friendship in new and glorious ways!

Jesus, you're the best friend I've ever had. Take me on an adventure. Let's laugh and play together with no worries. Your perfect sacrifice has liberated me. Teach me to live free, like a child—safe and happy, confident and unencumbered. With you, life is so much fun!

Commissioned

"But I call you my most intimate friends, for I reveal
to you everything that I've heard from my Father.
You didn't choose me, but I've chosen and
commissioned you to go into the world to bear fruit."

John 15:15–16

When we see ourselves not only as children of God but also as Jesus' most intimate friends, we can't help but smile. He doesn't just love us; He likes us! The King of all creation trusts us to carry out His mandate. He believes in us and calls us worthy. He wraps us in His robe of righteousness and places a crown upon our heads. He celebrates what we've yet to become, but it's up to us to embrace it.

The bondage of false humility will always disqualify us. It's unbelief to say, "I'm not worthy," when Jesus says, "You're without flaw, my love." The lies of accusation were silenced by the banging sound of nails piercing the Perfect One. There's nothing left to say but "Thank you," when He calls us worthy. There's nothing left to do but walk side by side with our best Friend when He tells us to represent Him to the world.

Jesus, thank you for being my best friend, for declaring me worthy, for looking into my eyes and cherishing what you see. I want all that you see within me to bring you glory. I yield myself to you without reservation.

October

Free from Shame

> "So the young son set off for home. From a long distance
> away, his father saw him coming, *dressed as a beggar,*
> and great compassion swelled up in his heart for his
> son who was returning home. So the father raced out
> to meet him. He swept him up in his arms, hugged him
> dearly, and kissed him over and over with tender love."
>
> *Luke 15:20*

No one is as compassionate and merciful as our Lord. He never pushes us away, even in our greatest sin. The enemy loves to remind us of our past and habits that we're still working on. He wants to clothe us in shame so we'll believe the lie that sin and failure define us. But Jesus not only holds the answer—He is the answer. Everything we need to live in victory is found in Him. When we truly crave freedom, He'll never disappoint.

Jesus has dug up the roots of our past and burned them in a holy inferno of love. Wrong choices become launching pads to discoveries of His love and mercy that we wouldn't know any other way. Our past doesn't define us. Shame is not our portion. We've been defined by the price of love.

Jesus, when all I see is my failure, you pull me close and wrap me in your righteousness. Even if I were to reject you, your love would remain. Fill every void with the fullness of who you are. Heal the wounds in my soul and strengthen me by your grace. Today I break my agreement with shame and choose a life of freedom in you.

Holy Boldness

But she came and bowed down before him and said,
"Lord, help me!" Jesus responded, "It's not right for a
man to take bread from his children and throw it out
to the dogs." "You're right, Lord," she replied.
"But even puppies get to eat the crumbs..."
Then Jesus answered her, "Dear woman, your faith
is strong! What you desire will be done for you."

Matthew 15:25–28

*P*owerful faith starts with radical encounter. When our lives have been touched by the reality of who Jesus is and how outrageously loved we are, holy boldness finds its way into seemingly impossible situations. Though life may try to get in the way of what's been promised to us, it doesn't stand a chance against a child of God who's full of holy boldness.

Faith isn't a rude, forceful, or prideful demand on the Lord's love. It's confident, humble, and absolutely surrendered to love in a way that completely ignores the barriers of conflicting facts. Convinced of His unconditional love and absolute power, we approach His throne with unshakable confidence and boldly receive what is rightfully ours.

Jesus, your love has given me boldness to run after the promises of your heart. I will not be denied the breakthroughs you've said are mine. Unfavorable facts are nothing but walls of convincing illusion, ready to crumble by the power of your Spirit inside me.

Healed

Then huge crowds of people streamed up the hill,
bringing with them the lame, blind, deformed, mute,
and many others in need of healing. They laid them
at Jesus' feet and he healed them all.

Matthew 15:30

Jesus is the same yesterday, today, and forever. If it was His will to heal when He walked this earth, it's still His desire to heal today. To deliver today. To set you free. Today. And today must be the day that you choose to embrace this truth. Agree with it. Give no place to the weight of fear pressing you down. Bow before no other than the Lordship of Jesus and believe He will come.

No matter what the doctors, symptoms, or abusive lies of the enemy try to convince you of, healing is Jesus' gift to you. There are times He chooses to release healing through doctors, but it's not your job to understand; it's your job to agree with healing. To reject fear. To stop rehearsing and analyzing the problem and nestle into Jesus' safe arms and find your peace.

Jesus, the power of your truth is like a breath of fresh air. Though I may not understand why some healing comes quickly and some takes longer to manifest, I choose to believe. To surrender fear. To rest in your perfect love. To believe that today is the day my healing has been released from heaven.

Embracing Vulnerability

"You always want to look spiritual in the eyes of others,
but you have forgotten the eyes of God,
which see what is inside you."

Luke 16:15

Jesus will never ask you to wear a mask and pretend everything's okay when it isn't. Though you may not want to be completely open with everyone, embracing vulnerability is both liberating and healing. It's important to start by accepting yourself and believing that, regardless of how messy, raw, and unguarded you are, Jesus loves you just the same.

Allowing yourself to be completely genuine means risking rejection. But it's much more freeing than pretending you're something you're not. The Lord created you to feel, and He isn't offended by your emotions. Though some may be uncomfortable around vulnerability, most people are drawn to it. Authenticity is beautiful and it helps free others to let down their guard. Acting spiritual, just so you appear to have it all together, denies your emotions a chance to find Jesus in the midst of them.

Jesus, I'm so happy you know exactly how I feel and never judge me for it. From now on, I won't hide how I feel from myself or you. Today, I strip off the mask that shields my emotions and invite you into every area of my soul that needs your healing. I'll embrace vulnerability and discover the joys of being me.

The Power of Praise

Simon Peter spoke up and said, "You are the
Anointed One, the Son of the living God!" Jesus replied,
"You are favored and privileged Simeon, son of Jonah!
For you didn't discover this on your own, but my Father
in heaven has supernaturally revealed it to you."

Matthew 16:16–17

Some of our greatest battles are won from an attitude of praise. The declaration of who Jesus is to us personally is a weapon that silences the lies of hell. The revelation that He is all-powerful, all-loving, and ever-faithful flows from the throne of God and straight into our hearts. It launches us into a lifestyle of unrestrainable joy and breakthrough.

Praise puts things in proper perspective. It crushes the hurdles of faith by clearing a straight path into His presence. Remembering who He is and how much he loves us leaves little room for negativity. A thankful heart keeps us free from anxiety and stress. It's so much easier to hear answers to prayer when our spirits and souls are in unity, which is what happens when our mouths declare His truth.

Jesus, I'm shouting with joy over your faithfulness toward me! Holy boldness explodes from my soul with a roar. Your plans for me are good. Your faithfulness is never-ending. Your mercy undeserved. Your glory dismantles the forces of hell and sets my heart ablaze with gratefulness.

The Power of the Word

"Heaven and earth will disintegrate before
even the smallest detail of the word of God
will fail or lose its power."

Luke 16:17

Jesus—the Word made flesh. Unstoppable. Insuppressible. Alive. A light unto your path. Sharper than a two-edged sword. There are many ways to describe the Word of God and the power it wields, but more important than describing it is living it and experiencing it for yourself.

As you abide in His Word and declare the truths contained within, you're not just strengthening your spirit—you're releasing life into your circumstances. His truth is infinitely greater than the facts you face. It sparks hope and life into the darkest situations. If you're going through a difficult time, find Scriptures to remind you of His will. Meditate on them and declare them over every storm. Truth will encourage you, release answers, dispel fears, and become a compass that guides your life.

Jesus, your Word is alive within me, directing my thoughts and anchoring my soul. Teach me the power of declaring your truth and reveal the mysteries of your precepts as I write them upon my heart. Your words are my greatest treasure and following them is life's greatest delight.

You Are Powerful

*"I will give you the keys of heaven's kingdom realm
to forbid on earth that which is forbidden in heaven,
and to release on earth that which is released in heaven."*

Matthew 16:19

You've been given authority to partner with the power of heaven's truth. Lies about who you are, circumstances that contradict sacred truth, upheaval upon the earth, and attacks against the innocent, all must bow to the authority of Jesus as you stand as His representative on the earth.

The keys to access your victory have already been granted. You unlock breakthrough when you unite with heaven and, from the position of bold love, declare the truth that cannot be overcome. The enemy is defeated, not because you scream louder but because peace and faith fill your heart. You are expected to stand against injustice, both personal and far-reaching, by declaring what Jesus has already decreed to be true. Agree with His Word and declare it into every situation. Let truth saturate your understanding and frame your world. You are powerful.

Jesus, when trouble raises its head, I will declare your Word and stand on its saving grace. I'll drench doubt and fear with declarations of hope and truth. I'll shift atmospheres and see people set free by the power of your Word. I am powerful, because of you.

Treasures of Truth

"There is so much more I would like to say to you,
but it's more than you can grasp at this moment.
But when the truth-giving Spirit comes, he will
unveil the reality of every truth within you."

John 16:12–13

The foundation of our faith is built upon the Word. Day by day, streams of glorious revelation flood our understanding. Ours is a journey of discovery that never ends. It's hard to imagine how much more truth is hidden within His Word—treasures waiting to be excavated. Life longing to be released.

Walking with Jesus must have been astounding for the disciples. Secrets never before disclosed were shared by the One who whispered them into existence. Through the unveiling of the Gospels, we learn, just as they did, when the Word became flesh. But it wouldn't be until the Holy Spirit came that we'd be taught *every* truth. Not just truth, but truth that already exists within us. How mind-boggling. How exciting! Pulsating within us are mysteries waiting to be unveiled since the beginning of time. Calling for our hearts to discover their rhythm.

⁑

Jesus, I want to live my life close to you, tucked within the very secrets of your heart. I want to spend my life uncovering your rich mystery, searching the depths of your reality and peeling back the layers of your love. In search of truth, I reach for more.

Never Alone

"Yet I am never alone, for the Father is always with me."
John 16:32

Loneliness affects everyone at some point in time. It doesn't play fair. Pays no attention to whether we're surrounded by people or isolated and alone. Its one goal is to cause us to retreat so far into ourselves that we become consumed with self and cannot see the One who extends the gift of companionship.

In order to see what's right in front of us, we have to take our eyes off ourselves and fix them on Jesus. It's only when we surrender our fear of being alone and unloved that we remember how near He is. How capable He is of healing our shattered hearts. Of loving us in a way no other person can. Of making Himself so real that we understand exactly what Jesus meant when He said, "I am never alone, for the Father is always with me."

Jesus, there's so much freedom in your love! Such peace to be found when I lift my head and see you smiling at me. I want to be known as an unwavering lover of God. One who gazes upon your face and trusts you even when I feel alone and confused. I feel you now, lifting my burden and drawing me to your side. Nothing can ever separate me from you.

Whispers of Peace

"And everything I've taught you is so that the peace
which is in me will be in you and will give you great
confidence as you rest in me."

John 16:33

Our entire life is a beautiful journey of discovery, where we find the reality of Jesus along the way. In our struggle. In our schedule crunches. In the waiting. He's with us. And this is what it's all about: not only facing the same difficulties as everyone else but also tapping into a source of life, peace, and joy that knows no bounds. Jesus is the Source, the One who isn't restricted by circumstances and doesn't want us to be either.

Sometimes we place the end result as the ultimate source of peace. We say, "When ___ happens, I'll finally be happy." But Jesus wants to give us His peace, even while circumstances aren't the way we'd like. As we rest in Him, stillness replaces chaos, and confidence outshines weariness. Though we don't have all of the answers, we know the One who does. And that gives us peace that passes understanding. A mystery that absolutely contradicts our understanding.

Jesus, you are my source of perfect peace, and it's in your presence that tranquility floods my soul. Give me grace to stay at rest, even when life feels out of control. To lean into your whispers—whispers that remind me to yield my frustrations and cares to you.

The Beauty of Surrender

"For in this unbelieving world you will experience
trouble and sorrows, but you must be courageous,
for I have conquered the world!"

John 16:33

In the driest, most painful seasons of our lives, we learn to find the Lord's presence in ways we wouldn't experience otherwise. When our soul is bowed low and words have turned to quiet, steady tears, He comes to soothe our deepest pain. With a love powerful enough to change the course of humanity, Jesus wraps His arms around us and reminds us who we are.

These are the moments that define us. Not because pain has brought us to our knees but because there we encounter His strength within us. His perfect love is like an injection of courage. Suddenly, the process of faith that momentarily felt unclear collides with certainty. We may not have all the answers, but we know the One who holds them. This is the beauty of surrender.

Jesus, in the midst of sorrow, I've come face to face with your kindness. Your love makes me brave. Your strength, displayed so graciously through my weakness, causes my faith to soar. Now I'm thankful for my trials because they teach me how strong I am when I rely on you. In my surrender, you've restored my roar.

The Glory Within

"Unveil the glorious splendor of your Son
so that I will magnify your glory!"

John 17:1

The glory of Jesus was a testament to the glory of the Father. A reflection. An infusion of radiant splendor that pointed to the brilliance of the Father shining through His Son. This is the lifestyle that we've been called to emulate. One that resonates His outrageous goodness to the world around us.

All that we are, every good, beautiful, and perfect aspect of our lives is an exhibition of His glory. When we're blessed, standing in our identity and experiencing His goodness, it magnifies Him. Jesus takes joy in unveiling our gifting, talents, and anointing. He wants us to walk in fullness, because He loves to bless us. When our lives are filled with glory, it causes us to celebrate and to magnify the One who has unveiled Himself in us!

❖

Jesus, magnify yourself through me. As I walk with you and encounter your goodness, I overflow with holy zeal. I want my life to be a living illustration of your outrageous kindness, tender mercy, and glorious goodness. Strip away anything that doesn't look like you. Free me of every earthly shadow that seeks to obscure your splendor in me.

Transformed

Then Jesus' appearance was dramatically altered.
A radiant light as bright as the sun poured from his face.
And his clothing became luminescent—dazzling like
lightning. He was transfigured before their very eyes.

Matthew 17:2

Glorious transformation. Brilliant light. Radiant splendor. Unimaginable change. All happening right before the disciples' eyes. It's hard to imagine what that moment was like for them. A wonder to think how much that one encounter must have transformed them.

That's what glory does. It changes us. Transfigures us to such a great degree that even our appearance changes. This same word, *transfigured,* is used by Paul to describe the renewing of our mind. When Jesus comes into our lives, we act different. Think different. Look different, because Life Himself is streaming to us and from us with even more brilliance than the sun itself. The glory of His mercy transforms the way we think, and changes us forever.

Jesus, hide me in the brilliance of your glory. Just one moment in your presence wipes away years of pain. One encounter with your love and my thoughts align with heaven. I'm not the person I once was. You've wrapped me in a cocoon of your love, and I've emerged a new creation. Transformed into your image. Changed by your grace.

The Joys of Heaven, Now

"... so that I may give the gift of eternal life to all those that you have given to me. Eternal life means to know and experience you as the only true God, and to know and experience Jesus Christ, as the Son whom you have sent."

John 17:2–3

Imagine now the joys of heaven. Limitless. Eternal. Satisfying in every way. To know and see the One who has loved us for so long. To look into the eyes that have never looked away from ours. To experience unclouded vision and joy unspeakable. This is what we've been promised: a life of never-ending bliss. An eternity that has already begun to unfold. A gift that's meant to be unwrapped and enjoyed by His children, starting now.

Though we won't fully experience all that Jesus has for us until we get to heaven, there's no reason to wait to enjoy the gift of eternal life. As we get to know the Father, Son, and Holy Spirit, we're encountering the beauty of His nature. Tastes of His goodness. Brushes with heavenly glory. It's these glimpses of His love that fill us with excitement and reveal what is to come.

✤

Jesus, I bow before your presence, undone by the beauty of your holiness. To think that one day I'll see you with unclouded vision sets my heart ablaze. At times, your glory is so overwhelming that I can hardly stand, and I wonder what it will be like when nothing stands between us.

Joyful Obedience

"I have glorified you on the earth by faithfully
doing everything you've told me to do."

John 17:4

Day after day, we're offered the opportunity to glorify God by submitting ourselves wholly to His will. To have nothing between us that would hinder us from being fully His. To live so close and so in tune with Him that we effortlessly live radical lives of joyful obedience.

It would be sinful to excuse ourselves from obedience simply because we're human. Jesus demonstrated what's possible for us when He became fully man and walked the earth. He gave us the tools to live in purity and power. Yes, we make mistakes and miss opportunities to be stretched in our faith, but the precious blood of Jesus wipes the record clean. He never condemns us when we fail, and He always gives us a fresh start so that we too can say, "I've done everything you've told me to do."

Jesus, I want your testimony of faithfulness to be mine. To be so in tune with you that I never question your will. To walk hand in hand with you and know exactly which way you're leading. And to live a life that pleases you in every way.

Our Need for Mercy and Grace

"No matter how many times in one day your brother sins
against you and says, 'I'm sorry; I am changing; forgive
me,' you need to forgive him each and every time."

Luke 17:4

Being able to forgive over and over again takes humility. It goes against our *right* to be angry. It's a strong reminder of our need for Christlikeness. Arrests our pride. Offers us opportunities to see our own stubbornness. Brings us face to face with our need for grace. Then we can stand before Jesus with a pure heart. Having nothing in us that would allow bitterness to poison our soul.

How many times has Jesus taught *us* the same lesson? If we're honest, we'll admit that we often run to Him with the same issues, needing forgiveness. Seeking His embrace. His strength. His love that never stops transforming. Forgiving others when it's hard keeps us humble and is a powerful reminder of our own need for mercy.

Jesus, I really need your grace so that unforgiveness won't poison my soul. I want nothing to do with bitterness. I desire to live before you with a pure heart and to be a true reflection of your mercy. In total and complete surrender, I yield my right to be angry.

Our Father

"Father, I have manifested who you really
are and I have revealed you to the men and
women that you gave to me."

John 17:6

Jesus loves to help us understand just how incredible our Father really is. It's His pleasure to unveil His nature so that truth will always lead us and expectation of His kindness will shield us from disillusionment. As our hearts are enlightened with truth, it transforms us and causes us to see with clarity the amazing plan He has for our life.

In order to understand who we are, we first must understand who God is. Until we're absolutely convinced of the greatness of His love and the reality of His Spirit inside of us, we'll never fully walk in our destiny. It's the goodness of God that leads us to repentance, but it's also His goodness that keeps us. When we know who we are and whose we are, it will overflow into every area of our life and into the lives of those around us.

✤

Jesus, you've unveiled my heart to the glories of our heavenly Father, but I long for more. Open my eyes so I can see the wonders of your ways more clearly. Pierce my heart with revelation truth. Take me from glory to glory.

Increasing Faith

Upon hearing this, the apostles said to Jesus,
"Lord, you must increase our measure of faith!"
Jesus responded, "If you have even the smallest measure
of authentic faith, it would be powerful enough to say
to this large tree, 'My faith will pull you up by the
roots and throw you into the sea,' and it will respond
to your faith and obey you."

Luke 17:5–6

Many of us can relate to the disciples as they said with sincerity, "Increase my faith!" But Jesus didn't respond to them by telling them how their faith could be increased. He answered by reassuring them that what may feel like insufficient faith, when authentic, is actually enough to do miracles. He was encouraging them to use the faith they had and to let go of excuses that would limit their effectiveness.

Let's be brave in our prayers and unflinching in our declarations of the Word over situations. When we trust in the One who lives in us, we're tapping into an unending source of power. We may not feel that our faith is enough, but when we agree with Him that it is, we'll see our breakthrough come to pass.

⁜

Jesus, fill me with holy boldness that isn't intimidated by the immensity of the problems I face. When I rest with confidence in what you've said, I will see things shift in my favor. Thank you for always encouraging me in my walk with you.

One Look Changes Everything

When Jesus stopped to look at them, he spoke these
words: "Go to be examined by the Jewish priests." They set
off, and they were healed while walking along the way.

Luke 17:14

One look, one instance of encountering Jesus, and our lives are altered forever. Think about the first time you experienced the reality of the Lord in your life. More than likely it left an imprint of His love that sealed your heart. Caused you to feel what you couldn't see. To know something words wouldn't describe.

All it takes is for Jesus to look in our direction. To speak words that awaken our hearts. Words that are alive. Able to heal and set us free. But freedom and healing are gifts that must be accepted. The lepers only had instructions from Jesus. They literally walked on nothing more than His words and went straight into healing. It took action on their behalf. They asked for healing, and though they had no physical manifestation, they obeyed as if they did. That was when healing happened.

Jesus, look in my direction and speak the words of life I long to hear. Instruct me and show me how to cooperate with your Spirit to see my prayers come to pass. Like the lepers, I will walk on the power of your words and see your healing and freedom manifest in my life.

Fully Yours

"My glory is revealed through
their surrendered lives."
John 17:10

The *yes* that's streaming from your heart is more powerful than the storm around you. That one word—the single commitment to seek Him first—wraps you with grace and fills you with glory.

This is your chance to honor the sacrifice Jesus made for you. To surrender every part of your life and hold nothing back. To lift your hands in seasons of doubt and bow your knees when questions plague your soul. Soon, His glory rushes in and revives your weary heart. When you say yes to Him, especially when it's the hardest, it invites His presence and strengthens your resolve. This is the joy of surrender—to yield every thought, hope, dream, and fear to the Lord, and know that even if no one else sees, He does.

⸸

Jesus, I'm not afraid to lay aside my will for yours because I know that your ways are higher than mine. May my life be a holy habitation for your glory, as every part of me becomes fully yours. There is nothing I have that didn't come from you, except for the yes that streams from my heart.

The Freedom and Power of Joy

"I pray that they will experience
and enter into my joyous delight in you
so that it is fulfilled in them and overflows."

John 17:13

*J*esus wants you to enjoy Him and to enjoy life! It's time to be free from the weighty burdens you've carried. To experience your breakthrough from heaviness and know what it's like to be carefree. But freedom is more than an answer to prayer. It's an eternal reality.

The God who freely laughs in the face of the enemy invites us to do the same. *His joy* is alive within us, and when we stir it up by faith, we're laying hold of what's rightfully ours. In order to break free from the power of anxiety, we must stop agreeing with it. Honestly, the last thing we want to do when we're stressed is to laugh. But the truth is, joy lifts not only our mood but our faith. So, let's laugh at every lie. Then laugh some more! Especially when we don't want to.

Jesus, I refuse to let stress steal from me any longer. You've destined me for a life of joy and happiness. I'm not going to wait for every detail of my life to line up perfectly before I start to enjoy myself. I choose to agree with the joy that's in me. Stir it up, Lord! Let's have a good laugh together!

Representing Jesus

*"I am not asking that you remove them from the world,
but I ask that you guard their hearts from evil."*

John 17:15

What a privilege we have to represent Jesus on this earth. To shine brightly in the midst of darkness. To walk in His overcoming power and see those around us set free. Jesus left us here to finish what He started. He's equipped us to take His place—trusts us to be His hands and voice upon the earth. You are called to labor in love with Jesus, and you don't need a fancy title to do it.

You are filled with the grace, anointing, and power to set the captives free. But while you do the job He's asked you to do, don't forget to guard your own heart. Keep yourself free from offense and stay before His throne of grace. Nourish and protect your relationship with Him. Tend the fires of holy passion that burn within and never let them grow dim.

Jesus, I want to represent you well. But in order to do that I need to tend to the garden of my own soul. Wrap me in your presence and strengthen me with your love. Fill me with desire to share your heart. Stop at nothing to make me wholly yours, so all I say and do overflows with the essence of you.

Because of Jesus

"And now I dedicate myself to them as a holy
sacrifice so that they will live as fully dedicated
to God and be made holy by your truth."

John 17:19

Jesus sacrificed Himself in order to consecrate us and set us apart. He showed us that complete dedication to God was possible. When moments of weakness grip our soul, He runs to us with kindness and understanding. Undergirds us with His strength. Acquainted with our trials and temptations, He happily reminds us that He's already won the victory on our behalf.

In our desire to live in absolute abandon, truth seals our hearts. It protects us from sin like a precious, powerful gift. When we dedicate ourselves wholly to His purposes, grace empowers us. Leads us. Clears a path for us to walk on. Because of Jesus, we are strengthened and empowered. We can do everything through Him!

Jesus, all that I am and hold dear, I submit to you. Your extravagant love has awakened me to life. Filled me with passion that cannot be quenched. Gives me the grace to endure. Seals me with holy purpose. You've taught me what true love looks like by paying the ultimate price. Your indescribable mercy has won my heart.

Kingdom Reality

Jesus responded, "The kingdom realm of God does
not come simply by obeying principles or by waiting
for signs. The kingdom is not discovered in one place
or another, for the kingdom realm of God is already
expanding within some of you."

Luke 17:20–21

This reality of God's kingdom is more profound than anything else we will ever experience. Though it's hard to describe, it moves us. Leaves us speechless. Blooms through our hearts with indescribable fragrance. Heals. Draws us close by the power of tender mercy.

His kingdom has found its home inside of us. It didn't come by works of flesh or religious law. It cannot be earned by our obedience and isn't offended by our disobedience. It's a gift—a living, breathing, life-altering gift within us. Though we look for signs or outward manifestations of this inward reality, we only catch a glimpse. It must be experienced from the inside out—the mystery of His kingdom inside us.

Jesus, I honor your presence within me. I love to hear your tender whispers and feel the warmth of your glory flooding my soul. The deepest cry of my heart is to live a life that reflects this beautiful reality into the world around me.

Spiritual Stamina

"God will give swift justice to those who don't give up.
So be ever praying, ever expecting."

Luke 18:8

aith. It's one of the most powerful words on the planet. A substance so dynamic that our entire belief system is built upon it. It's invisible, yet able to support us in the most difficult times. Though it shouldn't, it rises and falls and shifts according to the trials we go through.

This is where spiritual stamina comes in. The more we exercise our faith, the stronger we get. When we'd normally quit, we find ourselves holding on; declaring truth in the face of lies. Even when it feels like our prayers aren't being answered, we stir ourselves up and believe. We reject the fear, release the questions, and turn confusion into expectancy. We persevere because faith refuses to give up.

Jesus, I want faith that endures. Stamina to run this race with joy and expectancy. Strengthen me, train me, and fill me with your grace. Help me to never quit. To release every fear and hold on to faith. And if I begin to doubt, hold me close and breathe upon the embers of my heart. Bring me back to you.

The Honor of Unity

"I pray for them all to be joined together as one even as you and I, Father, are joined together as one. I pray for them to become one with us so that the world will recognize that you sent me."

John 17:21

For too long the church has been labeled by our differences. Separated by the things we don't fully understand. Pulled apart by pride instead of drawn together by humility and love. Jesus has a higher way. The way of oneness. The path of honor and deference. A symbol of wholeness for the world to see.

Instead of criticizing and focusing on what we don't agree with, let's see people the way Jesus does. Sense His love and excitement over the many different denominations that reflect Him, since it's impossible for one group to adequately represent the fullness of His magnificence. Other Christians may worship, pray, or interpret Scripture differently from you, but if their hearts are turned to Jesus, they've got the main thing right. It's time to forsake the theology of criticism and embrace the doctrine of love.

Jesus, forgive me for allowing the differences of others to steer my opinion of them. Teach me to embrace everyone, especially my brothers and sisters in you, with open arms. To honor others the way you do and to let our passion for you, unite us as one body. Give us grace to represent you well.

Sweet Surprises

"Go to the lake and throw out your hook,
and the first fish that rises up will have a coin in its mouth.
It will be the exact amount you need to pay
the temple tax for both of us."

Matthew 17:27

*J*esus loves to surprise us! He loves to prove how much bigger, greater, and more creative He is at solving our problems than we are. Too often we put Him in a box—expecting Him to answer our prayers in a way that makes sense. We make mental lists of how He may give us what we need (or how we could assist Him with breakthrough), only to be surprised by the unexpected way He comes through.

Jesus is so much bigger than our imagination. The ways He can answer are limitless. He isn't obligated to take care of our needs inside the confines of our boxes. He's a professional when it comes to thinking outside the box. It's time to lay our burdens at His feet, step back, and wait with joyful anticipation to see what He alone can do.

Jesus, forgive me for limiting you through my unbelief. For thinking that when you don't answer in a way I can understand that you must not be answering at all. Time and time again you've surprised me with your goodness, and I know you won't fail me now.

Humility

"Whoever continually humbles himself to
become like this gentle child is the greatest one
in heaven's kingdom realm."

Matthew 18:4

Jesus was the greatest man to ever walk the earth. Yet despite His magnificence, the King of kings became the world's most admirable servant. Such humility. Serving, honoring, and bowing low to prove His love. To leave us an example of pure humility and untainted authority.

He subjected Himself to controversy, pain, and death. Laid everything down so that He could be with you forever. You don't need to prove your worth. Jesus already did it for you. Now He asks that you live each day as He did. Overflowing with the same mercy He shows you. Continually humbling yourself. Embracing childlike faith. Loving well, even when you have every right to criticize. Knowing that you can stand as royalty in a fallen world and serve it, just like Jesus did.

Jesus, I want everything I do and say to reflect the beauty of the One who lives inside me. I want my smile to lift the burdens of others. I want my desire for greatness to be empowered by a humble heart. I want to be just like you.

The Perfect Partner

"Receive this truth: Whatever you forbid on earth
will be considered to be forbidden in heaven,
and whatever you release on earth will be
considered to be released in heaven."

Matthew 18:18

*Y*ou have been given the astounding privilege of uniting with the Lord in prayer. As His perfect partner, you're called to rule and reign with Him. To make His Words your own. To be intimately acquainted with the will of God and live so close to Him that you stand confident in every moment of prayer. To forbid on earth the things that He's already forbidden in heaven. To release on earth that which has already been declared in heaven.

Regardless of your fears, failures, moments of doubt, and bouts of pride, you're called to walk with and work alongside the King of kings. Declared holy, trustworthy, and powerful, simply because you carry His name. Never think little of yourself, because He certainly doesn't. Lay ahold of truth, speak it into every situation, and become the bride you're destined to be.

Jesus, pour the oil of your Spirit upon my heart. Let truth saturate my deepest parts so it bubbles up in every situation. Remind me of your Word when the noise of the world tries to distract me. You've empowered me to unite with you in prayer, and together we'll see the will of God released on the earth.

Children

> "I want little children to come to me, so never interfere
> with them when they want to come, for heaven's
> kingdom realm is composed of beloved ones like these!"
>
> *Matthew 19:14*

Can't you just hear the Lord's zealous love for these little ones? He didn't appreciate the disciples trying to keep them away. Jesus wanted everyone to know that children have a clear pathway to Him and that His heart was toward them. He didn't rush them away or show any sign that they were a bother. In fact, He calls them beloved.

Children don't have a lesser experience when it comes to the kingdom of heaven. The innocence and purity of their hearts opens them to glorious encounters in ways many adults struggle with. They don't reason away His glory. They simply embrace it. Jesus loves and celebrates them, and it's up to us to train them to partner with heaven, protect them from harm, and value their innocence. Let's encourage their relationship with the Lord and never put limits on how close to Jesus they can go.

⊹

Jesus, flow through me and bless the little ones. Let me hear your heart for them. Give me the wisdom I need to teach them, and the grace and compassion to reflect your heart. Make yourself so real to them that they will never question your love.

Loving Yourself

"Honor your father and mother, and love those
around you as you love yourself."

Matthew 19:19

*S*ometimes we put so much emphasis on loving Jesus
and loving others that we forget He wants us to love ourselves too. In order to do that, we must be radically impacted
by the way He loves us—completely and unquestionably.

Jesus is patient, kind, and considerate—extending grace
that enables us and mercy that washes us. He offers rest
when we're weary and hope when we're discouraged. He
calls us beautiful, even in our ugliest mess. He declares us
victorious and brave, even when we feel like utter failures.
Persistently gracious, He shows us how to love ourselves.

Today, cut yourself some slack. Don't be so hard on yourself. If you need rest, rest. If you mess up, it's not the end of
the world! If you're stressed, give yourself permission to fully
release your burdens and trust Him. If you need help, ask for
it. Take care of yourself!

✧

*Jesus, forgive me for being hard on myself, taking on more
than I should, and focusing on my failures when I don't get it
right. Help me to pay attention to my needs and love myself
the way you do. When I love myself, I'll be able to love others
with just as much understanding.*

November

The Desire for Holiness

Zacchaeus stood in front of the Lord and said,
"Half of all that I own I will give to the poor.
And Lord, if I have cheated anyone, I promise to
pay back four times as much as I stole."

Luke 19:8

One encounter with Jesus and our lives are transformed forever. His presence doesn't force us to change. It literally draws us into desire. Pulsates within us and creates an eagerness for holiness.

Purity births purity. The more time we spend getting to know the Lord, the greater our desire to be like Him. To live in a way that pleases Him. To consider our relationship with Him so precious that we don't want to do anything that may hinder it. Being in His presence softens our hearts, strips the veils from our eyes, and reveals the areas that we need to change. When we yearn for holiness, being confronted by our sin is actually freeing, because it's an opportunity to cleanse ourselves. Jesus is so patient with us—taking us from glory to glory as we grow in Him.

Jesus, come and let your glory fill this room. Draw me into a greater awareness of your presence. My heart is open to you. I desire purity in the deepest part of my being. Show me the areas that hinder the fullness of our relationship. Let the desires that drive my life be pleasing to you.

Deeper

"You must go and sell everything you own and give
all the proceeds to the poor so you will have eternal
treasures. Then come and follow me."

Luke 18:22

Too often we get stuck on the external—the *ways* of
doing, serving, and behaving. We hear words like the
ones Jesus spoke in this verse and focus on the actions
instead of the deeper matters of the heart. And these are the
essentials. The targets of Jesus' ministry—to make us think. To
feel. To come to terms with the things that are deeper than
surface obedience.

Jesus has and always will be concerned with the core of
our actions, and He wants us to be too. He wants us to recognize why we do what we do. He doesn't want us to try and
earn our way into His favor. We're already there. Salvation is
a gift. Now, all He wants is to be the center of our lives. For us
to rid ourselves of anything in our heart that competes with
our love for Him.

*Jesus, I want love for you to be the motivation behind all I
do. It's my pleasure to give my all in serving you, but I know
you love me despite it all. I can never be good enough, smart
enough, or holy enough on my own. The treasure of your love
compels me to follow after you.*

Trust

"For God can do what man cannot."
Luke 18:27

"I've done everything I can think of and nothing's changing." Does that sound familiar? Sometimes, we're so consumed with getting our breakthrough that we do more than our due diligence to see it happen. We slip into works of the flesh. Strive to make things happen, because we know with certainty that what we're going after is God's will. But sometimes our efforts actually hinder our answer from materializing. We take into our hands what must be left in His.

Jesus wants us to go after what He's promised. To believe with certainty that He's powerful. Faithful. Committed to us. But He also wants us to trust. And trust has a posture. It looks like rest. Sounds like praise. When we've done all we can think of to get the victory, Jesus steps in and takes the helm. He escorts us to the back of the boat to sleep while He steers us through the storm.

Jesus, forgive me for trying to force the breakthrough. Though I know the things I'm praying for are your will, I've allowed them to become the center of my attention. Do what only you can do. I place into your hands everything that needn't be in mine. Have your way. I trust you.

Promises Fulfilled

Jesus took the Twelve aside in private and told them,
"We are going to Jerusalem so that everything
prophesied about the Son of Man will be fulfilled."

Luke 18:31

Jesus is immensely interested in fulfilling every promise He's ever made to you. No one on earth is as faithful as He is. There are definitely times when it feels as though He's forgotten. Seasons when nothing seems further than the dreams you've envisioned and the prophecies you've received. But that's when faith comes in. When we need grace to keep believing.

When God has given you a word that speaks to your heart, it's yours. Whether it came through His written Word, a word of prophecy, or something He spoke directly to you, when it's a true word of God, He will bring it to pass. If there are specific promises rising in your heart right now, lift your voice and praise Him for bringing them to pass. Let's celebrate by faith what we've yet to see with our natural eyes.

Jesus, thank you for your faithfulness. Nothing can stop your unrelenting love for me. When my heart is toward you, I can almost sense your blessings chasing me down. I've done nothing to deserve your unyielding devotion to me. Every day I'm overwhelmed by your love. Expectant. Awaiting. Thankful.

Spiritual Revelation

> The blind beggar shouted, "Jesus, Son of David, have pity
> and show me mercy!" ... Jesus said, "Now you will see.
> Receive your sight this moment. For your faith in me
> has given you sight and new life."
>
> *Luke 18:38, 42*

*B*efore the blind man's sight was restored, he had spiritual insight. His cry wasn't one of entitlement, but of revelation. Calling on Jesus as the Son of David meant that he understood Jesus was the Messiah. These collisions with outrageous truth have a way of sparking life and boldness within us that cannot be silenced.

Jesus wants to show us things that are more real to us than anything we see. He wants us to be so convinced of who He is that external conditions come under the dominion of our internal reality. He wants the cry of our heart to have power behind it. This is when we experience our greatest breakthroughs and answers to prayer—when we simply believe He is who He says He is.

Jesus, give me spiritual revelation that far outweighs any natural understanding. Show me things I've never seen. Open my eyes to see the wonders of who you are. Give me boldness that's founded on the truth of who you are and the confidence of your love for me. I'll shout with joyful confidence, "My Messiah, will have mercy on me!"

More Than We Can Imagine

So he ran on ahead of everyone and climbed up a
blossoming fig tree so he could get a glimpse of Jesus as
he passed by. When Jesus got to that place, he looked up
into the tree and said, "Zacchaeus, hurry on down,
for I am appointed to stay at your house today!"

Luke 19:4–5

With Jesus, we always get more than we ask for. This extravagant One loves to surprise us. Never wants us to be satisfied with our current experience. Sees our passionate hearts that long for the depths of encounter few have ever had. Knows us by name. Enjoys our company. Has come to stay with us forever.

The truth is that sometimes it feels as if we need to climb a tree or make a great effort to show Jesus how much we love Him. But in reality, Jesus sees it all—the slightest turning of our hearts to Him causes Him to rush to our side. We've been granted much more than a quick glimpse of Him as He walks by. We've been offered the nearness of His love. The phenomenon of His Spirit within us.

Jesus, I can feel you smiling at me. Inviting me to join you on the adventure of a lifetime. To know you. See you. Hear the sweetness of your voice inside me. When I asked you for glimpses of your glory, you poured it out within me instead. You always give me more than I can imagine.

Life Has Come

Jesus said to him, "This shows that today life
has come to you and your household,
for you are a true son of Abraham."

Luke 19:9

Salvation does more than change our hearts; it's seen in our response to love. When we're drawn into the place of glorious encounter, our hearts tune into the frequency of holiness. We want nothing in us that's contrary to the purposes of God. Life has come.

Though we don't work to become holy, the desire to be righteous is a natural response to His nearness. It awakens areas of our soul that need His touch. His mercy. His life. His name. When we look into those eyes, ablaze with majesty, it's impossible not to be pulled into the flames. To long for their cleansing power and desire to be fully His. We have no need to hold on to complacency, sin, or hard-heartedness.

Jesus, I stand before your glory, wanting nothing more than to be fully yours. I know I don't have to do anything to gain your approval, but I long to live in a way that honors you. Come, breathe your life into my home, my thoughts, the secret musings of my soul. I invite your cleansing love.

When You're Faithful

"'Yes,' replied the king. 'But to all who have been faithful,
even more will be given them.'"

Luke 19:26

You never have to worry about being overlooked by Jesus. Every movement of your heart, each time you've resisted temptation, and every work of your hands has caught His attention. When others don't seem to notice, Jesus does. And He's the best at rewarding your faithfulness.

Everything you do in secret, to honor the Lord and serve others, touches His heart. It opens doors of favor that cannot be shut by the hands of man. When Jesus is the center of your life and everything you do is for the purpose of honoring Him, He finds ways to bring increase and blessing into your life. So, rejoice! He's the God of surprises, and though it may seem your efforts aren't noticed, when you serve Him with a right heart, you can rest assured He's got something exciting up His sleeve.

Jesus, I want everything I do to be pleasing in your sight. It's my joy to faithfully follow you. Though I know the blessings will follow, my heart is toward you. Bowed low in reverence. Overflowing with joy. Content to honor you in the secret halls of obedience and love. All I am is yours. All I do is for your glory.

A Shout of Victory!

They shouted over and over, "Highest praises to God
for the one who comes as King in the name of the Lord!
Heaven's peace and glory from the highest
realm now comes to us!"

Luke 19:38

Let a cry of freedom rise from within you until it roars with undeniable victory. Jesus came to set you free. It's time to shake off the heaviness and rejoice by faith for all that God desires to bless you with. Shackles of pain, rejection, and disappointment will effortlessly slide off of you when you drown your sorrows in a celebration of praise! Jesus loves to ruin a good pity party.

Heaven's peace and glory feels the most glorious when everything around you tells you not to be happy. When you look problems in the face and refuse to give them a place in your heart, you've already won half the battle. Remember how great He is, and your heart will soar high above the clouds of adversity. Stir yourself up and praise Him, especially if you don't feel like it. Joy is not meant to be surrendered!

Jesus, I want all of heaven and hell to hear my shouts of praise! You are good and faithful to your beloved. I'm done crying over things that I don't understand. It's time for me to roar with a declaration of victory! Nothing is too hard for you. Your joy is my strength!

Anything Is Possible

*"But what seems impossible to you
is never impossible to God!"*
Matthew 19:26

Impossibilities are only impossible when we judge them according to our frame of reference instead of God's. We determine something is possible or impossible based on what makes sense to us. Let's be honest, there isn't much about spiritual realities that make sense to our natural minds, so why pick and choose?

It's human nature to lean into dreams and ideas we think are more likely to happen. But it's God's nature to do things based on what's holy, praiseworthy, and reflects His nature. He's outrageously good—unlimited in what He can accomplish. We know that if He doesn't explode the boundaries, we'll fail, but our eyes are on Him. When we choose to trust Him and His ability to do the extraordinary, we step into impossibilities with expectancy. God flowing through frail human vessels, accomplishing the impossible. That's the exciting life of faith!

Jesus, I'm running after the impossible! I won't be limited by what I understand. I want to live with extraordinary confidence in your faithfulness and love for me. With boldness, I'll do what I can do and trust you to do the rest. You want me to succeed. Every impossible situation is possible when you're by my side.

Surrender

"For anyone who has left behind their home and property, leaving family—brothers or sisters, mothers or fathers, or children—for my sake, they will be repaid a hundred times over and will inherit eternal life."

Matthew 19:29

Jesus sees it all. There's no sacrifice you could ever make in honor of Him that will ever be overlooked. The times you've said yes to Him and walked away from people, places, or possessions didn't only move your heart, it also moved His. When you felt the greatest sting of sacrifice and wondered if it truly mattered, it did.

He told us beforehand that living for Him and walking the narrow path of obedience wouldn't be easy. But the most wonderful things in the world usually come at a price. The greatest blessings usually follow us down roads we thought we traveled alone. Such joyful rewards await us for the things we've yielded to Him. For the times we said yes through tears of heart-wrenching surrender and fathomless love.

Jesus, how could I ever compare the joys of your kingdom with the temporary sacrifices of love? You truly are my everything. Nothing I could ever surrender to your hands is worth struggling to hold on to. I yield my life to you—my All, my Lord, and my Friend.

Embracing Peace

"If only you could recognize that this day peace
is within your reach! But you cannot see it."

Luke 19:42

Right now, peace is within your reach. It's found by laying every worry, fear, and anxiety at the feet of Jesus and resting in the safety of His arms. When you turn your eyes to Jesus, His love fills your vision and protects your heart.

Peace defies reason, analytical explanations, and swirling circumstances. Even during life's most tumultuous times, it's possible to experience heavenly peace that's beyond our understanding. What we choose to keep in the forefront of our minds is our choice. It's imperative not to allow ourselves to become so overwhelmed by what's right in front of us that we cannot see what's available in His presence. His love has the power to settle both our hearts and our minds.

Jesus, I want to feel your peace infusing my mind and penetrating the depths of my soul. I refuse to have a pity-party, gluing my thoughts to the enemy's list of problems. I lay these burdens at your feet and ask you to give me eyes that see the path of peace. Take me by the hand and lead me into the secret place of your presence.

Yet, Will I Praise Him!

Jesus responded, "Listen to me. If my followers were
silenced, the very stones would break forth with praises!"

Luke 19:40

The crashing seas bellow, the birds sing their private love
song, the winds usher in His presence, and the stars
dance on the edge of His fingertips. All of creation has found
its voice. Surges with purpose for all the world to partake of
its God-given glory. Yet it's the praise of His beloved that has
the power to capture the attention of the Lord. We are the
ones who move His heart.

Don't let creation out praise you. Even when suffering
fights to silence your song, sing through your tears. Whisper
your words of adoration. Turn your heart to the One who created it. Your praise during times of great affliction, whether
weak or strong and intentional, is the highest form of worship.

*Jesus, my heart's overflowing, roaring with praise because
of all you've done and have yet to do. I won't let the stones
worship you in my place. Oppression cannot steal my praise. I
will rush to your gates with songs of deliverance, knowing no
enemy can stand in my way. You are good!*

Holding All Things Loosely

Jesus replied,
"You don't know what you are asking."
Matthew 20:22

Sometimes life makes us feel off-kilter. We believe we want one thing, ask for it, and get it, only to realize we really didn't want it. At times we pray for God to lead us in one direction, when really, He's trying to turn our attention in another. So how do we know which way is best? We hold all things loosely and trust Him entirely.

It can be frustrating and confusing trying to navigate our own lives instead of submitting ourselves to Him. He celebrates our dreams and encourages us to run after them, but only He sees the big picture, which often means letting Him tweak the details. Our journey is one of discovery. Each step of the way is an amazing adventure when we let Him lead. Yielding our desires to Him and asking Him to infuse each one with His perfect wisdom and guidance opens us up to an expansive, explosive, and joy-filled life!

Jesus, I believe you have the best in store for me. Come, let's journey through life together. Take the lead. All that I have, want, and desire, I submit to you, knowing in this place of total surrender I'm truly free.

The Gift of Compassion

Jesus was deeply moved with compassion toward them.
So he touched their eyes, and instantly they could see!
Matthew 20:34

Compassion is more than a feeling. It leads to action. Causes us to slow down and pay attention. Pulls at our heartstrings. Begs us to do more than take notice. Escorts us into opportunities to mirror our loving Savior.

Throughout the Gospels we read that Jesus, moved by compassion, did something to make a difference. It was as if compassion was a gift that enabled Him to recognize the heart of the Father. It revealed whom God wanted Him to reach out to. We never read that Jesus was moved by compassion and chose to ignore it. This is our example to follow. To pay attention to those moments of sympathy; the situations that stir our longing to *do*. Let's allow compassion to reveal His personality through us. To make a difference in someone else's life.

Jesus, I want my life to matter. I don't want one day to pass by that I miss an opportunity to show your love. Help me to be like you—always ready to act on the compassion that compels me. To do more than say the right things, to know exactly what you want me to do—and to do it.

Aquarium Believer

"You will lead by a completely different model. The greatest one among you will live as the one who is called to serve others, because the greatest honor and authority is reserved for the one with the heart of a servant."

Matthew 20:26–27

Jesus spoke these words to those who follow Him. The perfect model of Kingship, and the greatest leader of all time, demonstrated what a royal calling truly looks like— going low and serving others.

To walk with Jesus means we live in an entirely new way than the people around us. We model mercy, demonstrate humility, and express love in all that we do. At work, at home, at church, and everywhere we go, we are those who value friendships and treasure the relationships He establishes for us. Today, take the step of being an example for others. Become an "aquarium" believer—one whose life is transparent, allowing people to see what's swimming around inside of us. Find ways to exemplify Jesus and let them see Him shining through us.

Lord Jesus, your life is my example to follow. No one lived a life as pure and holy as you. Make me that servant who honors your example. Help me to find someone I can serve without expecting to receive anything for myself. I love your ways. Live your servant-life through me today.

The Answer

They stepped away and debated among themselves,
saying, "How should we answer this?"
Matthew 21:26

*J*esus alone holds the answers. Yet when we're faced with a problem we can't make sense of, we often run to others to help us understand. We rely on our own wisdom instead of leaning upon the Lord's. We try to navigate our way through the labyrinth of life, thinking we'll be able to grasp with our minds what's dictated by the Spirit.

We were created for a higher way of thinking. To experience the unpredictable with peace that passes understanding. To yield to the silence when our minds demand an answer. To rest. To know. To reject reasoning so it won't suffocate our faith. When we're feeling dry and our thoughts find no place to land, we turn to the source of wholeness and certainty. He alone is the answer we seek.

Jesus, questions are looming on the horizon of my mind. Sometimes it's hard to make sense of it all, so I won't even try. Instead of running to others or hiding inside my own thoughts, I step away from reasoning and choose to trust you. I lay every problem at your feet and rest in the faithfulness of your love.

Living to Honor Him

"We can clearly see that you're not one who speaks only
to win the people's favor, because you speak the truth
without regard to the consequences."

Matthew 22:16

Jesus was such a great example of how to be genuine. Of speaking the truth. His only concern was to honor the Father and set us free. We never read that He did or said anything because it was the popular or accepted thing to do. He cared only about revealing God's will to those who would accept it.

Lukewarm people are uncomfortable around burning hearts. Hearts that seek God's truth, presence, and favor above all else. Hearts that are unmasked. Souls that have been stripped of pretentious egos. Unafraid of what others think because they're secure in their heavenly identity. That means people aren't going to easily accept those who speak truth and live in purity. We're different—not for the sake of being controversial but because we live to honor the One who loves us despite the consequences.

Jesus, forgive me for wrong motives. For seeking to please anyone above you. For holding back when I need to speak with bold love. Help me not to ignore you as you gently tug on my heart, reminding me to be your mouthpiece. Your hands. Your vessel of honor.

Joyfully His

Jesus said, "Precisely, for the coin bears the image of the emperor Caesar. Well, then, you should pay the emperor what is due to the emperor. But because you bear the image of God, give back to God all that belongs to him."

Matthew 22:21

*U*nashamed. Uninhibited. Set free by holy hands that bear the mark of perfect love. We are His. We gratefully belong to the God who holds all things in flawless synchronicity.

When we invited Jesus into our lives, He not only wrapped us in His righteousness, but He also saturated every part of us with His divine nature. Our old attributes were swallowed up by His glory. Everything about us that was contrary to holiness has been made holy because of the sacrifice of Jesus. It isn't just our duty but our happy privilege to lay our lives at His feet. To be fully His. To bear our own marks of holy surrender. Refined like gold. Joyfully His.

Jesus, consume every part of me. I hold nothing back. All that I am and hope to be, every dream and goal, and each failure and fear, I surrender to your grace. I joyfully pour my life out for your glory. To see you. To hear you. To walk with you in sweet abandon. I am yours.

Worshipping Him with Our Thoughts

Jesus answered him, "'Love the Lord your God with every passion of your heart, with all the energy of your being, and with every thought that is within you.'"

Matthew 22:37

Loving the Lord with every thought is an act of worship that continues all day long, in every situation, conversation, and instance of boredom. Our mind is constantly running. Thinking. Imagining. Mental pictures materializing in the most unexpected ways. They cause us to feel. To ponder. To doubt or to believe. To turn toward His ever present love or to neglect it.

Worship is a lifestyle. A posture of heart that's heard in our words and recognized by what we do and don't do. It's reflected by what we allow ourselves to think about. An act of devotion as we learn not to dismiss our musings and invite Jesus into every one. To reject anything that leads us away from Him and recognize what doesn't sound like heaven. When we pay attention to our thoughts, we learn a lot about what's really going on in our mind and who's ruling our hearts.

✣

Jesus, I want every thought, word, and deed to reflect you, because you live inside of me. Teach me to pay attention to what I'm thinking about. Highlight thoughts that don't reflect your truth and beauty. May the meditation of my heart be a melody of worship to you all day long.

Listening to Our Hearts

"Outwardly you masquerade as righteous people, but inside
your hearts you are full of hypocrisy and lawlessness."

Matthew 23:28

*H*ave you ever pretended everything's okay when it
isn't? It's not that we need to open ourselves up to
everyone, but we do need to be open. To be honest. To pay
more attention to the health of our souls than the opinions
of others. We don't need to try and impress people with the
proper religious, scripturally correct answers when we're
dying on the inside.

When we're dealing with fear, temptation, and difficulties,
it's important to be vulnerable with others. Our righteousness isn't based on appearances or saying all the right things.
It's a gift that isn't contingent upon trying to impress anyone.
When our souls are afflicted, instead of putting on a mask of
religious piety, we need to go to someone we trust and ask
for prayer and counsel. To let people know when our hearts
are heavy.

*Jesus, I won't try to hide what I'm feeling because you see it
all. With you, I can be as vulnerable as I want to be and know
you understand. Help me to be honest with what I'm facing
and to never put on a mask of pretense. Surround me with
those who will counsel me with your wisdom.*

Radical Devotion

"When she poured the fragrant oil over me, she was
preparing my body for burial. ... the story of her lavish
devotion to me will also be mentioned in memory of her."

Matthew 26:12–13

*I*n Jesus' time it was customary to prepare bodies for burial with fragrant oils. Mary (Miriam) had no natural knowledge of Jesus' imminent death. Her actions were inspired by the Holy Spirit. I imagine she probably didn't understand the overwhelming desire to take her costly spikenard and lavish it upon Jesus. But she acted on it. Gave expression to the awakened love within.

That's what a lifestyle of radical devotion looks like. Responding to the sometimes irrational yet compelling tug of love that inspires us to do something that makes no sense. When we yield to the desires that rise from the overflow of our hearts, we tap into something greater. Significant. Prophetic. The seemingly ridiculous and often life-changing, yet never unnoticed by the One who sees it all.

Jesus, help me to never ignore the radical ideas that you place in my heart. To respond to the leading of your Spirit with absolute surrender and obedience without trying to analyze all the possible outcomes. To allow my heart to constantly lead me to you. And my life to be a testimony of awakened passion, just like Miriam.

Compelled

They confronted Jesus and asked him,
"We want to know right now by what authority
you're doing this. Who gave you the authority
to teach these things here in the temple?"

Luke 20:1–2

Man may tell you otherwise, but living as a light in this world doesn't require a special title. Jesus has called all of us to a lifestyle of ministry. Though many think being in the ministry requires years of theological training, Jesus never confirmed that. Ministry isn't something that only happens from behind a pulpit. It's a way of life. A belief that we're called for something greater. Something radical and contagious.

As we zealously pursue His presence, encounters with Jesus stir our compassion and zeal. We live and breathe the reality of His kingdom. We ignite hearts everywhere we go simply by expressing what's burning within. We look for ways to share the truth of His love by showing compassion, releasing hope, and obeying His gentle nudge. We're ministers of the gospel, not because of a title but because love compels us.

Jesus, I hear the call to live my love for you loudly—with radical faith that believes everyone wants to feel the reality of your nearness. Let my passion for you be seen in all I do and say. Experienced by every person I come across. Give me wisdom, courage, and insight. Show me how to share your love today.

NOVEMBER 24

Humbly Bow

"Everyone who falls in humility upon that stone
will be broken. But if that stone falls on you,
it will grind you to pieces!"

Luke 20:18

Repentance is a beautiful thing. And it's not something we do only once. It's a way of life. An indication of a heart posture. A pilgrimage of discovery that often leaves us undone—humbled by the glory He's bestowed upon us. It's not that we live in constant violation of His ways and need to repent for backsliding on a continual basis. But truly lovesick hearts yearn to be holy as He's holy.

Never hold your head so high that your knees can't find the ground. Little things matter. Don't tune out the quiet correction of His Spirit. Attitudes of heart, quiet criticisms, and impatient rumblings of the soul aren't to be ignored. The truth is that, despite your best efforts, you can't save yourself. You'll never be good enough. Holy enough. More perfect than He says you are. But you can humbly bow.

Jesus, I'm in constant need of your mercy. You're so patient and kind. I'm constantly pursued by your goodness and enduring love. You've made me in your image, and I want to be a true reflection of all you are. May I never take your mercy for granted and always bow my will to find the glory of your ways.

Say No to Fear!

"Don't panic or give in to your fears."
Luke 21:9

It must be pretty important to the Lord that we remain free from fear. He charged us not to fear multiple times throughout the Gospels. He must have known how often we'd need to be reminded of it. To have our attention redirected to His love, power, and faithfulness. To spark the fires of love that fuel our courage.

It's time to be bold and say no to fear. To invite infectious fervor and rise with the heart of a lion. To roar against oppression. To refuse thoughts that lead to spiritual disconnect, forcing us into the scrutiny of truth. Let's live from the place of extraordinary love that never lets us go. And believe that Jesus is more adamant about capturing us than the enemy is. We weren't created to live afraid, so let's keep our minds on Jesus and fear won't have a place to land.

Jesus, you didn't create me to be darkened by shadows of fear. When I stay focused on your love, I'm bold. Courageous. Determined to walk in your victory. Free to live as an overcomer. Confident in your ability to protect me. Today I choose to break my agreement with the enemy's lies. I say no to fear and yes to love!

Seasons

"Haven't you observed the fig tree, or any tree,
that when it buds and blooms you realize that
the season is changing and summer is near?"

Luke 21:29

*I*n every season of the soul, Jesus is by our side—loving, providing, instructing. At times His love is as refreshing as a warm spring day. The fragrance of His presence—unmistakable. At other times we enter in by faith as He whispers for us to seek and find. We battle the cold north winds of adversity. Drag our feet through the heavy snow just to get to Him.

It's important to be sensitive to His Spirit and to our own hearts. To recognize our season and to partner with Him to get the most out of each one. In a world where things always change, Jesus is the constant One. The eternal One within. Seasons are just that—seasons. They don't last, but each one serves a purpose. When we sense our spiritual seasons shift, let's run to Him and discover the beauty we've yet to uncover. Unwrap the lessons each one contains.

Jesus, help me to live with an open heart, able to recognize you in every season of my soul. When you feel far off and heaviness tries to force me inward to self, give me grace to find your presence. Teach me not to fight the things I don't understand but to glean truths from every lesson.

Because of Love

> "Be careful that you never allow your hearts to grow
> cold. Remain passionate and free from anxiety
> and the worries of this life."
>
> *Luke 21:34*

The light of Jesus' love guides, warms, nourishes, and strengthens. It not only highlights the areas that hinder us from walking in fullness, but it also pulls the "weeds" that dirty our garden. Accomplishes what years of striving cannot. Changes us from the inside out. All because we keep our passion for Him alive.

It's up to us to stoke the flames of holy adoration that burn within. To cry out for purity. To worship with total abandon. To bask in His light. To invite the brilliance of His smile into every dark crevice and heal every wound. We yearn for more—there's always more of Him. We lift our voices in praise. Sing our songs. Dance our passion. Paint the visions. Discover the limits of glory our bodies can handle. Until we're undone. Then we do it all over again because of love.

Jesus, I kneel before you, crying out for the grace to never let my love grow cold. I scarcely have the words to explain how intensely I love you. I can't imagine one day without you. I want to push the limits—to know how much of your glory I can handle. I want my heart to always burn with holy passion.

Remembering Him

Then he lifted up a loaf, and after praying a prayer of
thanksgiving to God, he gave each of his apostles a piece
of bread, saying, "This loaf is my body, which is now
being offered to you. Always eat it to remember me."

Luke 22:19

Communion is an invitation to remember Him. His sacrifice. His triumph. To invite into our hearts what we hold in our hands—the One who took on flesh for the sake of love. To ponder that love and to reflect on its limitless power. To feast our lives ever on His goodness. To allow the memory of sin to be washed away by this holy communion.

This is what it's all about. Remembering Him when we're faced with ourselves. Recognizing mercy has made us new. Letting our past stay in the past, where the expanse of love's reach absorbed our shame. When we remember, it turns fear into faith. Causes every ploy of the enemy to crumble and come to nothing. This is what Jesus did. He offered His body in place of sin. And this is what we remember: the price of love.

Jesus, I desire to know you more than any other person on the face of the earth. To live in remembrance of your love and not the sting of my past. To enjoy the beauty of fellowship and holy communion not just when I'm eating the elements but every day and for the rest of my life.

You Call Me Friend

"But I have prayed for you, Peter, that you would stay faithful to me no matter what comes. Remember this: after you have turned back to me and have been restored, make it your life mission to strengthen the faith of your brothers."

Luke 22:32

There's no one as kind as Jesus. Peter was about to deny his Lord. Instead of being reprimanded in advance, Jesus encouraged him. He not only prayed for Peter but gave him something to hold on to once the aftermath of his sinful decision was realized. Jesus let him know that he'd be restored, and that restoration would be the fuel he could use to strengthen others.

That's just how Jesus is. He knows ahead of time when we'll fail, yet He never treats us with disdain. He points us toward our destiny. Reminds us that He's already made provision for our mistakes. Jesus loves to nudge us forward so we don't get stuck in the guilt of past blunders. And He never looks at our sin as a wall that can keep Him out. He continues talking to us, as if we'd never sinned at all.

Jesus, I turn my eyes to you. Fill my vision with destiny and purpose. I pray that my heart will never grow cold or that I would slip and fall. Even in the pit of despair, you'll lift me to the highest place just to be near you. You revive my heart and flood it with new life. You call me friend.

Habits

Jesus left the upper room with his disciples and,
as was his habit, went to the Mount of Olives,
his place of secret prayer.

Luke 22:39

We've been called to a lifestyle of devotion. To create habits that are far more meaningful than simply fulfilling our religious duty. This is the invitation to divine union. One that shatters the mentality that we must work for His approval. To find such fulfillment in His presence that we become joyfully addicted to His glorious love.

When we make prayer our most valuable habit, it flows into every area of our lives—the way we approach stressful situations, the way we handle disagreements and even how we spend our time. This is the place where deep calls unto deep. Where the spiritual and natural realms collide, and the awareness of His presence influences our day. Sets the tone. Enables us to easily and joyfully become mindful of the Lord no matter what we're doing.

Jesus, lead me into the chambers of your holy presence. The place that has become my home. The secret garden where we meet each day. Whisper secrets, pour out the oil of your healing love upon my heart, and never let me long for anything else the way I long for you. May my time with you become my most magnificent and glorious habit.

December

December 1

Stand Guard

[Jesus] got up and went to his disciples and found them all asleep, for they were exhausted and overwhelmed with sorrow. "Why are you sleeping?" he asked them. "You need to be alert and pray for the strength to endure the great temptation."

Luke 22:45–46

There are times to rest in Jesus' strong arms, and there are times to press in with determination and stand watch. The Lord is so kind to pull us close and comfort us during times of exhaustion and sorrow. But sometimes He'll speak with earnest warning to draw from His strength and refuse to give in to disillusionment and discouragement. To be vigilant in prayer. To overcome.

When you're going through times of darkness, don't let your guard down. Refuse the heaviness that tries to lull you into complacency or spiritual laziness. Guard your heart at all times so it flows in unison with His Spirit. Pay attention to imaginations that contradict His truth. When the world feels dark, stay close to His presence. When you cannot see His face, you can still trust His heart.

Jesus, you're my strong shelter and place of safety. Though I feel weak, I'll draw from your strength. I'll roar with faith and laugh in the face of storms. I'll stand guard over my heart and yield every thought to you. I am courageous. Bolder than a lion when your love melts away my fear.

When He Speaks

Judas [was given] a large detachment of Roman soldiers and temple police to seize Jesus. ... Jesus, knowing full well what was about to happen, went out to the garden entrance to meet them. Stepping forward, he asked, "Who are you looking for?" "Jesus of Nazareth," they replied. He replied, "I am he." And the moment Jesus spoke the words, "I am he," the mob fell backward to the ground!

John 18:3, 4–6

Jesus always had the ability to stop His arrest and ultimate crucifixion. Here in the garden, He proved that. When the great I Am spoke His name, these strong men fell to the ground as a result of His great power. Jesus was in charge. He submitted Himself first to the will of our Father and then into the hands of cruel men.

He didn't run away while He had the chance. He stood His ground and offered Himself on our behalf. This wonderful Savior showed us what true love looks like. Ageless, unshakable, magnificent in power, yet bowed low to bring us high. Now our hearts have become the garden where His unending mercy and love blossoms.

Jesus, how can I ever express the gratitude that floods my heart? In power you've won me, in humility you became me. Yielded. Perfect. Surrendered. Rejected. Victorious. All because of the love that drove you. Now that love drives me, and I want nothing more than to worship you.

Freedom from Anger

Suddenly, Peter the Rock took out his sword and struck
the high priest's servant, slashing off his right ear!

John 18:10

All of us are growing into the person Jesus says we are. None of us are exempt from the great need for His mercy. Everyone has something the Lord's purifying in them. So, if anger is something you're working on, don't allow it to define you. Shame cannot exist where mercy and love have triumphed.

When we impetuously react in anger or frustration and lash out at people, it immediately cuts off their desire to hear us. It's definitely not God's way of communicating. The good news is that there's freedom from anger and the need to control. Soaking in His presence softens our hearts and tunes us into His. It's also important to surround ourselves with people who can encourage us on our journey—those who know how to walk in peace. Be encouraged; the more you hang around Jesus, the more like Him you'll become.

✣

Jesus, thank you for always seeing the value in me and not defining me by my weaknesses. Let the glory of your Spirit wash away any need I have for control. I surrender every wrong attitude, negative emotion, and impatient temperament so my soul will be free.

Unbearable

And one of the guards standing there said to him,
"Aren't you one of his disciples? I know you are!"
Peter swore and said, "I am not his disciple!"

John 18:25

Have you ever wondered what went through Peter's mind as the rooster crowed just the way Jesus prophesied it would? He'd betrayed Jesus with outright treachery and unfaithfulness. Turned away from the Lord the minute things became unstable. The pain of that moment must have been unbearable.

But that's what the cross was for. That's what love and forgiveness are all about: to lift the burdens we cannot bear. No one is too far gone. There isn't a person on earth who Jesus doesn't want to restore—not one single soul who has so offended Him and pushed Him away that Jesus isn't reaching out to embrace. His mercy covers every sin. His grace removes the stain of shame.

Jesus, you're so gracious and patient with me. No matter how I mess up, you're always standing with open arms, ready to draw me back into grace and mercy. I can cry out to you again and again, and you always come. I don't deserve your tender mercy, but I gratefully accept it. I happily choose to walk with you.

Staying Silent

"Have you nothing to say about these allegations?
Is what they're saying about you true?" But Jesus
remained silent before them and did not answer.

Mark 14:60-61

Jesus could have answered these men with truth that
would have no argument. He could have roared the
veracity of who He was and simply walked away. No one has
ever had more of a right to defend themselves than the King
of the universe. But He remained silent. Knew He was doing
the will of the Father.

Sometimes being quiet is our best defense. Like Jesus,
even when we're right, we need to learn to hold our tongue.
To know when arguing and defending ourselves will do more
harm than good. To trust Him with our reputation and not
always feel we have to stick up for ourselves. To stay committed to the will of the Father and exercise true humility. To lean
into Jesus, our shalom, the peace that passes understanding.
And allow Him to be our greatest defense.

*Jesus, I'm struck silent, not because you've rebuked me but
because I'm in awe of your humility. I'm undone by you, the
Savior of the world who held His tongue. You're beautiful. Perfect. You're more humble than anyone I know. I want to be like
you—free from the sting of pride.*

Forever with You

> "Then the King will turn to those on his right and say,
> 'You have a special place in my Father's heart.
> Come and experience the full inheritance of the kingdom
> realm that has been destined for you from before
> the foundation of the world!'"
>
> *Matthew 25:34*

You have always been on the Father's heart. The Trinity has always had you in mind, even before you were conceived in your mother's womb. Before time as you know it began, you were destined for glory. Loved. Anticipated. Worth the best heaven had to offer.

Your inheritance was assured the moment you said yes to Jesus. Though your feet are on this earth, you belong to a heavenly kingdom and are entitled to catch glimpses of it every single day. You don't have to wait until you get to heaven to experience it. Eternity has been placed in your heart. It's alive—a gift given by the King of kings. It calls to you. Can you hear it? It beckons you closer and it's yours to encounter, forever.

Jesus, I sense your presence all around me. You've clothed me in robes of splendor and drawn me into the glories of your kingdom. Open my eyes. Let me see what few have seen. I want to experience the bliss of your nearness now and throughout eternity. I want to spend forever with you.

Partnership with Jesus

"Then he will answer them, 'Don't you know?
When you refused to help one of the least important
among these my little ones, my true brothers and sisters,
you refused to help and honor me.'"

Matthew 25:45

Hospitality, compassion, service, intercession, and encouragement—there are many different ways to let our lights shine. We don't need a title, and we certainly don't need permission to help others. The ministry of compassion is a sign that we've been with Jesus. It's a natural outflow of our partnership with Him, as the bride.

Jesus, in His generosity, doesn't simply say, "Thank you for caring about those I care about," He takes your actions personally. He sees it all. Things like feeding the homeless or caring for the desolate are just as important as interceding for those He nudges you to pray for. So, keep your eyes and heart open. Look for opportunities to represent Jesus to those around you. And if it seems as if your actions aren't appreciated and your work goes unnoticed, remember that Jesus not only sees ... He's also thanking you, as if you've done it for Him.

❖

Jesus, fill me to overflowing with your generosity. May I always remain saturated with your presence, aware of your glory, and relevant to the world around me. I want every act of service to be genuine—done from a heart that truly cares. Together, let's look for ways to spread your love.

DECEMBER 8

Liquid Love

"This is my blood. Each of you must drink it
in fulfillment of the covenant. For this is the blood
that seals the new covenant."

Matthew 26:27–28

This is the blood. The sacred blood that flowed like liquid love in exchange for your soul. So much more than a symbol, this cup is an eternal covenant of love and commitment to you. A connection point. A holy moment where you partake of the mystery of covenant union.

As you drink the cup that represents the blood He shed for *you*, you're reminding yourself of the incredible price He paid to be with you. The worth of this most precious blood is beyond compare. It was the greatest gift the Trinity had to offer. And they did it all for you. The power of this blood has sealed you. Redeemed you. Cleansed you. Brought you near.

Jesus, as I partake of this holy cup of communion, I imagine your blood flowing through my veins. Healing every sickness, washing away wrong thoughts and sins, and making me whole. Saturate every fiber of my being with the glory of this liquid love. I'm so grateful for the price you paid to be with me. Thank you for the blood.

Man-Pleasing

Because he wanted to please the people,
Pilate released Barabbas to them.

Mark 15:15

The desire to please man is a dangerous ambition. It fuels pride, stirs greed, and incites competition. It drowns out common sense and, more importantly, the voice of God. Man-pleasing latches onto its prey like a nasty demon, driving us to do things that feed fleshly desires.

When being accepted by those around us matters more than God's will, we'll easily yield to temptation. The yearning for acknowledgment pushes us into self-indulgence, where anything that feeds our need for recognition feels good. Eventually, we're chasing after the temporary rush of acceptance, even if it leads to sin. The need for approval is universal. Everyone has it. But until you're assured of your worth to Him, the applause of mortals will always seem insufficient. For Pilate, man-pleasing resulted in the decision to crucify our Lord.

Jesus, may holiness and the desire to please you always lead my decisions. Forgive me for looking for man's approval when yours should be my primary goal. May every word, thought, and act be pleasing to you, fueled by the desire to feel you near with every movement of my heart.

True Love

> Then Pilate ordered Jesus to be brutally beaten with a whip of leather straps embedded with metal. And the soldiers also wove thorn-branches into a crown and set it on his head and placed a purple robe over his shoulders.
>
> *John 19:1–2*

We cannot rejoice in the beauty of our salvation without glorying in the sacrifice of Jesus. All of our hope, joy, and moments of holy bliss began on a road that led to death. It's not enough to celebrate our future and the blessings He's promised; we must ask Him for eyes to see the sacrifice, so it's clearly imprinted upon our souls. The brutality of what He endured must become an encounter that pierces our hearts.

The perfect One was crowned, not with the glory of kings but with thorns piercing His skull. Allow yourself to imagine it—our Lord, bowed low. The Son of God allowed Himself to be beaten and torn so badly, He was unrecognizable. Don't shun the pain of remembering. Allow the torture He accepted for you to be real. Cry your tears of thanksgiving, for this is true love.

Jesus, when I think about the pain you willingly accepted for me, my feeble words of thanks don't seem like enough. As I envision the gruesome torture you took—the holy, perfect Lord of all—just so I could be with you forever, I'm left undone. Humbled. Grateful. Loved. Left with no other desire than to offer you my love.

Here Is Our Lord

So when Jesus emerged, bleeding, wearing the purple
robe and the crown of thorns on his head, Pilate said
to them, "Look at him! Here is your man!"

John 19:5

Though Pilate saw a contrite man, we see a powerful
King. The One dripping with blood who won our heart.
What a heartrending picture of glorious love. Sacred blood
flowed like liquid love. Yes, He *is* our man. Our Friend and
our Savior.

He stood there, seemingly defeated, yet infinitely powerful. The beautiful One. The One who wore His stripes and
a crown of thorns as a glorious garment—the most perfect
symbol of triumphant love. It didn't strip Him of dignity;
rather, it clothed Him with the honor of redemption. Though
pained, mocked, and rejected, fiery love still flamed through
His eyes. This was the price He'd come to pay in order to
redeem us. Jesus is not just our man, He is our Lord.

*Jesus, you've ignited my soul with holy awe that drives me to
my knees. I bow before you with tears streaming down my
face. That you would take upon yourself the sin of the world,
and wear it to showcase perfect love, fills my heart with worship. You are worthy of my devotion and fully surrendered life.
I am yours without reservation.*

Clothed in Glory

> But his tunic was seamless, woven from the top
> to the bottom as a single garment.
>
> *John 19:23*

*J*esus' tunic was a symbol of holiness and righteousness. The Aramaic in this passage could be translated, "His tunic was entirely woven from above." As a believer, you are now robed in that seamless garment of righteousness in Christ. For all eternity you are clothed in radiant splendor, wrapped in the finest linens of extravagant love. You are the pure and spotless bride.

The priceless love and mercy of Jesus covers you everywhere you go. You are royalty. You move His heart, not just humanity as a whole but *you* specifically. As a royal bride, you must think differently. Align your thoughts with His. Let your speech agree with His, regardless of how outrageous it sounds. When you live in agreement with your identity, your words, spoken in agreement with His, will cause shifts in the atmosphere.

Jesus, you've lifted the cloak of sin and darkness and wrapped me in the brilliant radiance. I am not the person I once was. Every day I soar in your presence. I change—from glory to glory I ascend until I look and sound like you. You have clothed me in garments of glory, and I'm left awestruck by the wonder of it all.

Pierced by the Beauty of Love

They brought Jesus to Golgotha,
which means "Skull Hill."

Matthew 27:33

The revelation of Jesus isn't one we grasp with our intellect. Jesus was pierced at the place of the skull so that the revelation of heaven will pierce ours. These spiritual mysteries beckon us to dive into the depths that satisfy much more than the mind can comprehend. They are alive. Life-altering. Spiritually discerned. Truth that is experienced with the heart and then accepted by the mind.

An inferno of holy passion flowed from the cross that day. A love that cannot be compared to any other. Pure, transforming love poured into the deepest caverns of your soul. One kiss of revelation has the power to transform your entire life. To set you on a course of discovery that will last throughout eternity. Love has pierced your mind and raptured your heart.

✥

Jesus, pierce me with the beauty of your love. Let heavenly encounters of your glory greet me each morning and fill my visions at night. I'm not afraid of what I don't understand. You were pierced at the place of the skull so that I can have the mind of Christ. A heart that trusts. A spirit that engages with truth. A soul that wraps itself around the mystery of your love.

Our Sin, Our Savior

While they were nailing Jesus to the cross,
he prayed over and over, "Father, forgive them,
for they don't know what they're doing."

Luke 23:34

It was *our sin* that nailed Jesus to the cross. *Our sin* that pierced the precious body of Jesus. And it was *His* longing to be with the ones whose horrid pride, anger, lust, greed, and envy would need cleansing.

What love is this? A love so powerful it would redeem the world. This demonstration of forgiveness that has absolutely no limitation. Love so pure that it cried out with each blow for the very ones who beat Him. For you. For me. Love so perfect in vision that it saw the faces of those who would need a Savior, thousands of years later. So holy, it declared our forgiveness before we were ever born.

Jesus, thank you for taking my sin on that cross with you. For forgiving me, even before I did anything wrong. For not forsaking me, though you knew all the ways I'd mess up. For loving me even when I caused you pain. I am overwhelmed by your great love.

He Draws All Men

The criminal hanging on the other cross ... said, "I beg of you, my Lord Jesus, show me grace and take me with you into your everlasting kingdom!" Jesus responded, "I promise you—this very day you will enter Paradise with me."

Luke 23:40, 42–43

Jesus doesn't offer us ten steps to salvation. We don't have to beat our chests and sign up at the nearest church in order to earn His forgiveness. There is no sacrifice that puts us in His good graces. No penance could ever earn the gift that He offers. Salvation is ours the moment we turn our hearts to Him.

Jesus knows our iniquities. There's nothing hidden from His sight. Even the most heinous sins can slingshot us toward salvation, because His great mercy catapults us in love's direction. He only looks at one condition: the heart. And when that one soul turns to Him, He won't reject them. Many who we think died in their sins and didn't make it to heaven have turned to Him at the last moment, just like this criminal. Never stop praying for those you love. Mercy and love are magnets to a needy soul.

Jesus, set the captives free! Break the chains that have bound the weak and shackled them to a life of sin. Your mercy is never-ending. Your love knows no bounds. Let them come face to face with your relentless love. Roar against the enemy that has tried to barricade them in their sin and draw them to you.

DECEMBER 16

Honor

> So when Jesus looked down and saw the disciple
> he loved standing with her, he said, "Mother, look—
> John will be a son to you." Then he said,
> "John, look—she will be a mother to you!"
>
> *John 19:26–27*

*W*hat tenderness Jesus showed toward his mother. Though in agony, moments before His death, He considered her. Miriam (Mary) who was now a widow, would have no one to provide for her. Jesus deeply honored his mother by turning to His beloved disciple and placing her in his care.

The Word of God tells us to honor our father and mother, so that we'll have long life (Exodus 20:12). Jesus, the Living Word, gave us a beautiful example of just that. The truth is, however, no parent is perfect. We don't honor them because they've done everything right. Even if their actions were deplorable, we can respect their God-given position as a way of honoring Him. We must see them through the blood of Jesus that offers them the same mercy it offers us. Learning to love as Jesus loves begins with our families.

Jesus, thank you for considering your mother while you were on the cross. For giving us examples of righteousness and teaching us to honor others. For offering society examples to follow. Give me grace to honor the parents you've placed in my life, whether by birth or through those you've united me with.

Not Forsaken

And at three o'clock Jesus shouted with a mighty voice
in Aramaic, "Eli, Eli, lema sabachthani?"—that is,
"My God, My God, why have you deserted me?"
Matthew 27:46

The most painful trials are the ones where it feels like God has turned away and forsaken us. We've all felt the pain that leaves us feeling empty. The dark night of the soul—when it seems like God has abandoned us, just when we need Him the most. Suddenly, the nearness of His touch and sweetness of His voice are absent.

God turned away from Jesus so He never has to turn away from you. Confusion, fear, doubt, and shame—Jesus took the ugliness of it all upon Himself. Annihilated it on the cross. Opened the way for you to run straight back into the arms of love and find His presence again. You never have to frantically search for Him. Settle your soul. Quiet your mind. Be still. He is there, and you are not forsaken.

Jesus, though it feels as if I've been forsaken in this wilderness, I know you're here. You said you'd never leave me or forsake me. You'll use this season for my good—to soften my heart and remind me how much I need you. Forgive me for allowing these trials to steal my affection. I turn to your ever present love. You are here.

DECEMBER 18

My Bride!

When he had sipped the sour wine, he said,
"It is finished, my bride!" Then he bowed his head
and surrendered his spirit to God.

John 19:30

he very last words Jesus spoke on the cross was a cry of love for His bride and a decree of faithfulness to the Father. Everything that He had set out to do for His beloved was complete. A passionate roar against all that had stood in the way of our holy union bellowed from our Savior's bloody lips. It was finished, and He did it all for us.

The Hebrew word *kalah* is a homonym that can mean "fulfilled (completed)" and "bride." Here we have a better understanding of exactly what consumed His thoughts as He surrendered His spirit to the Father. As Jesus took His last breath, you, His glorious bride, were on His mind.

Jesus, the power of the cross has set me free. The strength of your love blazes through the depths of my soul. Ignites holy passion and consumes me to the marrow of my bones. I'm overcome by love. Set apart as your bride. Come, make your home within me.

The Birthing of Love

But one of the soldiers took a spear and
pierced Jesus' side, and blood and water gushed out.

John 19:34

We are born again by the wounded side of Christ. Just as a baby's birth is accompanied by the flow of blood and water, so Jesus gave *birth* to His children on the cross. Blood and water flowed from His precious dead body, giving life to those who would receive Him.

It's a wonder—that Jesus can be Lord, Friend, Savior, Brother, and *Father*. That the Trinity can be three distinct persons yet one and the same being. The way we're in Christ, yet filled with His Spirit. The way invisible truths are the substance we feast on. Live by. This is the mystery we've been honored to partake of and dive into, unafraid of the perplexity of it all. Free to enjoy what makes no sense to our minds, but somehow makes perfect sense to us in the deepest parts of our being.

Jesus, your love has birthed a revival in me. It's incited a longing to know you more. To be a part of a kingdom that I cannot see yet somehow know it exists. I want to feast on the glory that satisfies yet leaves me longing for more. To look into your eyes and see the Father, Son, and Holy Spirit smiling back.

You're Invited into His Chambers

And suddenly in the temple the thick veil hanging
in the Holy Place was ripped in two!

Luke 23:45

Such a powerful image of the tearing of the veil! As God tore the curtain from top to bottom, He extended the invitation into the holiest place of all—the chambers of the King. Never again would we have to stand outside of His holy presence. The death of the Perfect One, our Beloved, removed the veil so that we could look Him in the eyes.

Today, the holy place is within us. When we say yes to Jesus, He happily steps over the curtain of separation and walks straight into our hearts. We are His, and He is ours. In perfect unity we live as one. Our souls are flooded with the substance of His love, and each day we're invited to dance with Him in His holy chambers.

Jesus, thank you for this invitation to divine intimacy. For making a way for us to be together when there was no other way. You didn't lift the veil of separation. You completely ruined it! I feel you tugging at my soul, drawing me into your holy chambers. I have no power to resist you, and by your grace nothing will ever come between us again.

Resurrection Life

The women were breathless and terrified,
until the angel said to them, "There's no reason
to be afraid. I know you're here looking for Jesus,
who was crucified. He isn't here—he has risen
victoriously, just as he said!"

Matthew 28:5–6

Jesus is the victorious One! He paid the ultimate price to prove his love. Neither death nor the grave could keep him away from you and now He wants you to experience a life of resurrection power.

Radical encounters with His glory are yours for the taking. Every day is an opportunity to discover aspects of His character you've never known. To walk, laugh, and relish in the joys of kingdom living. To live a life worth imitating. A life of unquenchable devotion and obedience to His every word. To pour yourself into every moment and to find Him there. To experience the absolute fullness of this gift of resurrection life.

Jesus, I don't want to live for myself; I want to run with passion after you. Breathe your resurrection life into all that I do. Open my eyes to see the wonders I've yet to behold. Surround me with your holy angels and wrap me in your love. Let me experience the glory of life with you.

Rejoicing in Brokenness

Along the way, Jesus suddenly appeared in front
of them and said, "Rejoice!" They were so overwhelmed
by seeing him that they bowed down and grasped
his feet in adoring worship.

Matthew 28:9

Have you ever been so totally overwhelmed by life that it feels like you'll never shake the heaviness? No matter what you do, you can't seem to crawl your way out of that sticky swamp of doubt and confusion. Then suddenly, Jesus appears out of nowhere, bringing encouragement. Illuminating the shadows of hopelessness with His glorious light, He tells you how to find your way out of that pit; He tells you to rejoice!

Our life of faith has its ups and downs. When we're going through heartrending trials, it's not easy to lift our hands in praise. Jesus doesn't tell us to rejoice over our pain, but rather over the One who rose in resurrection power in order to free us from it. There's nothing more precious to the Lord than the fragrance of our worship in the midst of brokenness.

Jesus, I know that even in the midst of my deepest sorrow and greatest pain, you are still worthy. Though I don't feel like rejoicing, I choose to lift my voice and declare your goodness. To praise you for who you are and dance in your rays of glory. I offer you my brokenness. I offer you my love.

Finding Love, Throwing off Fear

Then Jesus said to them,
"Throw off all your fears. Go and tell my brothers
to go to Galilee. They will find me there."

Matthew 28:10

Throw off your fear like a wet slimy cloak. You weren't meant to wear it. Jesus paid the price for you to be free from fear, but it's up to you to part with it. To treat it like a plague and refuse it residence in your life.

Fear no longer needs to smother you. It has no right and no hold on you now that Jesus has confronted the enemy and won. When you're stuck staring at your fears, it's hard to find His presence. That's because Jesus isn't in the fear. He's in the glory—in the place of freedom, where He's called you to join Him in perfect love. You can choose to receive that freedom today—to throw off your fears, run to Him, and embrace the love that remedies every fear.

Jesus, sometimes I step away from the awareness of your love and end up enslaved to fear and anxiety. Yet over and over again you come to rescue me from bondage. To remind me that freedom is a choice. A step. An action. A movement toward you. A glorious invitation to find your love.

Eyes that See

All at once their eyes were opened and they realized
it was Jesus! Stunned, they looked at each other and said,
"Why didn't we recognize it was him?"

Luke 24:31

Once Jesus opens your eyes, everything changes. Things that seemed lifeless and dull become filled with joy and wonder. You see Him in every sunrise and hear His voice in the breeze that brushes your face.

It's hard to fathom how we ever could have missed the glories that are so evident. How this priceless, beautiful love was overlooked. But that's part of the beauty of revelation—it's revealed when the Lord knows we're ready. All along the way, He imparts nuggets of truth. Draws us. Softens our hard hearts. Woos us into His presence. Longs to make His touch known. Learning *about* Him isn't enough. He wants you to experience His reality. When He wraps you within the power of His embrace, there's no denying it.

Jesus, give me eyes to see your wonder. A heart to discern your voice. Let me see you in every person I meet—feel your nearness, every moment. I'm not content with what I know or with what others have taught me. I want revelation that I cannot get from anyone but you. Unfold the mysteries of your love and take me deeper, until all that I am is consumed by all you are.

The Humble Lamb

"You will recognize him by this miracle sign:
you will find a baby wrapped in strips of cloth
and lying in a feeding trough!"

Luke 2:12

The cradle of our Messiah was the same place where Passover lambs were situated after birth. These lambs, which couldn't have bruises or broken bones, were wrapped in cloth and placed on soft hay in the feeding trough in order to keep them from hurting themselves. The Lamb of God, who entered the world in lowliness, was the final Passover lamb.

Today, our King is still known by the miraculous way He stoops down and lives in gentleness toward all mankind. He loves to be near those who, like Him, have a humble and contrite heart. He didn't enter the world with fanfare but in quiet significance. Religious actions and words that seem holy but carry no power have never impressed Him. Like Jesus, let's live in humility but pour it out with redemptive power.

Jesus, thank you for the way you clothed yourself in humility yet wrap me in your righteousness and treat me like royalty. Help me to represent you well—to live with compassion and humility yet confidently releasing the glory of the One who lives inside me.

Holy Passion

"Didn't our hearts burn with the flames of holy passion while we walked beside him? He unveiled for us such profound revelation from the Scriptures!"

Luke 24:32

When you're near Jesus your heart burns with holy passion. It's difficult to describe but easy to feel. His nearness ignites a flame that causes every part of us to blaze with unquenchable fire—the passion, the boldness to go even closer. To be consumed by His perfection. To be cleansed by His purity.

The more time we spend adoring this radiant One, the greater our zeal for holiness. We want nothing to come between us. We yearn for Him to consume anything that doesn't resemble Him. Bowing before His majesty, we invite the fires of His cleansing gaze. We cry out for purity and holiness, and Jesus, in His great mercy and tender affection, reveals the areas that need our attention. Nothing is hidden from His sight.

Jesus, I want to walk with you in the revelation of holy passion. Where all of me is consumed—undone by the glory that streams from your smile. To be saturated in more than knowledge of your Word but to become one with its reality. Draw me into your holy fire. Burn your purity into the depths of my being so I'll never stray.

Cast Your Cares

"Be at peace. I am the living God. Don't be afraid.
Why would you be so frightened? Don't let doubt
or fear enter your hearts, for I AM!"

Luke 24:37–38

"Be at peace." That was not a suggestion. Jesus' instruction carries with it the power to make it happen. We choose which kingdom to agree with. Which truth to focus on. Even when it feels like we just can't get a grip, the truth is that peace is a choice.

When our minds are stuck on the trial, fear has entered our hearts. It has overridden faith and caused us to forget that the great I AM is able to do *absolutely anything*. Jesus asks the question, "Why would you be so frightened?" He knows that as long as the great I AM fills your heart, there's no room for fear. The solution is to completely saturate yourself in His presence. A practical way to do this is to play your favorite worship music and, with every other distraction out of the way, stay in that place of worship until peace has come.

⚜

Jesus, I long for the peace that your presence alone can bring. I surrender every overwhelming fear, doubt, and concern and lay them at your feet. As I worship you, I believe you're bringing the victory. I breathe in the peace of your presence. I feel you here.

Destiny

"Yet what I want is not important,
for I only desire to fulfill your plan for me."
Matthew 26:39

Jesus cares about your future and the call upon your life even more than you do. There's no secret formula for discovering your destiny. It simply unfolds as you live in total and complete submission to Him and pay attention to the stirring of your heart. Learn to listen to the desires that spring up or blossom slowly within you, as they'll escort you toward true and sometimes unexpected opportunities.

You don't have to be afraid of missing your destiny. Nothing—not setbacks, opposition, or failure can stop what He's placed in motion. These things will only serve as prophetic declarations of your soon-coming breakthrough. It's impossible to miss His will, because like a baby safely tucked away in the womb, so you are in Christ. Profoundly protected, your destiny will be released in its ordained season.

Jesus, I want to come to the point of such blissful abandon and such absolute trust in your care for me that I don't fear missing your will. I believe that the sacred secrets of your heart are mine. I trust in your eternal purpose for my life. Nothing will stop you from working on my behalf!

Conquering King

After saying these things, Jesus was lifted up
into heaven and sat down at the place of honor
at the right hand of God!

Mark 16:19

*J*esus is our conquering King! The magnificent One seated in victory. No one will ever love us the way that He does. No one can look at the darkness of humanity and say they've paid the price for its redemption.

He is all and fills all. For every ploy of evil, He is its destroyer. For every sorrow, He is the joy that fills us. His healing hands still heal. His forgiveness is unlimited. And the lost have a Redeemer who extends His love to the suffering heart. The joy that we desire, the peace that calms the raging storms, and the hope that overwhelms hopelessness is found in Him. He is perfected beauty. Glorious love. Unrelenting devotion.

And He is ever present with you, every day.

Jesus, I glorify you today, not just for who you are to me but for who you are for the entire world. I honor you for the way you rule with might and power yet treat me with such compassion. For encouraging me when I'm discouraged. For laughing with me and walking by my side. For empowering me to be all that you created me to be. For loving me. You are my Conquering King, and I am yours.

Redemption

After they had breakfast, Jesus said to Peter the Rock,
"Simon, son of John, do you burn with love for me more
than these?" Peter answered, "Yes, Lord! You know
that I have great affection for you!"

John 21:15

Our Lord is a redeeming Lord! His love for us is unmatched by any other. While we may not know how to heal a wounded soul, He knows exactly what to do. Despite denying Jesus three times, as Jesus predicted, Peter was one of the disciples He purposefully sought out after His resurrection. No lectures. No guilt-trips. Though that may be the way of religion, it isn't the heart of Jesus. Jesus brings restoration by reminding us of our identity and true affections.

Jesus knew exactly how to silence Peter's tormenting memory of denying the Lord. Three times Jesus asks him if he loves Him, and three times Peter confesses his deep love for Christ. The declaration of Peter's true affection brought healing, and once the sting of his denial was gone, he was ready to begin his ministry.

Jesus, your mercy is so tender toward me. Thank you for never leaving me to wallow in my failure. For constantly offering me the chance to see myself the way you do. You are the God of restoration. Heal my memories that seek to drag me back into self-reproach, and I will release that healing to others.

Your Destiny

"As you go into all the world, preach openly
the wonderful news of the gospel to the entire human
race! ... And these miracle signs will accompany those
who believe: They will drive out demons in the power
of my name. They will speak in tongues. They will be
supernaturally protected from snakes and from drinking
anything poisonous. And they will lay hands
on the sick and heal them."

Mark 16:15, 17–18

Y ou don't have to look any further than the Gospels to discover your destiny. It starts and ends with Jesus, and what a powerful destiny it is! The same authority Jesus had when He walked this earth—to heal, save, and deliver—has been given to you. Yours is a *supernatural* life waiting to be lived.

It's time to live with a purity and zeal for Jesus that ignites desire in others. Adorn yourself with a radical faith that cannot be denied. Heal the sick. Love well. Comfort the hurting and lonely. Make a change in your society. Carry the awareness of His love always. Be the voice of hope!

Jesus, when all is said and done, I want to stand before you with a pure heart—a heart that believed I was powerful and anointed enough to carry out your great commission. May I have crowns to lay at your feet and a heart united in love.

About the Authors

Dr. Brian Simmons is known as a passionate lover of God and the lead translator of *The Passion Translation*, a new heart-level Bible translation that conveys God's passion for people and His world by translating the original, life-changing message of God's Word for modern readers. Brian and his wife, Candice, travel full-time as speakers and Bible teachers.

Gretchen Rodriguez has co-authored three devotionals with Brian Simmons. Her heart burns with one main message: intimacy with Jesus and discovering the reality of His presence. She is also a dancer and ballet teacher. She and her husband invested nine years as missionaries in Puerto Rico, along with their three daughters, and now make Redding, California, their home.